I DON'T LIKE MONDAYS

MIRROR BOOKS

1

Published in Great Britain and Ireland in 2026 by
Mirror Books, a Reach PLC business.

www.mirrorbooks.co.uk
@TheMirrorBooks

Print ISBN 9781917439671

Editing and Production: Christine Costello, Nick Webster
Cover Design: Chris Collins

Photographic Acknowledgements: xxxx

Printed and bound in Great Britain by
CPI Group (UK) Ltd, Croydon, CR0 4YY

MIX
Paper | Supporting responsible forestry
FSC® C013604

I DON'T LIKE MONDAYS

THE TRUE STORY BEHIND AMERICA'S FIRST MODERN SCHOOL SHOOTING

N. LEIGH HUNT

MIRROR BOOKS

CONTENTS

To Penny, Molly, and Scarlett: thanks for being perfect.

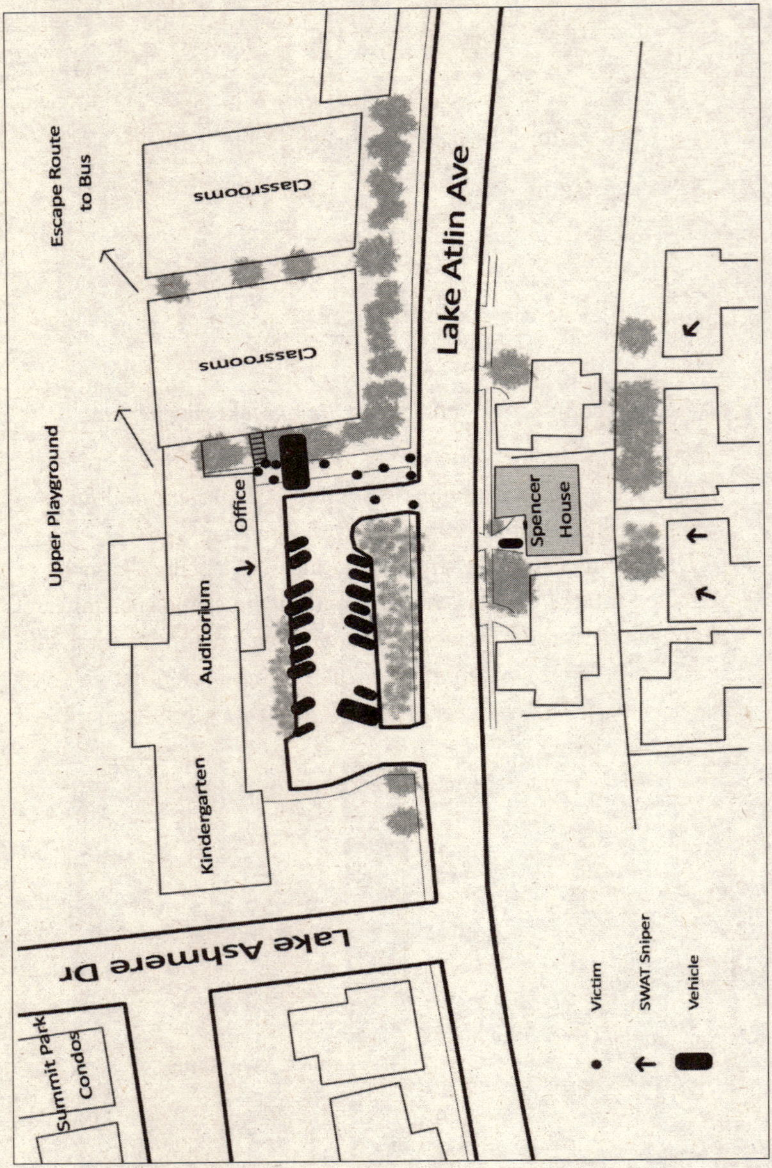

Crime scene layout at Cleveland Elementary School

PREFACE

WHILE THERE ARE conflicting statistics on the amount of school shootings since Brenda's case, figures from multiple sources suggest there have been more than 1,300 shooter incidents in schools in the United States since 1970. The FBI started their statistics in 2000 and news outlets like CNN did not start keeping records until 2008. There are many online resources who have a multitude of numbers differing by political motivations.

Definitions can range from shootings on a school campus to targeted attacks or gang violence within the school perimiter. It has been hard for any single source to give a definitive total with varying definitions. Columbine High School shooting in 1999 has been used as the cornerstone for what a school shooting is today. One thing is for certain; the attacks have increased in force and preparation which has led schools and institutions to create mechanism to keep children and staff safe.

Alert, Lockdown, Inform, Counter, Evacuate (ALICE) training was devised in Ohio to deliver lifesaving training for staff and students. Run, Hide, Fight is another. Both are used in many parts of the United States but they are only two of many courses faculty can choose from. Artificial Intelligence is often used today for behavioural pattern analyses and real-time weapon detection. In the most recent presidential election, both candidates were pro-gun. Neither had pledged to change the current gun legislation. All efforts still seem to be on mental health rather than restricting access to weapons.

Lockdown training is nothing new to many schools in America. There are some schools who do bi-yearly drills for active shooters, or amend their fire drills to incorporate plans in case of an event. There is no national standard for these types of precaution and they often differ by district and county. Some schools in rural Texas, where gun ownership is high may not have any training in school, whereas some in high population areas with low gun ownership may have a yearly drill and metal detectors at the front of the school. It is a perplexing issue.

It is virtually impossible to calibrate how many victims there are from school shootings. Deaths, wounded and witnesses can all be determined victims of this phenomenon. The age ranges begin at time you start attending school (five) and until you graduate (18). This does not include school staff and faculty who are often in the firing lines. The vast majority of gun violence at schools is limited to a few victims but events like Columbine, Sandy Hook and Uvalde were designed by the shooter to create dozens of victims.

FOREWORD

MENTION THE CLEVELAND Elementary school shooting to most San Diegans, and you'll get a blank stare. Tell them it happened here in 1979, that a 16-year-old girl opened fire on children from her front door, that she inspired a hit song with her motive for murder – 'I don't like Mondays' – and watch disbelief cross their faces. Despite living in this city for nearly three decades, I only know Brenda Spencer's name because I evaluate violent offenders. Even in my threat assessment training, her case was a footnote in training materials.

This collective amnesia speaks to something deeper than mere historical oversight. It's a kind of protective forgetting about one of the earliest moments when violence found its way into our elementary schools. While Columbine is seared into national memory, Cleveland Elementary has faded like an old photograph, its edges worn away by time and perhaps by our inability to process what it meant. N. Leigh Hunt's remarkable book is an important reminder. Brenda Spencer didn't just commit the first modern school shooting; she provided the template that we failed to read.

THE FIRST MODERN SCHOOL SHOOTING

What happened on January 29, 1979, wasn't a crime of passion, a targeted assassination, or gang warfare spilling onto school grounds. This was something new: a child shooting children she didn't know, from her home across the street, for no reason that made sense. When a journalist asked why, her "I don't like Mondays" response became infamous precisely because it revealed the motiveless malignancy we would see again and again.

Spencer shattered every assumption we might have made about who commits such acts. Female school shooters remain vanishingly rare; she was one of the first. She was 16, living in suburban San Diego, not urban decay. She used the rifle her father had given her for Christmas, foretelling our ongoing debates about access to weapons and troubled teens. She telegraphed her intentions, telling others she was going to do something big, something to "liven up the day". Revisiting this case is like digging up an origin story to understand our roots; it speaks to a pattern that began that day in 1979.

WHY THIS BOOK, WHY N. LEIGH HUNT?

To excavate a buried story requires both the detective's persistence and the storyteller's art. N. Leigh Hunt brings both to this forgotten tragedy, along with something rarer: the dual perspective of insider and outsider. Originally from San Diego but now based in the UK, Hunt occupies that valuable space between proximity and distance that allows for both intimacy and objectivity.

As a crime historian and broadcaster, Hunt understands that true crime, at its best, isn't about sensationalism. It's about sense-making. His approach to the Spencer case reflects this ethos. Over years of meticulous research, he's assembled not just facts but perspectives; from law enforcement officers who responded that day, from survivors still carrying physical and psychological scars, and remarkably, from Brenda Spencer herself. Their ongoing correspondence, revealed in these pages, provides insights unavailable elsewhere.

This isn't just professional interest for Hunt; it's personal archaeology. He's excavating a case that touched his own family's history. His father, the editor of the Evening Tribune, immediately sent his reporters to the house. He got a front-row seat to the media coverage of this tragedy and law enforcement's response to this unprecedented crime. Yet his years in England provide crucial distance; he can view this watershed event with the clarity of someone who lives outside our daily normalisation of violence.

Hunt's greatest achievement may be his restraint. In an era of true crime sensationalism, he lets Spencer's words and actions reveal more than any analysis could. He presents her concerned correspondence about gophers and hedgehogs alongside her evolving excuses for mass murder, trusting readers to grapple with these jarring juxtapositions.

When Hunt presented this case at Crime Con UK, British audiences were stunned. How had they never heard of this? Why hasn't this case been revisited as the beginning of a predictable pattern, a search for clues that might foreshadow future school shootings? Perhaps these questions should mirror our own.

WHAT THIS CASE TEACHES US

The leakage. That's what strikes me reviewing this case. Spencer told her classmates what she was going to do. She showed off her father's guns. Talked about shooting police officers. Today, these behaviours are recognised as warning signs. In 1979, they were dismissed.

In my work evaluating violent offenders, Spencer's case reads like an early version of some of the findings I uncover today. The broken home, the alleged abuse, the previous arrests, the suicidal ideation. The changing stories.

Hunt's evolving relationship with Spencer parallels her evolving explanations for what happened: abuse, drugs, hallucinations, an attempt to commit suicide-by-cop. After 46 years, she's still changing her story. Or maybe she's finally finding language for something she couldn't articulate at 16. That ambiguity is what makes this case so unsettling.

Having evaluated hundreds of violent offenders, I recognise this pattern of shifting narratives. Sometimes it's manipulation, sometimes it's genuine insight emerging over time. Hunt presents these contradictions without forcing a conclusion, which is precisely what makes his account so valuable.

MORE THAN TRUE CRIME

Hunt refuses to give us the simple narrative we might crave. There's no straightforward monster here, no easy evil to dismiss. Instead, through meticulous research and unprecedented access, he presents something far more unsettling: a fully human story of how ordinary dysfunction can metastasize into extraordinary violence.

The book's strength lies in its multiple perspectives. We hear from Cam Miller, shot at age nine, who still attends every parole hearing, still carries the trauma in his body and mind. We meet the families of Principal Burton Wragg and janitor Mike Suchar, the heroes who died trying to protect children. We follow the officers who risked their lives establishing the response protocols we now take for granted. Each voice adds complexity to a story that could have been reduced to sensationalism.

Most remarkably, we hear from Spencer herself, not the 16-year-old of 1979, but the woman now in her 60s. Her letters to Hunt reveal someone simultaneously self-aware and self-deluding, remorseful yet minimising, institutionalised but still hoping for freedom. We encounter something I often see in my own work: the jarring coexistence of casual kindness and devastating violence in the same person. She is neither the monster of our imagination nor the victim she sometimes portrays herself as.

Hunt chronicles every parole hearing with courtroom precision, showing us how a moment of violence reverberates over decades, how trauma passes through generations, how a community's forgetting may be its way of surviving. He asks whether justice means eternal punishment or allows for the possibility of redemption, even for acts that seem unforgivable.

WHY READ THIS NOW?

In February 2025, Brenda Spencer was again denied parole. Three more years. She still insists she aimed the gun over the children's heads, a claim contradicted by the physical evidence. Commissioner Kozel's words are telling, "This denial gives the board no pleasure, especially after all these years."

For those of us hoping to prevent violence, we naturally spend more time studying incidents with higher casualties; it's a practical allocation of limited training time. But Hunt's book made me rethink what we might learn from this first case. Not because we've ignored it, but because we may not have had the framework to fully understand it until now.

The Wragg family's impact statement includes these six words: "We do not forgive school shooters." After 46 years, their clarity is absolute and understandable. I have seen too often how victims' families navigate the impossible territory between justice and healing. The Wraggs remind us that some acts create wounds that time alone cannot heal.

Brenda Spencer became the first name on a list none of us wanted to start. Hunt's careful documentation ensures we understand not just what happened, but why it matters. Her name belongs in our memory—not as a cautionary tale we failed to heed, but as the beginning of a conversation we need to finish.

Dr Joni Johnston
Forensic psychologist, private investigator, and crime writer

AUTHOR'S NOTE

THIS BOOK WAS written for all the victims of the Cleveland Elementary School shooting in 1979. They are the Wraggs, Suchars, Buells, Clarks, Hardys, Millers, Robles, Selvigs, Stites, Verners, and Robbs. The school's 300 plus students, faculty, and all of their families should also be considered victims.

Long before Columbine or Sandy Hook and the dozens of school shootings in the United States, there was Brenda Spencer. Who is she? Why did she shoot up an elementary school? I hope to explain as much as I can within this book.

Spencer is often referred to as the first modern school shooter in US history, but the events leading up to the shooting have never been fully documented. It is my intent to catalogue as much information as possible to understand her motive. I believe that her story and the way she was glorified in song, greatly contributed to the phenomenon of school shootings.

Will publishing this add to her fame? Maybe, but better understanding Brenda could stop future rampages. She is still relevant and should not be forgotten. I was a 10-year-old San Diegan at the time of her attack on the school, and it greatly affected my life. "I don't like Mondays" is a phrase that took on an entirely new meaning that day.

In researching this book, I was immediately struck by the number of assumed facts. These "facts" have been repeated over and over by journalists, podcasters, and psychologists. I respect that categorising different types of psychopathy is a fundamental part of analysis.

But the evidence shows it has done little to stop the growth of the active shooter phenomenon.

I corresponded directly with Brenda in prison and spoke with neighbours, witnesses, police, and journalists to capture as much as possible. Officer Robb was the only victim I communicated with, and I was careful not to involve victims unnecessarily. They have suffered enough.

1

MONDAY MORNING

MONDAY, JAN. 29, 1979, was a colder than usual day, with a bit of frost on the ground. The sky was slightly grey, but it promised to warm up by midday.

A little after 8am, parents in San Carlos, a pleasant suburb of the California seaside city of San Diego, started the drive to drop their children off at school. Older students began walking.

The day began not unlike any other winter morning in the small community. Most children wore coats they could easily shed once the mid-morning sunshine burned away the low clouds, as it always does in southern California.

Parents would often drop their kids off early at Cleveland Elementary School to avoid kerbside congestion. The school covered a full square block, surrounded by miles and miles of housing estates matching one another. Children would also enter at the rear gates and play with their friends in the back playground away from the street waiting for the bell to ring.

Soon more parents would be filling the street with drop-offs, kissing their kids goodbye for the day. They often would double park, blocking the entire road for a moment because kerbside space was limited. The front of the school was the only no-parking zone along Lake Atlin Ave., but that did not stop parents from momentarily stopping.

The main office was set back from the road about 40ft with a parking lot immediately in front of it. Kids would congregate near the car park or walkway leading to the classrooms, waiting for the principal to open the school gate. At 8:15am, the first bell rang for the kindergarten classes – five to six-year-old – giving a warning to the youngest children in the school who were let in 15 minutes before the regular school starts its day.

At 8:30am, the bell would ring for kindergarten to start and the main school to open. Some meandering students would shuffle in past the main office, believing they had ample time before school started at 8:45am. Others rushed like wild animals. If they weren't running late, they had only 15 minutes from the time the gate opened to scurry to the classrooms and get settled before the bell sounded to start the school day.

Ten-year-old Linda Selvig walked to school each day. She got a late start this Monday and would just make the 8:30am bell after the eight-minute walk from her house.

Normally, her nine-year-old sister Monica would travel with her. The sisters had started the walk together, but Linda decided to stay back to meet friends. So, Monica ventured by herself.

Monica Selvig walked alone on the sidewalk with the avenue on her left. The school's south side is lined with ivy covered fencing that blocks it from the road. She rounded the corner of the fence and onto the school's main walkway just next to the parking lot.

As she walked with her back to the road, she felt a sharp pain in her left side as a bullet struck her.

She was thrown to the ground after the shock of the impact. Monica had only made it about ten feet up the school walkway and was still more than 30ft from the safety of the main office building. The sound of gunfire was not immediately recognised as anything other than a backfiring car if it was heard at all.

Just moments later, a bullet struck eight-year-old Mary Clark in the left side of her stomach as she walked up the school path with her six-year-old sister, Amelia. The girls had just been dropped off by a parent. The bullet went straight through her and bloodied her white top as she fell to the ground.

Mary, described as incredibly shy, did not want to cause a fuss. She rose to her feet, made her way into the school and was eventually herded to safety with a group of other students. At the same time but from the opposite direction, Greg Verner, aged eight, had just wandered across the car park and was about to step onto the east walkway and up the short concrete stairs to his classroom building.

The parking lot was directly in front of the school and the only access to the main entrance. From here students could either go up the stairs to the classroom building or head into the covered walkway that takes you all the way to the back playground. He was struck through his green Toughskins brand jeans into his right upper backside. The bullet hit his pelvic bone, sending him to the ground on the driveway.

The children were far too young to know what was happening and were probably preoccupied with getting to class on time. Many parents were safely in their cars and making their short trip back home without hearing anything out of the ordinary.

Some children began to run for cover, while others stood still watching and waiting for instruction. It was unclear where the danger was coming from as the small popping sound of gunfire was not immediately recognisable. The ricocheting bullets echoed through the covered walkway that ran through the middle of the open-air school. These shots could not be heard by the congregation still in the car park at the front of the school.

Crystal Hardy, dressed in baggy green shorts, boots, and a cream patterned cardigan, was ten years old. She was with her younger brother, being dropped off by her mother in front of the school.

She saw some friends she wanted to chat with and walked up the main walkway.

"I heard shots, but I thought boys near me just had firecrackers or something," she later recalled.

As she looked around curiously, Crystal was struck through her right wrist. The bullet only just missed the bone and all vital tendons and exited as she walked. She fell to her knees and began to cry, blood pouring from her arm. She got up and made her way to the nurse's office and was given paper towels to stem the bleeding. Crystal's brother Matthew, five, witnessed the shooting and began to panic, not understanding what had happened, but he was not shot.

Moments later the youngest victim, seven-year-old Audrey Stites, snatched at her right arm as she walked up the driveway with her older sister Madeline. They both stopped and saw Monica and then Greg on the ground. Audrey was struck from behind through her bright puffy green ski jacket and into her right elbow. They stood in shock for a moment before noticing other students running for cover and hearing screams all around.

Madeline avoided injury when bullets passed through her coat pocket and were stopped by her binder and pencil case. Audrey ran crying and bleeding to her classroom. She had not noticed a second bullet had burned the inside of each thigh near her crotch.

It was still unclear exactly where the shots were coming from, but it was apparent they were not from the school. The shooter was obviously targeting students on the walkway.

Almost all the students in the parking lot and on the driveway had instinctively gone into a safe hiding spot. They jumped under parked cars or ducked into the main office and under the window. Some made it up the stairs next to the office entrance and hid in a classroom, while others were stranded in the bushes that decorated the parking lot and looking around for where the danger was coming from.

In less than three minutes, five children had been shot as more unsuspecting students were arriving on foot. Some were being dropped off right in front of the house across the street. The parents and students still arriving had no idea of the existing threat.

Peggy Whiteside dropped off her kids, Lisa, five, and Joey, eight, sometime after 8am and went home.

Later, she said, "I heard shots. I just thought it was some kid with firecrackers. It happens all the time."

Her daughter had gone into the kindergarten, and her son was safely playing in the playground behind the school. Twelve-year-old Michael McDaniel was just arriving and heard gunshots from down the road.

"I heard shots as I walked towards the front of the building, and there were little puffs of dust on the embankment next to me," he would recount later that day. "My teacher called to me to come into the principal's office, and I just started running... It just didn't seem real."

Burton "Bert" Wragg, who was in his first year as Cleveland principal, was not at the entrance gate as he usually would be.

Principal Wragg had just fed his chickens and kissed his wife, Kathe, goodbye. He left his home about 7am and arrived at the school by about ten past that morning.

He was having coffee with sixth-grade teacher Daryl Barnes in the main office. They could see little Monica and Greg on the ground as the sound of bullets whistled through the ivy near the main office.

They watched the surreal events unfold from the window facing the walkway. It was only then that they realised with horror that a sniper had opened fire on the school.

"We heard two shots and Wragg immediately ran out into the crowded school grounds to help children," said Barnes.

Wragg made a beeline for the first child on the ground with

Barnes closely in tow. The pair ran directly onto the walkway and right into the view of the shooter.

"Duck, you guys! Crystal, run!" was the last thing Principal Wragg said as he was shot twice in his chest. He fell to the ground and spun into the ivy patch near the walkway.

Barnes stopped in his tracks and was standing over the principal as shots flew past his head and against the building behind him.

"Almost immediately there were two more shots, and I ran out to find Wragg lying on the ground. There were children running everywhere," Barnes remembered. "He was badly wounded in his chest. I opened his shirt. He appeared dead."

With the principal on the ground, Barnes continued down the drive and gently picked up the two wounded children, Monica and Greg. He turned his back on the shooter and made his way back to safety.

"I grabbed two and rushed into the nurse's office with them," he said later.

Barnes could see the blood coming from Monica's abdomen and calmly rested her on the bed in the nurse's office. The nurse started to treat the injured child as best she could while Barnes considered going out front again to collect more of the injured.

Instead, he ran to tell school secretary Mary Smith to call the police ASAP. Smith's desk faced the school's front window and could see the carnage as it unfolded. She could also see where the shots were coming from and had already started calling the police.

As Wragg, the new principal, career educator, and World War Two veteran, lay bleeding just steps from the office doors, three other wounded children remained outside. Through the office window, Barnes could see head janitor Mike Suchar dart past.

Affectionately known as Mr. Mike, Michael Suchar had been one of the most popular figures at the school for ten years. He was a sturdy Navy man who served during both World War Two and in Korea before coming to the school. Students saw him as a big strong protector who would do anything for the school.

Barnes shouted to Mr. Mike as he dashed into the line of fire.

"I looked up and saw Suchar running from his office. I rushed to the window, but I was too late," said Barnes.

Standing in his bright blue long-sleeve work shirt over the wounded Principal Wragg, Mike Suchar was knocked to the ground as he lowered a blanket to help his friend and boss.

Barnes recalled Mr. Mike saying, "My God, I've been hit!" as he fell into the shrubbery and bushes next to the walkway.

"I saw him lean over Wragg and almost immediately two bullets hit him, spinning him around and to the ground," Barnes said.

Eleven-year-old Kathy Voeks had wandered up the walkway within feet of the victims. She turned to look at her "close friend" Mr. Mike as he gasped and said, "Oh God! Oh God, go get the police!"

Kathy heard Barnes's cries for children to take cover as she ran unharmed up the steps and into her fifth-grade classroom.

Jennifer Engle, 10, was another student walking up.

"I saw the principal, and he was lying flat on the ground," she would recall. "He wasn't moving or anything, and I saw two holes in his leg, and then I saw the janitor, and he was groaning. Mr. Barnes told me to start running, and I started running, and I heard this shot from a gun."

Children, unaware of danger, continued to arrive at the school.

Carolyn Hewitt stopped her car to drop off her son Matthew, eight, in front of the school as the bell rang, then made her way home. She later said she may have heard cracking noises but thought little of it.

"I don't know where my woman's intuition was. When I pulled up, he got out of the car, and I heard three shots. I never connected it with a gun."

The weapon being used was a 10/22 Ruger semi-automatic rifle. It is not an explosively noisy gun and with the car engine running and car windows up on a cold morning, the sound could have been muffled.

It was reported that one mother dropped off three of her children at 8:35am, which would have been the middle of the heaviest gunfire. She knew nothing of what had happened till she was back at home and told by a friend. For whatever reason, the shooter did not fire at the parents or at their cars.

Eleven-year-old James Lira saw the two bodies and a wounded girl when he reached the school. "She was lying in the street, and I turned her over," he said, "but a teacher told us to run, so we ran into the teachers' lounge."

His mother said, "I saw a man lying on the ground, and I thought he had a heart attack. Then I saw another little girl on the ground. My kids were getting out of the car, and I tried to yell at them, but at that time, the bullets were flying"."

Elaine Fournier had dropped off her five-year-old at 8:15am, then returned home to bed.

"I'm pregnant, and it's the only chance I get to sleep," she said. "One siren I can ignore but not that many!"

In her classroom, teacher Miyoko "Mickey" Miyashita was two buildings away and unaware of what was going on.

"I was in my room preparing to greet the kids when I heard the bang-bang, like firecrackers, but never gave it much thought," she said.

A colleague ran from the scene and alerted her to what was going on.

Mrs. Miyashita and her good friend, teacher Katherine Keith, went looking for as many students as they could find.

"We immediately grabbed any kid that was outside and pulled them into classrooms," she said.

She guided as many children as she could see in the playground behind the main office into her classroom.

"We were going to celebrate Chinese New Year, so I had brought some almond cookies."

1979 was the year of the goat in the Chinese Zodiac, and there were small celebrations over the previous weekend. Is it possible that some informed students thought the gunshots were fireworks? Fireworks were illegal in California, but their sound would easily be mistaken for a small calibre weapon.

"After all the kids were secured, I locked my door and closed the shades. We stood closely together in the back part of the room away from the windows," Mrs. Miyashita told me.

The fire alarm suddenly sounded at the lower part of the school, pulled by a staff member or possibly hit by a stray bullet. This caused a problem for children arriving. Children had always been instructed to go straight to the assembly point through the school gates when they heard the fire alarm so many arriving students stopped where they stood to await orders from teachers and the principal.

Teacher Wanda Carberry began to blow her whistle to attract the attention of the arriving children. In the madness, she was trying to direct traffic and keep them out of the line of fire.

"The sniper seemed to pick them off easily as they ran towards the school," Carberry said.

Christy Buell was a nine-year-old, who walked the few blocks to school. She was playing with a classmate on the slippery grass near the walkway in front of the school. Looking left and right and hearing the whistles and commotion, she heard a popping noise and was shot in the stomach and lower back in rapid succession. She fell to the ground and began to vomit as blood began to soak her Winnie-the Pooh T-shirt.

"All of a sudden, it felt like my whole body was falling asleep," she remembered, "like pin pricks all over. We just heard someone shouting, 'Run! Run!'"

Cleveland Elementary was an open-air, single-story campus with multiple stucco buildings. Christy crawled up the walkway as low as she could and was able to reach an external classroom door. The teacher heard her crying, "I want my daddy, I want my daddy!" and let her in as bullets were hitting the door. Christy's father was Norm, the well-known owner of the popular local Chicken Shack Restaurant. She had three siblings who all attended Cleveland Elementary at one point or another.

Christy was struck twice, but she narrowly missed being shot a third time, later finding a bullet hole in her hood.

Barnes and other teachers tried to rescue other children as the bullets kept flying.

"Five shots came in with three of them just over our heads," Barnes said.

The fire alarm continued to ring and the kindergarten class, unaware of the dangers in the front of the building, began to assemble in an orderly line at the door. They were stopped moments before streaming into the direct vision of the sniper and taken to a protected school building.

Ten-year-old Julie Robles heard all the noise and commotion as she walked to the entrance of the school with a schoolmate. As she turned to look at Wragg lying on the side of the walkway in the vegetation, a bullet passed through her right side and her glasses fell from her face.

She was able to maintain her footing, picked up her specs and immediately ran into the school to hide. Julie was wearing a large brown coat with fluffy cuffs and collar that kept her warm.

"I saw Mr. Wragg lying on the ground," Julie said later. "Then felt a little nip, but it didn't hurt that much." She was in a classroom when she saw the blood. "I started to cry, but I knew that wasn't going to do any good." The thought of getting to the hospital was out of the question. The school nurse tried her best to tend each victim one by one.

It was now clear to everyone at the scene that the shots were coming from a house across the street. But the students crossing the road or at the other end of the parking lot were still unaware of the imminent danger . The small calibre shots coming from across the road would not have been heard over the fire alarm at the school.

The teaching staff in the main building began to filter as many children as possible into the auditorium through the rear entrance. It was the largest room with minimal front-facing windows, and it could hold a large number of students requiring attention. Children were still arriving straight into the line of fire, and others were just standing still, wondering what was going on.

Charles A. Miller III was only nine and went by the name "Cam" – his initials. All the school faculty knew Cam well as he was often called upon to help the principal with errands and tasks around school.

Michael Guerrero, the assistant janitor, who worked at the school when he wasn't in classes at nearby San Diego State University, remembers him as a nice, chubby, little boy.

Cam's mother, DeLois Miller, normally dropped him off at Cleveland Elementary's side gate by the playground. But this was a cold morning and she thought he should get him inside quickly. So, she drove to the front of the school.

They both heard what they thought was a car backfiring as she drove away. Cam strolled up to the school thinking everyone was messing around and continued to walk towards the entrance gate. The boy was dumbfounded by what he saw as he arrived at the main office.

With a smile on his face, he was struck with a bullet that tore through his left shoulder. He was standing with his back to the road when the projectile only just missed his heart. Cam fell forward, toward the fallen principal and janitor. He stumbled but regained his feet.

He said he felt an "electric shock" in his shoulder and with the help of another student he managed to get around to the back of the school.

He saw his teacher and told her, "I think I've been shot." The teacher opened his puffy blue vest and saw blood all over his clothes.

Almost all the remaining students had the same feeling as Cam's first thoughts on arriving as they walked across the parking lot or rounded the corner into the driveway. Someone was fooling around, surely? The fire alarm was going off amid the sound of firecrackers. This was a Californian suburb in the late 70's; what could be that big of a deal?

2

SAN DIEGO POLICE DEPARTMENT

THE FIRST EMERGENCY call came into the main city police station at 8:25am. At the time, the city of San Diego had one main station located in downtown, and all dispatches originated from here. It was openly broadcast on police frequencies as a red alert. Virtually all available units were given the 11-6 call – the police code for gunshots – to attend Cleveland Elementary School. It was a rare broadcast at that time in San Diego.

America's 911 emergency call system was not widespread in 1979, unlike the 999 system used in the UK since 1939. So, the original call from the school office was transferred to the police dispatcher by a telephone company operator.

It is uncertain which police officers arrived at the scene first, but local veteran policeman Sam Cater and rookie officer Patti Berneathy were there soon after the first flurry of shots. Cater was Berneathy's field training officer and she was to shadow his every move. They were quickly separated in the school parking lot, searching for a suspect as shots rained in from across the road.

Officers Larry Griffin and Sharon Amos arrived around the same time or soon after. Griffin focussed on tending to the students and securing the school buildings. Amos tried to make her way to the fallen principal and janitor.

As all units rushed to the area, Officers Dennis Doremus and Robert Robb were dispatched to the main San Diego police station to deploy their white police ambulance. The city of San Diego did not have formal paramedics at the time and police provided first-responder services to Cleveland Elementary, with non-emergency ambulances coming from local hospitals.

"The San Diego Police Department performed basic emergency medical transportation in converted station wagons and vans equipped with minimal medical supplies," a report on local paramedic history by the San Diego Fire-Rescue Department says. "The service was little more than loading the patient and driving as fast as possible to the hospital for medical attention."

Officers Doremus and Robb took the call from the downtown central police station. It was usually the case that emergency medical technicians and young police officers drove the police ambulances. After restocking their ambulance van following the graveyard – or overnight – shift, Doremus and Robb received the radio call reporting a shooting at a school.

They thought there wouldn't be any officers in the area because the graveyard shift was reporting off duty at the same time the morning shift was loading up. Robb and his partner were the first officers to head out on the street from downtown, even though he says, "we weren't really ready."

Robert Robb, 28, had finished his police academy training just weeks earlier and was still nursing foot injuries from attending the scene of what at the time was the worst airline disaster in American history. On Sept. 25, 1978, a Boeing 727 jetliner, Pacific Southwest Airlines Flight 182, collided in mid-air over San Diego with a small Cessna.

Both planes smashed into the ground over the central city area of North Park, killing 144 people and destroying 22 homes on the ground.

While in the academy, Robb was called to the scene and worked the crash site with other police recruits when the heat of burning wreckage melted the asphalt and his shoes at the same time. He realised he had first and second degree burns only when he arrived home and found his melted socks stuck to his feet. Despite his injuries, Robb says he still was instrumental in preventing looting during the mayhem in North Park.

Calls on police radio said children were being shot, with two people down. The calls reported that graveyard shift officer Cater had turned around before coming off duty and had gone to the scene first. He put out the call and was giving updates from Cleveland Elementary.

"He was telling everyone to *not* come in at the front of the school because that was where the shooting was going on," a frantic radio call reported.

As Robb recounted, he and Doremus "threw all our stuff in the Ford police van/ambulance and went."

It was "one hell of a ride, and I was driving". Racing through morning rush hour traffic Robb drove through the middle of centre dividers and down the wrong side of the road. Robb said he did every "freakin' thing you could imagine to get there."

Robb and Doremus arrived at the back of the school off Lake Angela Drive and went through the gates into the playground. Parking the ambulance right up against the back of the building on the tarmac of the playground, they grabbed the gurney, oxygen tanks, and first-aid kits and went running down the main outdoor walkway.

Both officers wore small white bullet protectors. They could hear bullets passing by their heads and bouncing off the walls.

"At the end of the hallway was a bunch of kids huddling with a teacher behind a chain-link fence area covered with ivy. You could hear the bullets flying through the ivy, so we got the kids and teachers into a nearby classroom that was right there."

Once they were sure the students were safe, they looked out to the right and saw Principal Wragg and the janitor, Mr. Mike, lying motionless on the ground.

Robb said he "saw a police officer laying out there in the middle of the ground, hiding. So, I turned to my partner, and I told him, I'm going out there to see what I can do to help them. Before he could say anything, I grabbed the first-aid kit, ran down the steps, and headed for the parking lot.

"There was a little planter area there with a big tree in it, and that's where I was going to go. But it just so happens that at the same time I was heading for that tree – a female officer who had arrived on the scene from the other side was heading for that same tree. And there was only room for one of us. So, I let her have the tree, and I just dove for cover down on the ground."

The female officer was Sharon Amos (now Amos-Newberry), who had already started to evacuate children to safety. Amos and Cater were still trying to identify the location of the shooter as they knelt for cover.

As Robb hit the ground his first-aid kit broke open and all of its contents flew in different directions. There was a short break in the shooting with Robb assuming the shooter was reloading. He started to roll back and forth between the victims, checking their wounds and making assessments. At the time Robb believed they had several gunshots in their chests. He checked in with the other officers nearby; all said they were fine.

Robb started to pick up the contents of his spilled medical bag, which had fallen into the sidewalk and plants in the small area. "I was looking for the chest-wound sealers, and I was going to slap them on."

As Robb turned and looked down, he was hit by a bullet that went straight into the right side of his neck.

"At the time I didn't know it, and I'd thought I'd just been grazed. But in actuality, the bullet had gone into my neck, nicked my carotid artery, bounced off my shoulder blade, and lodged against my fifth thoracic vertebrae. Well, it took me a few seconds, but I shook it off and went back to work trying to patch people up."

Robb continued giving treatment to the fallen men and "luckily, I didn't get hit a second time".

Patrolman Doremus began to shepherd scared children into an open door and said, "You could hear bullets ricocheting off the fence." Doremus could see Robb had been shot, but he did not know how badly.

"He was wearing a body protector, and he thought a bullet had ricocheted off it," Doremus told reporters. Robb told me he was actually shot straight into his neck but was so full of adrenaline he mistook the shot for something bouncing off his bullet protection vest.

As Officer Ted Kasinak headed to the school from his beat in North Park, he received calls from the dispatcher saying continued shots were being fired.

The 27-year-old officer arrived to the east of the school. He stopped to put on his white bullet-proof vest over his tan polyester uniform. In the 1970s these vests left much of the neck, shoulders, and lower midsection completely exposed.

"The old vests back in 1979 did not offer as much protection as the newer vests that were issued over the years," Kasinak told me.

From his position on the slight incline he could see SDPD ambulances driving across the playground to the rear of the school buildings. Kasinak could also hear the gunfire.

"I heard SDPD officers calling out over their police portable radios that they needed 'Cover now,' and they were being 'Shot at' in front of the school. I immediately responded to their calls for help and drove southbound."

As Kasinak approached he saw a large white refuse truck with a blue "Sanitanier" sign on the side. His first thought was "this truck was bigger than my police vehicle and would provide a bigger shield for the officers at the front of the school."

The truck was already travelling east towards the school, so Kasinak waved down the driver. He told him he needed the truck *now* because of a shooting down the road!

The driver pulled the emergency brake and jumped from his seat with the engine running. Kasinak jumped into the truck and put it in gear. He was joined by his colleagues, Officers Mike Blakely and Dennis Christensen, who had seen the exchange and came to support.

"I told Officers Blakely and Christensen to ask the driver how to release the emergency brake. They told me to look for the yellow knob." It took Kasinak a moment, but he found it on the large centre dashboard.

With the truck in gear and rolling, Blakely jumped on the running board, and Christensen ran alongside this beast of a vehicle. As they drove they could now hear the gunshots coming from the south side of the road.

With the school coming up on the left and the shooter on the right, Kasinak ducked down behind the huge centre compartment in the truck, turned left into the east driveway of the school and narrowly avoided a van parked in the first space.

From the driver's seat, Kasinak could see officers Robb, Amos, and Cater lying on the grass near the principal and janitor. He bumped the truck over the kerb and walkway, deep into the grassed area.

With shots still being fired all around him, Kasinak had successfully blocked the shooter's view of the school entrance. He shut down the truck and took a position by the left rear wheel with Blakely and Christensen. The manoeuvre had successfully provided a shield to officers and protected the evacuation of the victims.

"At this time, a volley of shots was fired at us in the front of the school. I saw the rounds striking the front of the walls of the building and around us," Kasinak said. He remembers waiting for the shots to end.

"I went over to where the victims were lying with gunshot wounds. I assisted other officers in placing victims on gurneys for transportation to the hospital."

He assumed his hiding place at the rear wheel of the garbage truck to try and scout the shooter's location. From this position, he could see Officers Griffin and Berneathy pinned down behind parked cars in the front parking lot. Kasinak did not know Berneathy at the time as she was a new recruit, but he would come to know her well during her turbulent time with the SDPD.

"We then noticed movement at the front door of a house directly across the street from the school and believed it to be the location of the suspect."

This information was immediately radioed to the dispatcher who broadcast it to present and arriving officers. Kasinak remained at the rear of the trash truck, giving as many details as possible to the dispatcher.

Officer Robb managed to rise and get back up the nearby stairs, and with Doremus's help, brought the gurney down. Supporting officers helped load Wragg on the gurney and strapped him down ready for transport. Robb grabbed what was left of his first-aid kit, and Cater grabbed the oxygen bottle. They all started to move towards the steps leading to the walkway and their police ambulance. As they went past the truck the gunfire started up again when the team came into the view of the shooter for a brief moment.

Doremus was pulling the gurney on one side while Robb was treating the victim and trying to keep his own end up. Cater was holding the oxygen tank on the other side trying to steady the equipment. While travelling up the stairs, Robb's right arm gave out on him, and he dropped his end of the gurney.

"Luckily, I caught the gurney with the belt buckle of my gun belt, so he didn't fall all the way down," he said about the victim he was transporting.

Robb screamed in pain, and Cater took his side of the gurney. They and Cater continued down the covered walkway with Robb's right arm hanging to his waist. Arriving back at the ambulance, they loaded up Wragg and shut the doors. Robb managed three steps around the side of the vehicle and was heading for the driver's side door when he collapsed.

Doremus picked Robb up and loaded him into the back with the victim. He then jumped in the driver's seat while Cater jumped in the back with Robb and Wragg. The full ambulance started racing the four miles to Alvarado Hospital.

The team radioed ahead to the hospital and just before arriving, they started CPR. Robb tried to begin chest compressions despite his injury, and Cater assisted with the airbag as they rolled into the loading bay. The doors flew open, the attending medical staff grabbed the gurney and pulled Wragg out as Doremus continued CPR.

Cater helped Robb from the back of the ambulance and helped him into the emergency room. Once inside, Robb was put on his own bed but appeared to refuse treatment.

"They cost like $40 for a damn uniform shirt and 50 bucks for a pair of pants," he complained to the nurses. He was already missing his service weapon and did not want anyone cutting off his uniform. Disoriented and confused, Robb removed his own uniform and police belt, only releasing it to his sergeant. He was finally sedated and taken to the operating room.

3

LIVENS UP THE DAY

AS THE POLICE and ambulances raced to the scene, San Diego Evening Tribune police reporter Frank Saldana was picking up the police calls on his scanner from his base at the station. Frank was a seasoned and personable correspondent, intentionally placed at the main cop shop to grab breaking stories.

He immediately recognised this as out of the ordinary and called it into the newspaper's head office. Chief assistant city editor Bernie Hunt took the call and awaited more details. Frank was an "action man, sent to the scene for immediate impact," Hunt would later say.

Hunt is a lifelong journalist from the UK and also my father. I visited the Evening Tribune building often and know many of the reporters from that bygone era.

On the fourth floor at the Tribune's impressive building in Mission Valley the editors were reaching their deadlines for the first afternoon edition. Having received the information of the shooting from Saldana downtown, city editor Mike Walker and Hunt sent all available reporters to the scene to get the story.

With all active reporters already out tramping their usual editorial beats or hitting the streets for this story, Hunt walked down to the "politics corral" and threw a phone directory to Steve Wiegand.

It was shortly before 9am, and Wiegand was in the office early. Steve was a 27-year-old politics writer who had finished his master's degree in mass communication in San Jose only about 18 months before. The Tribune was his first newspaper job, and he already had been a city hall and general assignment reporter before the shooting.

Wiegand would later say he "looked as goofy as you'd expect a 27-year-old San Diego surfer to look in the late 70s. I was 6ft tall and on the thin side, with curly blonde-brown Afro-style hair, a porn-star moustache and wire-rimmed John Lennon-style glasses."

Hunt told Wiegand about the breaking story and pressed him into service to start calling houses near the school to see if he could track down witnesses to the events.

The first number Wiegand called was the house across the street from the incident.

"When you are fishing for witnesses through the directory, you get very few results," Steve recalls. "So, just getting someone to answer the phone on my very first call was a bit of a win, since we were on a pretty tight deadline."

Wiegand was surprised that someone answered and slightly more surprised when it was the voice of a young girl.

It was just after 9am, and the person identified herself as "Brenda."

Wiegand asked if she had heard the shooting or if she knew anything about the incident.

"Yes, I saw the whole thing," she replied.

Wiegand did not know that Brenda had paused her shooting spree to answer the phone.

This break in the action was what Kasinak was waiting for as he hid behind the trash truck. Officers on the scene started their removal of victims and finished rushing others to safety. Officers Griffin and Berneathy would have sneaked a peek and seen the shooter was not at her post by the front door. They slipped stealthily out from behind the cars in the parking lot and into the school.

Wiegand recalled thinking, "cool, I can get something to the city desk quickly."

He asked "Brenda" if she knew who did it and where the shots were coming from. She said she saw everything – it was a 16-year-old kid, and the shooting was coming from 6356 Lake Atlin Ave.

"Isn't that your address?" he asked, thinking she may have been confused by the question.

"Sure, who do you think did it?" she responded with a laugh, before hanging up the phone.

Wiegand immediately thought she was fooling around since that was the address he had just called. He immediately called back, thinking it was a joke, and would ask if an adult was available to speak with.

The young woman answered the phone fairly quickly, and Wiegand was able to establish that he was a reporter and wanted to ask a few questions. Brenda asked if she was being interviewed and agreed to chat for a little while. She said she started shooting about 8:30am, just as school started. She said she used a 22-calibre rifle her father gave her for Christmas. She also said she told her dad she was too sick to go to high school at nearby Patrick Henry.

Only a month prior, Brenda received a shiny new rifle for Christmas. Her father thought she was ready for her own gun, and her brother bought her a matching trigger lock for safety. For years she practiced shooting with her trusty pellet rifle on cans and other small targets in the backyard or on trips to the mountains. She had become a brilliant shot. Her family in Arkansas took her hunting while on vacation and saw no reason why she didn't have a weapon already.

Her father, Wally thought she deserved a reward for her hard work at school. He gave her a 10/22 Ruger carbine semi-automatic rifle with a scope and 500 rounds of ammo. She had already proven she was adult enough for such a gift and promised to take care of it. Brenda cherished the weapon and always kept it cleaned and in its case.

The Ruger 10/22 rim fire semi was more than half her height with an 18.5in barrel and hardwood stock. Weighing only five pounds, even with its four-power magnification scope it was easy to hold and load its 10-round rotary magazine. These weapons were first produced in the mid-60s and were immediately popular.

Ruger advertised it as the perfect gift for an inexperienced or young shooter. With virtually no recoil and inexpensive ammunition, it quickly became America's most popular rifle. Ruger have sold well over a million since it was introduced.

"I just started shooting. That's it. I just did it for the fun of it," she continued. During this longer conversation, Wiegand stood up at his desk, realising he actually might be speaking with the sniper. He made hand signals for city editor Walker to come over.

"I just don't like Mondays. Do you like Mondays? I did this because it's a way to cheer up the day. Nobody likes Mondays," Brenda said calmly.

When Wiegand asked why she opened fire on people she did not know, she responded: "What's so different about that?"

The girl spoke about her father, giving his full name and place of work but said she did not know what he did there. She said he was Wallace E. Spencer, and he worked at San Diego State University, but she did not think he was a professor.

Brenda added that she was worried about what her father would think and what would happen when he found out about the shootings.

"My dad's going to kill me when he gets home and finds out about this. He's going to flip. This will really blow him away," she said.

Walker arrived and sat next to Wiegand as he continued his conversation with the confessed sniper.

On the phone, Wiegand told the girl she might have shot three or four innocent people.

"Is that all? I saw lots of feathers fly," she responded with disappointment. She said she was sure she had hit more people.

In the middle of a sentence, she stopped herself to say, "Oh oh, somebody's moving around outside. If he gets close enough, I'll shoot him too."

Moments before hanging up for the second time, Brenda said: "I nailed me a good pig, and I want to shoot some more."

Wiegand said, "her demeanor during both calls was calm and quiet, no shouting or hysteria in her voice. There was no slurred speech, or much emotion at all. While in the first, I was pretty sure it was just a teenager putting me on, I believed what she was saying in the second phone call."

After she hung up, Wiegand turned to Walker and said he was pretty sure he had just spoken to the sniper. All reports coming in were saying the point of origin was the house across the street from the school. Wiegand had definitely spoken with the shooter.

Walker decided to have Wiegand start writing the story and get something out for the first edition. The fast-approaching deadline was just 25-30 minutes away. As Wiegand started writing up his notes in story form, Clarence A. "Gus" Stevens was given the number and told to call back again and keep the girl talking.

Stevens was slightly older than most reporters at the Tribune and well known for reaching deep into the personalities when reporting. He was a sober reflective man with wire-rimmed glasses and a patchy beard.

Hunt brought him in to help cover the story from his normal post in features because he was available and competent. In his free time, Stevens wrote more than 100 romance novels, and perhaps he was the right person to delve into the mind of a teenage female shooter?

Stevens took Wiegand's place and rang back at about 9:15. Brenda answered again.

Stevens introduced himself and to his surprise she was still interested in talking.

She said she had never shot anyone before but that she had been in some fights.

"They usually don't last long. I usually open up their skulls with a cleaver," she said.

Stevens then asked her why she was shooting at people.

"I don't know. It just popped into my head. About last Wednesday, I think," she said.

Stevens prompted her, and Brenda began a short story about her older brother and sister; she also spoke about her mother and father being separated.

Brenda made it clear that she was alone in the house.

"Do you think I would be doing it if someone was home?"

Brenda continued her story as Stevens frantically made notes.

She said she had been in trouble with the police before for burglary and shoplifting saying, "But it never went to court. I always got off."

Stevens considered his questions carefully and asked if she had chosen her victims at random or shot at particular people. Brenda responded, "No one in particular. I kind of like the red and blue jackets," before hanging up for the final time.

It was about 20 minutes past 9am, and Brenda did not fire another shot.

As Stevens was trying to call back and continue the interview, city editor Walker told him to "knock it off". Wiegand and Stevens were never directly contacted by the San Diego police during any of the conversations with shooter Brenda Spencer.

It would have been a small scandal if the public knew the Trib reporters made contact with the suspect before the cops. Wiegand believed the police had been in contact with Brenda between their calls, and she rumbled them. The police had contacted the newspapers telling them they were interfering with an investigation and to clear the line immediately.

Confusion strained the relations between San Diego police and the Tribune that day. The newspaper reported that it had alerted police that its reporters had spoken "with a possible suspect." But rumour had it that the police chief was "pissed off" that Spencer's line was busy when cops tried to call her.

But what is clear is that first responders and school staff carried out a military-style operation during these calls. While Brenda was clearly entertaining herself by bragging to Wiegand and Stevens, potential victims were sneaking off to safety. These calls fall exactly at the same time as most of the evacuations from the front of the school. Perhaps the combination of the truck blocking her line of sight, and the phone ringing was the reason she gave pause to the attack?

Wiegand went on to work the political desk at the SF Chronicle and Sacramento Bee. He has authored a number of historical books like U.S. History for Dummies and The Mental Floss History of the World.

Gus Stevens became the TV and radio critic for the Union-Tribune and passed away in 2011. As well as the romance novels he wrote a book about home safety. Neither journalist has written about Brenda Spencer after 1979.

4

SWAT

DURING THE THREE phone calls from the Tribune reporters lasting about 20 minutes, the police and teachers were scrambling to rescue injured students. The nurse's office was now full of half a dozen of the injured, and Principal Wragg had just arrived at the hospital.

The janitor, Mr. Mike, who was now safely shielded by the garbage truck, was loaded up and rushed off to Alvarado hospital. The police were arriving in numbers and neighbours were coming from their houses to see what was going on.

Children were hiding in classrooms with a few teachers taking refuge in the windowless bathrooms at the end of the building blocks. The cafeteria's southern wall faced the shooter, but it was a solid brick building and the largest enclosed space in the school.

Dozens of children arrived there from the playground or ran up the walkway and around the corner as instructed by teachers evacuating the main entrance. Teachers rested a piano with tables and chairs against the southern wall as protection against the gunfire. Students were positioned on the floor and huddled together awaiting instruction from the police.

"We barricaded the exposed wall with tables and chairs and pushed the piano across the door. The kids lay face down on the floor. They were terrific, just terrific," said Wanda Carberry, the fourth-grade teacher, who had 23 years' experience at the school.

Once police HQ had established it was a sniper situation, senior officers assembled the SWAT team and assigned San Diego Police hostage negotiators and detectives. In 1979, SDPD had three murder teams, and with a death toll unknown, Homicide Teams II and III were assigned to investigate and began building the background of the case.

Sgt. John Kennedy headed Team II, and because Sgt. Paul Ybarrondo was on vacation that week, Sgt. Ted Armijo headed Team III. The two teams met at a hastily established command post in the nearby Navajo Shopping Center. Patrol officers briefed both teams, and it was decided that the different teams would take opposite sides of the road when the scene was secured.

Police contacted Brenda's father, Wallace 'Wally' Spencer, at his workplace at San Diego State University and directed him to return to the scene. Detectives also located her mother, Dorothy "Dot" Spencer, working as an accountant with the Andy Williams Golf Tournament in Torrey Pines on the San Diego coast. She first said she was unable to leave because Fuzzy Zoeller had just won the tournament the night before, and she had a table of money to count. Eventually, Dot gave in, and an officer drove to Torrey Pines to collect her.

It was about 9:30am, and for the next 90 minutes the police would slowly give way to the incoming SWAT team. The acronym SWAT stands for Special Weapons and Tactics, a military-style police formation of specially trained officers. They arrived at different times from all over San Diego.

Marty Duitz, a member of the SWAT sniper team, remembers, "We were regular patrol officers who carried all our SWAT gear with us and when a 'Code 10' was broadcasted, we stayed free of calls until it came out as a 'Code 11,' then we reported to the command post."

In 1979, SWAT members were regular uniformed officers given special additional training each month. In Duitz's case, he did monthly sniper team training.

Some years later, SWAT membership would become a full-time job with many police officers seeing it as a holiday of working out, SWAT training and shooting with the occasional journey to a crime scene.

"Wow, what a gig," said Duitz. If only he had known things would change, he said, he would not have transferred into investigations in the 80s.

With the help of a couple on-duty detectives, SDPD set up the first command post behind San Diego Glass and Paint in the southern corner of the Navajo Shopping Center. This large parking lot and semi-secluded area was about three blocks northwest of the scene, on the corner of the street which ran parallel to Lake Atlin with the school's playground in between. This was the perfect location for officers to reach the school's rear safely and still give quick access to the hospital and freeways.

In the upper-level classrooms, teachers were huddled with students.

"No more shots were heard, but we remained there for a long time before a policewoman escorted us into the girl's restroom, very crowded," recalls Mrs Miyashita. "I had brought my portable radio with me, so we sat on the floor, ate cookies, and listened to reports on what was happening."

She recalls the tiles and high windows of the surroundings but remembers the freezing students most on that cold January morning.

"I heard radio stations airing the tragedy and speculating whether there was more than one shooter. I opened the door slightly and was shocked to see the SWAT team coming down the ramp," she said.

Mrs Miyashita remained as calm as she could so the children did not start to panic. Before long, the police asked her to turn the radio off to shield the kids from the news that was about to break.

At Alvarado Hospital the "General Blue" alert sounded just after 9am. This alert meant police ambulances would soon be arriving with casualties. Memories were stark for emergency room staff of the last "General Blue" alert – the horrific PSA crash a few months before. Everyone braced for the worst.

Principal Wragg was the first to arrive and was taken to surgery just after 9:15am. He died 35 minutes later. His wife, Kathe, was contacted by the police and rushed immediately to the hospital. Sadly, she arrived shortly after he passed away.

"No, no, no, don't tell me that he's dead!" she cried. "He can't be dead. He's not dead."

"Mr. Mike" Suchar was pronounced dead on arrival. His wife, Tina, was also called to the hospital and taken to one side to be told the sad news. She broke down in tears and cried in her German accent, "No, no, he can't be dead. Please come back to me."

Reporters gathering in the emergency room heard the distraught wives. But families declined to speak with the journalists.

The injured Officer Robb was carried into an adjoining room, refusing to let medical staff remove his uniform. He was left alone for a minute to undress and remove his police belt. He realised his service weapon was missing and asked his partner Doremus to help him recover it.

The nine-year-old Cam Miller arrived in the same ambulance as Suchar. He already knew Mr Mike was dead, remembering that at one point, the janitor's lifeless body rolled onto the boy as the ambulance rounded a corner at speed.

Cam was given the gurney, and Suchar, presumed dead by hospital staff, was taken into the hospital on a stretcher. The boy's mother arrived later, and he asked her what had happened to Mr Mike, confirming what he already knew.

Cam had been in the auditorium awaiting medical attention, still not sure he actually had been shot.

"My left arm and shoulder went numb, my entire body trembled," he recalled. Cam was lucky, as the bullet passed straight through him, entering just under his shoulder blade and missing vital organs.

Cam's father, Charles, heard on his car radio of a shooting at his son's school. He returned home, where neighbours said his son was one of the victims.

"On the way back, I was doing a little praying," Miller told reporters. "I didn't think it would be right to pray that it would be someone else other than my son, but I prayed that at least it would be minor, and my prayers were answered."

The other nine-year-olds – Christy Buell and the first victim Monica Selvig – arrived at the hospital at the same time. Both were in critical condition with internal bleeding and abdominal wounds. They were rushed straight into surgery with all the operating rooms now taken. After surgery, both their conditions were downgraded to stable.

Christy's father, Norm, had walked up to the blockade near the school where police told him his daughter was on her way to the hospital. "Which hospital?" Norm was heard asking.

He arrived at Alvarado with one of Christy's dolls for good luck. Norm knew his way around the hospital. He lost Christy's mum to leukaemia there six years earlier.

Monica's father, attorney Lee Selvig, burst into the emergency room, beseeching, "Is there somebody here who knows about my daughter?"

The distraught father then pushed past social workers on duty, saying, "Pay me the courtesy of finding out how my daughter is." A doctor told Selvig that Monica would recover from her abdominal wounds after surgery.

Wilfred Suchar, Mr Mike's son, was told of the shooting by his wife who was listening to the radio and called him at work. He quickly raced home, grabbed his wife, and went to his mother's house. Wilfred found her singing to herself while gardening in the backyard.

The Suchars called ahead to get news of Mr Mike's condition, but the hospital was unable to give details over the phone. Worried, shocked, and fearing the worst, the trio raced to Alvarado. They learned he was declared dead on arrival and his body had already been moved into the basement morgue.

For about 30 minutes from 9am, "the information desk handled about 150 calls from parents, other relatives and friends of children who attend the school," hospital social worker Don Berk told Tribune reporters. "Fortunately, no one who called us had children involved in the tragedy." Police and hospitals, with help of school secretary Mary Smith did all they could to make sure all victims' families were notified as soon as possible.

Officer Sharon Amos had spent the last half hour getting children to safety and settling the situation for teachers. Behind the trash truck, she was able to collect the injured 4th grader, Greg Verner, as he was struggling to walk after being shot in the buttocks.

With Crystal Hardy in the front seat and Greg lying face down in the back of her patrol car, Officer Amos set off rapidly for Alvarado Hospital. En route she was told to report instead to Grossmont Hospital.

She arrived about 9:20am. Both children were clearly in pain but were not crying. Crystal walked quickly to medical staff outside the ER entrance and was greeted by a nurse. Medical staff lifted Greg from the back seat and carried him, facedown and stiff as a board, into the emergency treatment area.

Shortly after, ten-year-old Julie Robles arrived in a police ambulance driven by Officer Bob Sylvester. Smiling, she was strapped to the gurney, still in her brown coat with fluffy cuffs and collar, Sylvester in his uniform, sunglasses, curly black hair, and moustache.

At about 9:45 a.m., the youngest victim, seven-year-old Audrey Stites, arrived at Grossmont still holding her lunch bag. She was a little behind the others because she had wanted to see her teacher first and introduce herself to police officers.

Television news crews filmed the arrivals, looking for all the world like some scene straight off primetime TV.

About an hour later, all the children at Grossmont were reported in good condition and out of danger. They were readied for release and were taken home, one by one.

Crystal Hardy was released fairly quickly considering the bullet went straight through her wrist. But it did not hit the bone or injure anything major. With a huge bandage on her right hand and a surgical glove blown up like a balloon, she made her way to her mother's arms. They stopped to chat with a news crew from San Diego's TV Channel 8.

"We are just praising the Lord," Liane Hardy said as she bent down and kissed her daughter on the cheek.

Julie Robles was released to her father, Refugio, at about 11am. With her father next to her and his arm around her, the girl spoke with reporters. She retold her story and tried to smile as her father pulled her closer.

Greg Verner was later transferred to Kaiser Hospital in La Mesa on his parents' instructions.

5

CALLING ALL UNITS

RECORDED RADIO DISPATCHES show the San Diego Police Department sent more than 90 uniformed officers into San Carlos that morning.

Among other things, police established a command centre and created traffic and crowd control points on surrounding streets. As the radio contact continues and police negotiators begin to take positions, officers radioed in to say they are 10-97 – arrived at the scene.

DISPATCHER - "39 TOM, GO AHEAD."

39T - "DO WE HAVE SOME BEHIND THIS BROWN HOUSE TO SEAL THIS GUY UP, DO WE?"

DISPATCHER - "THAT'S AFFIRMATIVE, 42 ZEE IS BEHIND THE HOUSE. THE HOUSE BEHIND IT HAS BEEN EVACUATED AND HE IS IN POSITION."

42Z - "42 ZEE I'M ON THE ROOF OF THE WHITE HOUSE BEHIND." 42Z - "42 ZEBRA."

DISPATCHER - "42 ZEE."

42Z - "I KEEP POKING MY HEAD OVER THIS ROOF WATCHING THE BACK DOOR."

DISPATCHER - "42 ZEE, WHAT'S YOUR ETA BACKUP?"

Police officers took various positions to keep the perimeter contained. Locking the scene down to not let anyone in or out was standard procedure. Eventually the SWAT team would arrive and take control. Police radioed in as much information as they could while also keeping a keen eye on the shooter's house.

DISPATCHER - "39TOM, ARE THEY STILL FIRING?"

39T - "NO, NOT SINCE THAT LAST FLURRY, I'LL TELL YA."

DISPATCHER - "10-4."

The last shot fired was one at the trash truck, or perhaps Officer Kasinak as he stood behind the left rear wheel. He was not hit, but the building school behind him was struck many times as the shooter desperately sought a target.

Traffic units and supervising lieutenants started to radio in looking for assistance in blocking the roads and using their vantage points to identify civilians at risk. By now, all officers were aware of the success of the trash truck maneuver, and a local sergeant suggested commandeering another large vehicle. He was told it could help but was deemed unnecessary.

DISPATCHER - "10-4 ON THAT."

Just after 9am, the San Diego police checked with the County sheriff's department and requested the use of their aircraft program. In 1971, the newly appointed Sheriff John Duffy had rolled out the Law Enforcement Helicopter Patrol.

Named the Aerial Support to Regional Enforcement Agencies in tribute to Astrea, the Greek goddess of justice, the unit was free of charge for all public safety agencies in San Diego. The sheriff's department had two Bell 47 model choppers, one of which it dispatched to San Carlos. San Diego police also would dispatch its reconnaissance plane. Separate radio frequencies used by the two aircraft would spark a small concern.

ASTREA (HELICOPTER) - "THERE IS A DOG IN THE BACKYARD, SUSPECT'S BACKYARD. ASK THE UNITS AT THE

REAR IF THEY SAW ANY ACTIVITY AT THE WINDOW BECAUSE THE DOG, AH, STARTED WAGGING ITS TAIL LOOKING AT THE WINDOW, FOR A MOMENT."

42Z (OFFICER ON THE HOUSE BEHIND) - "NEGATIVE ON THE SIDE WINDOWS AND NOTHING AT THE BACK DOOR. AND I CAN'T SEE ANY OTHER WINDOWS BECAUSE THERE'S A TREE IN FRONT OF ME. BUT IF YOU SEE ANOTHER MOVEMENT, BE SURE TO LET ME KNOW"

ASTREA (HELICOPTER) - "10-4."

DISPATCHER - "743, ARE YOU 10-97." - (CODE FOR "ARRIVED AT SCENE")

743 - "I'M AT THE COMMAND POST BEHIND THE GLASS AND PAINT COMPANY."

DISPATCHER - "10-4. CAN YOU ADVISE IF THEY NEED A PRIVATE ARMORED TRUCK TO GO OUT THERE? "

743 - "ASK 732, HE'S AT THE SCENE AND HAS A BETTER VIEW OF WHAT'S GOING ON."

DISPATCHER - "732, CAN YOU ADVISE IF YOU NEED A PRIVATE ARMORED TRANSPORT OUT THERE?"

710 - "USE THE SWAT VAN, IT'S ARMORED, THAT'S WHAT IT'S OUT THERE FOR."

With all the known victims either arriving at or en route to the hospitals, concern arose about possible overcrowding. But three hospital emergency rooms were virtually equidistant from Cleveland Elementary.

753 - "ALVARADO CAN HANDLE EVERYBODY, LET'S BRING THEM ALL HERE."

DISPATCHER - "10 -4. BRING ALL THE 11-41S TO ALVARADO, ALVARADO CAN HANDLE ALL OF THEM. WE HAVE 51 HENRY TO ALVARADO WITH TWO." - (11-41 IS CODE FOR "AN AMBULANCE NEEDED")

10S - "10 SAM, WE HAVE AN AMBULANCE ON ROUTE TO ALVARADO WITH TWO, AND THERE WILL BE A POLICE CAR EN ROUTE WITH TWO MORE SHORTLY. 10 SAM, AS FAR AS I KNOW, THAT'S ALL THE VICTIMS ARE EN ROUTE TO HOSPITALS NOW."

DISPATCHER - "OK, CONFIRMING ALL THE VICTIMS ARE GONE FROM THE SCHOOL NOW AND TO THE HOSPITAL."

10S - "10 SAM, AFFIRMATIVE. ALL OF THEM THAT I KNOW OF ARE EN ROUTE TO THE HOSPITAL NOW. (INAUDIBLE) AH, ALL OF THEM, ONE TO GROSSMONT BEFORE THAT."

DISPATCHER - "10-4. IS THE 11-44 STILL THERE?" - (11-44 IS CODE FOR "POSSIBLE FATALITY")

44J - "44 JOHN, ALL THE 11-41S ARE GONE AND THE 11-44, THERE IS STILL ONE GIRL. AH, STAND BY."

This victim taken from the school to the hospital would turn out to be seven-year-old Audrey Stites.

32D - "32 DELTA ON ROUTE TO ALVARADO WITH TWO."

DISPATCHER - "32 DELTA TO ALVARADO WITH TWO."

Cops had established a clear safety zone behind the school, and officers began to converge on the known origin of the shooting. First thing was to establish a good line of sight to the suspect and first responders had entered the house next door to the east.

Until this point, police had not openly communicated who the suspect was or how many there might be. In fact, all police transmissions described the suspect as male, although Mike Walker at the Tribune had long since passed the information that the shooter was a young female to desk officers at the main police station.

It was clear that there was someone in the house, but it was not clear if other suspects might have escaped and be on the run. Even though the shooting had stopped some time ago, the threat was still apparent. The next 10 minutes of radio dispatches were almost frantic.

732 - "CAN I GET ONE OF MY UNITS NEAR THE SCHOOL TO START COMMUNICATING WITH ME SO I CAN GIVE BETTER INFO?"

DISPATCHER - "UNIT 30 DELTA… UNIT 30 DELTA. OK, UNIT 39 TOM."

30D (KASINAK)- "30 DELTA."

DISPATCHER - "UNIT 30 DELTA, ARE YOU STILL AT THE SCHOOL?"

30D (KASINAK) - "AFFIRMATIVE, BEHIND THE TRASH TRUCK."

DISPATCHER - "31 LINCOLN."

31L - "I ASKED IF WE HAVE ANY OFFICERS ON THE HOUSE NORTH OF THE SUSPECT'S HOUSE."

DISPATCHER - "OK, UNITS FOR THAT ARE URGENT. STANDBY FOR A MINUTE… UM, COMMAND POST 743?"

732 - "CAN YOU GIVE ONE UNIT AT THE SCHOOL SO WE CAN COMMUNICATE DIRECTLY? "

DISPATCHER - "I HAVE SOME INFORMATION REGARDING A POSSIBLE SUSPECT. IS THERE A UNIT CLEAR TO COPY? 743? 732? WE HAVE A POSSIBLE SUSPECT DESCRIBED ONLY AS BEING BRENDA. A WHITE FEMALE. 16, SHE'S A STUDENT FROM PATRICK HENRY. HER LAST NAME POSSIBLY IS SPENCER. I HAVE A PHONE NUMBER. IS THE COMMAND POST SET UP SO YOU CAN CALL FROM THERE?

743 - "NEGATIVE, BUT I'M SURE THAT (INAUDIBLE) AND THAT COMMAND POST NEXT DOOR SHOULD BE ABLE TO GET TO A PHONE. "

DISPATCHER - "(INAUDIBLE) YOUR UNIT NUMBER?"

753X - "753, WE ACTUALLY HAVE TELEPHONES, CHANGING FACILITIES, EVERYTHING HERE."

DISPATCHER - "10-4. CAN YOU COPY THIS NUMBER? 461-2345, HER NAME'S BRENDA. A POSSIBLE SUSPECT IN ALL THIS."

753X - "10-4, I'VE GOT HER… CAN WE HAVE A NEGOTIATOR?"

DISPATCHER - "753 X, DO WE HAVE A NEGOTIATOR?"

753X - "NO, THAT'S WHY I'M ASKING YA."

24S - "24 SAM, CAN WE GET A SHOTGUN FOR THE EAST SIDE OF BUILDING FOR THE UNITS THAT ARE UP THERE. WE AT LAKE ANGIER AND LAKE ADELINE" (HE MEANT LAKE ANGELA AND LAKE ATLIN).

DISPATCHER - "44 JOHN."

44J - "OK, ALL THE 11-41S (AMBULANCE IS NEEDED)

ARE GONE. 11-44 (POSSIBLE FATALITY) IS GONE. RIGHT NOW, THERE IS AN 11-48 (FURNISH TRANSPORTATION) A SMALL GIRL, ON HER WAY. THEY HAVE BEEN REMOVED."

DISPATCHER - "10-4. ALL THE VICTIMS ARE OUT OF THE AREA. HAVE ALL THE RESIDENCES IN THE AREA BEEN ALSO EVACUATED AND SECURED?"

Bill Palm was the SDPD negotiation supervisor at the main command post in the Navajo Shopping Center. He sent two of his team, Det. Paul Olson and Det. Chester 'Chet' Thurston to the scene to set up their own command post nearer the shooter. They were driven up Lake Atlin Ave. in a SWAT van and set up shop in the house next door.

Det. Thurston began calling the suspect with his bullhorn and Olson got on the house phone and began calling Brenda. Rescue operations continued.

NEGOTIATOR THURSTON - "I'M ABOUT 20 YARDS AWAY FROM THE WINDOW WHERE THIS WOMAN'S LOCATED. - I HAVE RANG NUMEROUS TIMES, AND NO ONE HAS ANSWERED IT."

732 - "CAN YOU GET ME ONE OF MY UNITS THAT'S BEHIND THE SCHOOL THAT'S PRETTY WELL ON TOP OF THE SITUATION THAT I CAN COMMUNICATE WITH?"

DISPATCHER - "UNIT 51 HENRY CHRISTENSEN GO AHEAD WITH UNIT 732. AND I NEED THE NUMBER FOR THE COMMAND POST, 753X DO YOU HAVE THAT AVAILABLE?"

31H (DOREMUS, OFFICER ROBB'S PARTNER) - "31 HENRY ALVARADO EMERGENCY."

DISPATCHER - "31 GO."

31H (DOREMUS) - "YOU WILL HAVE TO TAKE THE REST OF THEM TO GROSSMONT AS ALVARADO IS FULL. "

DISPATCHER - "10-4, ALL THE REST OF THESE 11-41S (AMBULANCE IS NEEDED) ARE GOING TO GROSSMONT. ALVARADO IS FULL."

45K - "45 KING. ARE YOU AWARE, I HAVE ONE 11-41 AT THE REAR OF THE SCHOOL IN THE PARKING LOT?"

DISPATCHER – "NEGATIVE, WE ARE NOT AWARE OF THAT. YOU KNOW 122 CAN YOU HANDLE? IS THERE AN AMBULANCE FOR ANOTHER 11-41 TO THE REAR OF THE SCHOOL?"

24H – "24 HENRY, WE ARE ON LAKE MURRAY AND JUST GOT THE INTERSTATE 8, AND WE'LL CAN RESPOND."

DISPATCHER – "DO I HAVE A PHONE NUMBER YET FOR THE COMMAND VAN? "

753X – "753 X, IT'S 461- 2181."

DISPATCHER – "10-4."

DISPATCHER – "FOR ANY AMBULANCE WHO ARE JUST NOW MOVING INTO THE AREA OR FOR ANY UNITS. THE SNIPER IS GOING TO BE ON LAKE ATLIN ACROSS THE STREET FROM THE SCHOOL. AVOID THAT AREA. THERE'S GONNA BE A 11-41 TAKEN OFF… TO THE REAR OF THE SCHOOL. THEY WILL DIRECT YOU IN FROM THERE."

DISPATCHER – "510, 10-4. WHAT YOU NEED?"

510 – "ONE FEMALE VICTIM WITH A SHOT IN THE SIDE NEEDS IT."

DISPATCHER – "YEAH, 53 X."

53X – "OK, THE DAUGHTER IS ALONE IN THE HOUSE, THIS IS HER FATHER HERE. HER FATHER IS COMING ALONG WITH THURSTON TO THE COMMAND POST. THEY HAVE 500 – 600 ROUNDS OF AMMUNITION, AND IT'S A 22 SEMI-AUTOMATIC RIFLE SHE HAS."

DISPATCHER – "I AM REPEATING THIS INFORMATION. OK, THE FATHER OF THE SUSPECT, KNOWN ONLY RIGHT NOW AS 'BRENDA', IS EN ROUTE TO THE COMMAND POST. HE ADVISES THAT SHE'S GOT 5 TO 600 ROUNDS OF AMMO INSIDE THE HOUSE."

DISPATCHER – "44 JOHN, GO AHEAD."

44J – "JUST TO ADVISE YOU, WE DO HAVE A SWAT OFFICER OUTSIDE OF THE SCHOOL (INAUDIBLE) WHO IS GOING TO HANDLE IT."

Almost all empty police ambulances were making their way back from Alvarado Hospital. Any injured would go to Grossmont hospital, the closest to the scene, until further notice.

Astrea, the Sheriff's helicopter, was asked to set down at the command post in the Navajo Shopping Center. The incident would alarm onlookers and give rise to worries by concerned residents and parents with children in the local schools. Officers were forced to move motorists and rubberneckers out of the area.

Moments later, traffic sergeant Gary Morris read out assignments for traffic and crowd control.

Most of the official traffic stop locations Morris read out were already being manned, but he had a lengthy list of local street intersections that needed to be double checked.

Police worried the sniper, who had been quiet for a while, might pick a new target and begin firing again. They feared the large, newly built Summit Park Condominium complex could be within easy range. The complex had a stretch of dwellings directly behind the kindergarten and slightly elevated over the school. The area was very difficult to control with balconies and a large parking lot in view of the shooter. The condos were filled with young adults and new families.

Meanwhile, crowds of onlookers – terrified parents of children at the school, journalists, and so-called lookie-loos drawn to the scene by news coverage – were growing and becoming difficult to control. Officers feared they, too, might prove a possible target. Community service officer Nancy Kaiser had her hands full.

At the corner of Lake Atlin and Lake Angela, parents pleaded with police for information. Ruth Ann Miller was frantic as she waited for news about her two children in the school, Dawn, 13, and Brett, 10.

Jennifer Engle told reporters her oldest daughter had called her saying she was in the playground. So, the mother made her way down to the school. Engle's daughter, Jennifer, 10, had walked right through the danger zone and was rushed to safety by a teacher. Her father later called the hospital and was told his daughter was not among the injured.

Teresa Neal arrived with her mother and asked reporters in reference to the shooter, "Who are they? Who are they? I have three kids in that school!" and "This is horrible… Where is this man!"

Her mother tried to help by saying, "It could just be a rumour."

A father of a 10-year-old at the school named Robert Stephens was addressing the situation slightly differently. He held up a Budweiser can to a *San Diego Union* reporter just after 10am and said, "This is my nerve-satisfier." He was standing in his driveway a small distance from the school and out of harm's way.

"It's weird man, I tell ya," he said, while shaking his head side to side.

Radio calls continued as police prepared for an evacuation of the school. In all the confusion, children went many directions to avoid danger. Some ran straight home the way they arrived; others hid in the large playground in the rear.

Police first had to account for as many children as possible, working with teachers to identify their full classes. Officers made the decision to evacuate from the rear of the school to Pershing Junior High School nearby, when it was safe to do so. They believed this was the most logical place for parents to assemble and await their children. If the situation required the SWAT team to unleash gas at Cleveland Elementary, the kids would be safely far away.

510 – "WE'RE TRANSPORTING SOMEBODY ABOUT EIGHT, FROM THE REAR OF THE SCHOOL THAT NEEDS SOME PROTECTION."

DISPATCHER – "UNIT 130 MARY."

130M – "WHERE DO WE ADVISE PARENTS, WHO WANT TO CHECK ON THE WELFARE OF THEIR CHILDREN, TO GO?"

DISPATCHER – "ALL THE 11-41S, ALL THE INJURED, ARE GOING TO BE TRANSPORTED OR ARE ALREADY TRANSPORTED TO ALVARADO AND THEN TO GROSSMONT. CHECK THOSE TWO LOCATIONS. "

130M - "ALSO, A FAIR FEW HAVE BEEN ASKING IF THE SCHOOL HAS BEEN EVACUATED?"

UNKNOWN - "(INAUDIBLE) ALL THE STUDENTS ARE, APPARENTLY, ON THE FLOOR INSIDE THE SCHOOL. I THINK THERE'S TWO OFFICERS - ALSO A COUPLE WOUNDED INSIDE THE SCHOOL?"

DISPATCHER - "10-4. THE SCHOOL HAS NOT BEEN EVACUATED; THE CHILDREN ARE INSIDE AND DOWN ON THE FLOOR. THERE ARE OFFICERS INSIDE TO MONITOR THAT SITUATION."

UNKNOWN - "THEY ARE DEFINITELY CODE 4 (NO FURTHER ASSISTANCE IS NEEDED) IN THAT AUDITORIUM. THERE'S A BRICK WALL AND THEN THE WALL TO THE AUDITORIUM AND THEY ARE ALL LAYING ON THE FLOOR."

DISPATCHER - "ASSURE THE PARENTS YOU'VE GOT THERE THAT IT'S DEFINITELY CODE FOUR INSIDE. THEY'RE IN THE AUDITORIUM AND THERE'S BRICK WALLS THERE. THEY'RE INSIDE AND DOWN ON THE FLOOR."

WITHOUT MISSING A BEAT, THE DISPATCHER CHANGED DIRECTION TO SEE WHERE THE OTHER CHILDREN MAY BE.

DISPATCHER - "YA KNOW, 510, WHERE DID YOU TAKE THOSE CHILDREN AND PEOPLE YOU HAVE? THE ONES THAT WEREN'T INJURED."

510 - "I HAD ABOUT EIGHT KIDS THAT WERE EXPOSED AT THE REAR OF THE SCHOOL. THEY WERE TRANSPORTED OUT ON AH… IT'D BE THE WEST SIDE OF THE SCHOOL AWAY FROM THE AREA."

It was announced that all ambulances responding to the area were using TAC or tactical communications. TAC was the term used for on-scene communications without using the dispatcher. In other words, they would be speaking ambulance to ambulance so they would not disturb the police operation going on at the school.

DISPATCHER - "42 Z IS BEHIND THE SUSPECT HOUSE. THE HOUSE BEHIND HAS BEEN EVACUATED, AND HE'S BEEN TRYING TO WATCH THE REAR OF THE HOUSE… 42 Z ARE YOU STILL AT THE REAR OF THE HOUSE?"

42Z - "I CAN HAVE A VIEW OF THE WHOLE BACK OF THE HOUSE, (INAUDIBLE) AND I LET YOU KNOW IF ANYTHING MOVES BUT I JUST CAN'T KEEP MY HEAD POKED OVER THE ROOF. "

DISPATCHER - "42 Z IS ON LAKE ARIANA BEHIND THE HOUSE."

42Z - "42 Z, ALSO THIS WOULD BE A GOOD SPOT FOR A SWAT OFFICER IF WE COULD GET ONE OVER HERE."

DISPATCHER - "YEAH, 42 Z."

42Z - "CAN SOMEONE GET A SHOT BACK OVER HERE UNTIL WE GET A SWAT GUY UP HERE? "

DISPATCHER - "CAN SOMEONE GET THE SHOTGUN BACK TO THEM? THEY'RE BEHIND THE HOUSE… ON LAKE ARIANA."

120J - "SHAUN, I'M A SWAT OFFICER, AND I HAVE A SHOTGUN."

42Z - "ABOVE PATROL UNIT 479, IT'S THE HOUSE RIGHT BESIDE IT."

120J - "WHERE'S THE AREA ON ARIANA, DIRECTLY BEHIND THE HOUSE THAT NEEDS A SHOTGUN?"

ASTREA 14L (HELICOPTER) - "HE'S ON THE ROOF OF THE HOUSE TO THE REAR AND THE WEST BEHIND THE SWIMMING POOL. RIGHT, THE HOUSE RIGHT IN FRONT OF UNIT 479."

120J - "120 JOHN. 10-4."

Sgt. James McFadden (751x) was the leader of the SWAT team and placed himself at the east end of Lake Atlin and began to formulate a plan to end the siege.

His first move was to understand the layout of the terrain and possible hazards. He called out to anyone with a view of the scene and collected intel from them.

ASTREA 14L (HELICOPTER) - "14 LINCOLN TO 751 X, I HAVE A GOOD SIGHT OF THIS HOUSE … (INAUDIBLE)"

751X (MCFADDEN) - "10-4. HAVE HIM ADVISE ME, HOW MUCH SHRUBBERY OR WHICH SIDE OF THE HOME HAS THE MOST SHRUBBERY?"

DISPATCHER – "WHICH SIDE OF THE HOUSE HAS THE MOST SHRUBBERY, 14 LINCOLN?"

ASTREA 14L (HELICOPTER) – "IT'D BE CLOSEST TO THE NORTHEAST. RIGHT IN THERE IS A WOODEN FENCE WOULD BE (INAUDIBLE) TO THE BACK YARD OF THE HOUSE. OVER."

DISPATCHER – "NORTHEAST SIDE. YEAH, FROM THE NORTHEAST SIDE SEEMS TO, AND THERE'S A WOODEN FENCE IN THE BACK AND SIDE OF THE HOUSE."

751X (MCFADDEN) – "10-4. THAT'S NORTHEAST SIDE, UM, IS THAT THE FRONT OR THE REAR OF THE HOUSE?"

ASTREA 14L (HELICOPTER) – "REAR OF THE HOUSE."

751X (MCFADDEN) – "10-4. OK, THAT'S ONE TEAM NOW, ASK 14 LINCOLN FOR THE SECOND TEAM IN THE FRONT SO WE COORDINATE. "

ASTREA 14L (HELICOPTER) – "WE'VE GOT TWO OFFICERS DOWN AT THE HOUSE NEXT DOOR ON THE EAST SIDE (INAUDIBLE) WHO WERE PLACED OFFICERS, BUT THEY DON'T HAVE GOOD VIEW."

DISPATCHER – "THEY WANT A LOCATION IN THE FRONT OF THE HOUSE FOR A SECOND TEAM, 14 LINCOLN."

ASTREA 14L (HELICOPTER) – "BEST PLACE IN FRONT OF THE HOUSE WOULD BE THE SHRUBBERY ACROSS THE STREET IN THE SCHOOL YARD PARKING LOT BUT THERE'S NO OTHER COVERING ANYWHERE."

751X (MCFADDEN) – "IS THERE ANY HIGH GROUND OR ON TOPS OF BUILDINGS IN THE AREA SO WE CAN HAVE A VIEW DOWN RATHER THAN STRAIGHT ACROSS INTO THE OTHER HOMES?"

ASTREA 14L (HELICOPTER) – "THE ONLY HIGH GROUND HERE IS THE SCHOOL DIRECTLY ACROSS FROM THE FRONT OF THE HOUSE."

510 – "GET AHOLD OR TO TELL ALL THE SWAT UNIT, APPARENTLY, THEY… AH… ASKED THAT IF SOME OF THE KIDS WERE MAYBE MOVED FROM THE SCHOOL. WE HAVE, APPARENTLY, ALL THE KIDS ARE OUT WITH THE EXCEPTION OF ABOUT 75 WHO ARE EITHER IN THE AUDITORIUM OR BACK WITH SUFFICIENT MANPOWER GUARDING BOTH LOCATIONS. I ADVISE THAT WE DON'T REMOVE THEM ANYMORE."

DISPATCHER - "510, 10-4."

A FEW MINUTES LATER:

DISPATCHER - "510, GO."

510 – "OK, WE HAVE ALL THE KIDS THAT ARE REMAINING, THAT REMAIN AT THE SCHOOL, AT THE BACK OF THE SCHOOL IN EITHER THE BATHROOMS OR SECURED AREAS THAT WE DO HAVE SUFFICIENT OFFICERS HERE TO GUARD."

DISPATCHER – "OK, 10-4, 510. ADVISING, IT'S CODE FOUR (NO FURTHER ASSISTANCE) AND FIVE (STAKEOUT) AT THE SCHOOL. ALL THE CHILDREN ARE PROTECTED NOW."

10S – "10 SAM, WE HAVE ONE MORE 11-48 (FURNISH TRANSPORTATION). I ASSUME WE HAVE A CAR HERE TO TAKE IT OUT. WE SHOULD HAVE ONE MORE AMBULANCE COME IN OFF LAKE ASHMERE, ALL THE WAY ACROSS THE SCHOOL TO THE EAST SIDE OF THE PLAYGROUND AND DOWN BY THE SCHOOL IN CASE ANYTHING HAPPENS, WE WILL HAVE ANOTHER AMBULANCE AVAILABLE AT THIS LOCATION."

DISPATCHER – "10-4, ALL THE AMBULANCES ARE ON TAC RIGHT NOW WITH SGT KRAL. 4 HENRY IS 10-4, AND I'LL GET THE INFORMATION TO THE REST OF THEM."

10S – "WE HAVE ONES IN THE CORNER, AH, OF THE STREET IN FRONT OF THE SCHOOL. WE NEED ONE ON THE SCHOOL GROUND. ONE MORE WILL DO IT."

DISPATCHER – "711 IS HANDLING THAT INCIDENT ALL THE OTHER AMBULANCES ARE ON TAC."

10S – "10 SAM, WE HAVE ONE MORE 11-48, SUPERFICIAL WOUNDS. I'LL TAKE IT OUT TO LAKE ASHMERE AND WILL GRAB AN OFFICER THERE 11-48 IT."

DISPATCHER – "4 HENRY SHOULD BE BEHIND THE SCHOOL NOW, 4 HENRY?"

10S – "SAVE HIM, THIS CAN BE A MANNED 11-48 (INAUDIBLE)."

DISPATCHER – "10-4 THEN, ONE PATROL UNIT TO GO BEHIND THE SCHOOL UP ON LAKE ASHMERE FOR AN 11-48 (FURNISH TRANSPORTATION), A SUPERFICIAL WOUND OUT OF THE AREA, IDENTIFY… ONE PATROL UNIT TO IDENTIFY TO ASSIST 10 SAM 11-48 OUT OF THE AREA FROM BEHIND THE SCHOOL."

The dispatcher was fully aware that Sgt. Frank Kral was at the scene and overseeing the police ambulance activity in the area. Kral had been a sergeant for more than 10 years and was a key figure in SDPD ambulance patrol. He was the trainer in the Academy for Advanced First Aid and did most of the EMT training for new SDPD officers. He was someone all the attending officers would have known and respected.

6

ONLOOKERS

WORRIED PARENTS WERE starting to congregate at all traffic stops on or near the scene. The corner of Lake Atlin and Lake Angela, along the fence line of the school and one of the school's exit points for children, was just 500 yards west of the Spencer house; parents, reporters, and onlookers crowded in. Sgt. Dave Kelly was assigned to secure the scene and prepare for SWAT to arrive from the east.

Local resident Gordon Dale assisted with crowd control as he focused his binoculars on the school, hoping to spot his five-year-old grandson. He was uninjured and was eventually reunited with him later in the day.

130M - "130 MARY, PARENTS ARE ASKING IF THEY CAN PICK UP THEIR KIDS WHEREVER THEY HAVE BEEN EVACUATED TO. WHERE OR WHAT DO I ADVISE?"

DISPATCHER - "OK, IF THEY ARE OUT OF THE AREA THEN THEY HAVE BEEN 11-48'D HOME, AT ONE OF THOSE HOSPITALS, OR THEY ARE SAFE INSIDE. THEY ARE NOT GOING TO TAKE MORE OUT. "

130M - "10-4. BUT DO YOU WANT ANY PARENTS GOING OVER TO TRY AND PICK THEM UP IN ANY LOCATION?"

DISPATCHER - "NEGATIVE FOR NOW, THEY ARE ALL TAKEN CARE OF OR SAFE INSIDE. THEY DON'T WANT ANY OTHER PEOPLE INTO THE AREA."

130M - "10-4. BUT DO YOU KNOW WHAT LOCATION THEY ARE BEING EVACUATED TO?"

DISPATCHER - "THE LOCATION TWO BLOCKS NORTH OF THE SCHOOL, SOME OF THE TEACHERS TOOK THE CHILDREN UP THERE."

700 - "700 KELLY. THE PEOPLE AT 6400 LAKE ATLIN, SOME OF THEM ARE STARTING TO COME OUT OF THEIR HOUSES SO WE ARE SENDING TWO UNITS, CORRECTION TWO OFFICERS, TO ADVISE PEOPLE TO STAY IN THEIR HOUSES.

DISPATCHER - "THE UNIT WHO IS ON LAKE ATLIN, THE EAST END, IDENTIFY!"

700 - "700 KELLY, I'M AT THE EAST END."

121A - "IF SGT. KELLY CAN MOVE AROUND TO THAT END, WE CAN MOVE OUT TO THE WEST END".

Sgt. Kelly was asked what he thought of onlookers as he patrolled the cordon.

"It's a vicarious thrill. What would they be doing now, watching 'Days of Our Lives'?" he mused.

Kelly's experience told him that people like to see blood, and some onlookers would be prepared for a long day.

"As long as she talks, we wait," he said.

As the injured continued to become known, police swiftly moved to get them to hospitals. Audrey Stites, the seven-year-old who was the fifth person shot, was found hiding in the school. Officers were finally able to transport her to the hospital by police car.

508 - "I'M MAKING AN 11-48, ACTUALLY AN 11-41 (AN AMBULANCE IS NEEDED) FOR A FEMALE. SHE'S GONE TO GROSSMONT. SHE'S GOT AN ELBOW, A HURT ELBOW."

DISPATCHER - "508, 10-4. WHERE DID YOU TAKE ALL THOSE OTHER KIDS THAT YOU TOOK OUT OF THE AREA? "

508 - "WE MADE AN 11-48'D THEM HOME."

DISPATCHER - "10-4. SOME OF THESE CHILDREN HAVE BEEN 11-48'D TO THEIR HOMES."

Audrey was taken to Grossmont Hospital where her father met her.

"She won't say very much about what happened… she is kind

of in shock. It's hard to say what is going on in her mind," Frank Stites told reporters. Audrey, the youngest person injured in the shootings, was treated and released in less than two hours.

The SWAT team continued to radio in with a direct instruction from Sgt. James McFadden:

751X (MCFADDEN) - "ONE POLICE OFFICER TO 10-87 AT LAKE ARIANA AND LAKE MURRAY BLVD., MAKE IT CODE 2 (URGENT). GET SOMEONE OVER HERE WHO CAN DIRECT US BY WALKING INTO THIS SITUATION SO I CAN POSITION MY PEOPLE."

DISPATCHER - "120 JOHN, CAN YOU HANDLE THAT? YOU'RE ALREADY ON LAKE ARIANA; JUST GO DOWN TO LAKE MURRAY AND DIRECT THEM IN?"

120J - "10-4. DO THEY WANT TO GO IN THE BACK OR THE FRONT?"

731 - "CAN YOU TELL 751 X-RAY THAT I HAVE THE GIRL'S FATHER IN MY CUSTODY, AND I CAN BRING HIM TO HER. SO THAT WE CAN ESTABLISH COMMUNICATIONS IF HE DESIRES."

751X (MCFADDEN) - "751 X-RAY. DISREGARD ON THAT AND HAVE HIM HOLD HIM AT THE CP AT THE PRESENT TIME UNTIL I GET MY PEOPLE IN POSITION."

731 - "731 IS 10-4. IF HE NEEDS HIM, HE CAN CHANNEL REQUESTS THROUGH TO ME."

751X (MCFADDEN) - "10-4."

Almost an hour since the last shot was fired, the SWAT team learned the family next door to Brenda Spencer's house had not been evacuated.

39T - "309 TOM, THE HOUSE NORTH OF THE HOUSE WE ARE INVOLVED WITH, IT'S A WHITE HOUSE HAS NOT BEEN CLEARED. YOU MIGHT NOTIFY THE SWAT OFFICERS TO THAT FACT."

DISPATCHER - "IS THAT NEXT TO THE SCHOOL ON LAKE ATLIN STILL?"

39T - "IT'S RIGHT ACROSS THE STREET FROM THE

SCHOOL, IT'S A WHITE HOUSE. HAS NOTHING PARKED IN THE DRIVEWAY, AND IT'S JUST NORTH OF THE… BROWN HOUSE THAT WE ARE INVOLVED WITH?"

32D - "32 DELTA, THE ADDRESS IS 6368"

DISPATCHER - "WE'LL TRY AND CALL THEM."

At Alvarado Hospital, Officer Robb was fighting for his life. Once he was on the operating table, his partner, Dennis Doremus, discovered that his service revolver was missing. Doremus radioed in from the hospital as soon as he realised it was missing.

31H (DOREMUS) - "CAN YOU FIND OUT IF ANY UNIT AT THE SCENE HAS PICKED UP A HANDGUN FROM OFFICER ROBB?"

DISPATCHER - "ANY UNIT AT THE SCENE PICK UP A HANDGUN FROM OFFICER ROBB? "

30D (KASINAK) - "30 DELTA, ASK HIM IF HE WAS OVER AT THE 11-41S JUST IN FRONT OF THE SCHOOL?"

31H (DOREMUS) - "OUT IN FRONT OF THE SCHOOL."

No record exists to say Officer Robb's weapon was ever found.

As SWAT officers continued to form their plan to end the situation, they called on the sheriff's aerial support for help. Officer McFadden appears to be well-known to the pilot as they map out where his team is to be positioned.

Kasinak and Christensen stayed on the scene near the trash truck that impeded Spencer's view to keep an eye on the suspect's house and offer as much support to SWAT as possible. They are fully aware that once the SWAT team arrives, they are to surrender their positions.

ASTREA 14L (HELICOPTER) - "TO 751X. JIM, ARE YOU AWARE THAT WE HAVE TWO PATROL OFFICERS IN THE HOUSE NEXT DOOR, DIRECTLY ACROSS FROM THAT PLACE.

DISPATCHER - "751X, HE'S TELLING YOU THAT YOU GOT TWO OFFICERS RIGHT NEXT DOOR. BUT YOU KNOW THAT, THEY SAID THAT THEY DID NOT HAVE GOOD POSITION AT ALL."

751X (MCFADDEN) - "ARE THEY ON THE GROUND FLOOR OR THE ROOF?"

ASTREA 14L (HELICOPTER) - "THEY ARE ON THE GROUND IN THE HOUSE TO THE EAST. "

751X (MCFADDEN) - "I'M GOING TO HAVE ONE TEAM GO UP ON THE ROOF WHERE THE POLICE OFFICERS ARE THAT ARE TO THE NORTH AND THE WEST OF THE RESIDENCE IN QUESTION."

UNKNOWN - "SGT. MCFADDEN, ARE GOING TO MOVE IN ON THE FRONT ALSO?"

Occupants of the house next door said the SWAT team cleared them safely from their house and escorted other occupants on Lake Atlin to safety.

DISPATCHER - "THEY SAID THAT THEY DIDN'T HAVE GOOD COVER FROM THE FRONT. THE ONLY PLACE WAS A SHRUBBED AREA ACROSS THE STREET AT THE SCHOOL. IS THERE A SWAT TEAM 10-97 AT THAT LOCATION?"

751X (MCFADDEN) - "751 X-RAY, WE ARE PRESENTLY LOOKING OVER THAT SITUATION TO PUT THEM IN THE BEST SPOT. SO, STAND BY."

710 - "710. 751 X-RAY, I'M UP ABOVE SO IF YOU GOT ANY PROBLEMS LET ME KNOW."

UNKNOWN - "SGT. MCFADDEN, ARE YOU AWARE WE HAVE AN OFFICER DIRECTLY CROSS THE STREET BEHIND THE TRASH TRUCK?"

DISPATCHER - "30 DELTA, IS THAT YOU BEHIND THE TRASH TRUCK DIRECTLY ACROSS THE STREET?"

30D (KASINAK) - "AFFIRMATIVE."

51H (CHRISTENSEN) - "CHRISTENSEN'S ALSO THERE, 51 HENRY."

UNKNOWN - "SGT. MCFADDEN, ARE YOU AWARE HE HAS VERY GOOD OBSERVATION FROM THE TRASH TRUCK, THERE?"

DISPATCHER - "39 TOM, IS THAT A GOOD POSITION FOR A SWAT TEAM. IS THERE PROTECTION THERE?"

39T - "VEHICLES WOULD PROVIDE GOOD PROTECTION; HOWEVER, THE VIEW IS HINDERED SOMEWHAT."

DISPATCHER – "751X. 39 TOM AND 32 ALPHA SAY THEY ARE DIRECTLY ACROSS THE STREET FROM THE HOUSE IN QUESTION IN THE PARKING LOT OF THE SCHOOL. CARS THERE WOULD PROVIDE COVER; HOWEVER, THE VIEW WAS HINDERED, THEY SAID."

With civilians now under lockdown and away from harm, SWAT officers had suited up from the gear in the trunks of their cars and prepared to carry out the plan drafted by McFadden to end the crisis and capture the sniper.

Ready to move in from their group location on the west side of Lake Atlin at Lake Murray, officers called for a police ambulance to give them cover as they made their way to their assigned positions.

Police radio reports continued:

510 – "OK, ALL OF THE TEACHERS AND ALL OF THE CLASSMATES, AH, HAVE BEEN ACCOUNTED FOR WITH THE EXCEPTION OF THE VICTIMS AND ALSO ABOUT SIX OR SEVEN OR EIGHT THAT WERE TRANSPORTED FROM THE REAR PARKING LOT. AND I BELIEVE IT WAS 51 HENRY AND 508 WAS ALSO INVOLVED IN THAT, AND I BELIEVE HE SAID THEY TOOK THEM HOME."

DISPATCHER – "THAT'S AFFIRMATIVE. 508 DID SAY THEY TOOK SOME HOME. 508, HOW MANY DID YOU TAKE HOME?"

508 – "WE TOOK HOME FIVE."

DISPATCHER – "REPEATING IT IS CODE 4 INSIDE THE BUILDING, AND EVERYONE SEEMS SAFE INSIDE NOW. PROTECTED FROM ANY FURTHER FIRING."

Once all the children were confirmed safe, the police units began to clear the wider area.

The shooter had always been the main threat, but the arriving SWAT teams readied for a possible gunfight as they drew near the sniper's position. They needed innocent civilians out of the immediate area.

44J – "44 JOHN, DO YOU THINK THAT ASTREA COULD GET ON THE PA AND GET THOSE PEOPLE IN THE APARTMENTS JUST WEST OF THE SCHOOL TO GET DOWN? THEY ARE RIGHT IN THE LINE OF FIRE LOOKING OVER THE FENCE. THERE'S ABOUT 15 OF THEM."

DISPATCHER – "ASTREA, CAN YOU BROADCAST THAT?"

710 – "710, DON'T HAVE ASTREA ON THE LOUDSPEAKER!"

DISPATCHER – "IS THAT A HOLD OFF?"

751X (MCFADDEN) – "751 X-RAY, JUST GET THE PEOPLE OUT OF THERE WE DON'T WANT ASTREA TO TELL THE PERSON WHERE THE CIVILIANS ARE."

751X (MCFADDEN) – "751 X-RAY, ADVISE THE SNIPER TEAM ONE THAT WE ARE ON LAKE ASHMERE AND WE ARE GOING TO MOVE SNIPER TEAM TWO INTO POSITION, AND WE WILL ADVISE THEM OF THEIR LOCATION."

723 – "CAN YOU CALL MCFADDEN? I WAS WONDERING WHAT HIS PLANS WERE FOR THE FRONT OF THE BUILDING. THE SCHOOL IS STILL PROBABLY THE BEST LOCATION FOR OBSERVATION?"

751X (MCFADDEN) – "751 XRAY, I AM AWARE OF THAT, AND I AM 10-97 (ARRIVED AT SCENE), AND I AM DEALING WITH THAT. STAND-BY."

Moments later Sgt. McFadden made a call for all SWAT teams to switch dispatch communications and go onto a special frequency called CLEMARS, the California Law Enforcement Mutual Aid Radio System. It was normal procedure to use CLEMARS when SWAT needed a frequency unavailable to others when different police agencies worked together.

751X (MCFADDEN) – "751 XRAY, PLEASE BE ADVISED THAT THE SNIPER TEAMS, THE GAS TEAM AND MYSELF WILL BE ON CLEMARS PORTABLE."

DISPATCHER – "10- 4. SNIPER TEAM ONE, 751X IS GOING TO BE ON CLEMARS PORTABLE."

SNIPER TEAM ONE – "10-4. WE ARE THERE ALREADY."

As Brenda's mother was brought to the police command van near Lake Angela, the desk captain at the main police station in downtown San Diego managed to procure a floor plan of the Spencer house.

Sergeants at the scene asked the SWAT team if they already had the house plan or needed it. One copy was given to dispatch, and another was physically transported to the area command post from downtown. It arrived 30 minutes later, long before the interrogators made direct contact with Brenda. A rough layout of the house had already been described by her father, who had been at the scene for about 45 minutes.

The dispatcher began to give out final instructions to the officers before SWAT officers began taking over the scene. She had a number of outstanding issues or concerns to double check. There was still the problem of Robb's missing gun and the rubberneckers in harm's way at the apartment complex and neighbouring houses. Reporters' presence also caused a concern.

DISPATCHER – "THE SUSPECT'S MOTHER IS ALSO KNOWN TO THE COMMAND VAN NOW, FOR INFORMATION."

DISPATCHER – "39 TOM, WE HAVE IT THAT THE OCCUPANTS OF THE WHITE HOUSE THAT YOU WERE ASKING ABOUT BEFORE ON THE LINE, AND THEY HAVE BEEN ADVISED TO KEEP INSIDE AND UNDER COVER."

DISPATCHER – "FOR YOUR INFORMATION FOR UNITS IN THE AREA, IT LOOKS LIKE THE SHOOTING HAS BEEN DONE THROUGH THE FRONT DOOR. THAT'S PER UNIT 754."

DISPATCHER – "AND FOR YOUR INFORMATION ALSO, 11 SAM IS NOW HEADING TO THOSE APARTMENTS TO THE EAST (SHE MEANT NORTHWEST) TO TRY AND GET THOSE PEOPLE OUT OF YOUR WAY."

DISPATCHER – "SO, ALVARADO IS OPEN AND CAN ACCEPT MORE VICTIMS. ALVARADO IS ACCEPTING MORE VICTIMS."

DISPATCHER – "DID ANY OFFICER PICK UP ROBB'S GUN FROM THE HOSPITAL?"

30D (KASINAK) – "30 DELTA, YOU ASK HIM WHERE HE POSSIBLY DROPPED IT."

DISPATCHER – "DID HE DROP IN FRONT OF THE SCHOOL PICKING UP THOSE VICTIMS?"

700 – "700 KELLY, I HAVE ROBB'S PARTNER WITH ME, AND AS SOON AS IT'S POSSIBLE, WE WILL GO DOWN AND MAKE A SEARCH FOR IT."

30D (KASINAK) – "30 DELTA, IF YOU HAVE SOMEONE AVAILABLE YOU MIGHT WANT TO SEND THEM UP BY THOSE PEOPLE AGAIN. THEY ARE SITTING ON TOP OF CARS WATCHING THE WHOLE INCIDENT... THE POLICEMAN WHO IS STANDING THERE IS ALSO VULNERABLE."

DISPATCHER – "11 SAM IS THAT APARTMENT COMPLEX AND IS ABLE TO HANDLE IT. 11 SAM, THEY ARE APPARENTLY IN THE DIRECT LINE OF FIRE; AND DON'T USE ANY KIND OF A BROADCAST."

732 (COMMAND POST AT SAN DIEGO GLASS & PAINT) – "ANY MEDIA SHOULD BE REFERRED TO THE COMMAND POST. IF THERE IS ANYTHING DIFFERENT, PLEASE ADVISE."

700 – "STAND BY, THERE IS A LOT OF MEDIA HERE AT LAKE ATLIN AND LAKE ANGELA. EVERYTHING BEEN HANDLED ALL RIGHT THOUGH."

DISPATCHER – "10 -4. THEY'VE GOT THE MEDIA AT A DIFFERENT LOCATION, AND THEY SAID IT'S BEING HANDLED OK AT THAT POINT AT LAKE ATLIN, THAT'S PER 700 KELLY.

700 – "700 KELLY, RIGHT NOW I HAVE A BIG PROBLEM. THERE ARE PEOPLE ON THE FENCE, ON THE NORTH SIDE OF LAKE ATLIN. LOOKS LIKE THEY ARE AT THE REAR OF THE CONDOS. THERE'S A COMMUNICATIONS TRUCK UP HERE WITH A DISC MIC. THEY ARE RIGHT IN THE LINE OF FIRE IF SOMETHING GOES DOWN."

7

NEGOTIATIONS

AS TRAFFIC UNITS and sergeants fought back the media, onlookers, and concerned parents at a number of barricades, SWAT teams moved into place and relieved regular officers from their positions.

Officer Ted Kasinak, the police hero credited with saving many lives by commandeering the garbage truck and maneuvering it into position in the sniper's line of fire, fell back to a safer position at the rear of the school.

Marty Duitz, a 26-year-old SWAT sharpshooter on Sniper Team 2, entered the school from the rear so he was never in any view of Brenda until he took position in a small office space near the kindergarten.

"We were on the ground floor of the school and had clear sight of the house door and windows," he said of him and his assigned spotter.

SWAT snipers often were given spotters to help with the surroundings, so the sharpshooter can focus on the target without interruption. The previous September, Duitz had received a commendation for his heroism. He spotted smoke coming from a crashed and partially submerged vehicle. With gasoline leaking into the water and the engine burning, Duitz went chest deep into the flammable water and pulled a trapped driver to safety. He gave the unconscious man CPR and saved his life.

Four months later, he is in his SWAT gear across the street from an active shooter awaiting a clear shot at his target.

"This was one of two SWAT incidents in which I was given a 'green light' (authorization to shoot the suspect on sight)," Duitz recalled.

Negotiators Paul Olson and Chet Thurston did not arrive at the command centre until about 9:45am, some 45 minutes after the last shots. Police officers on the ground held the area secure while SWAT rolled in and took control.

The second command post was established in the SWAT van now parked in front of a neighbour's house and in the house itself. Negotiation supervisor Bill Palm and the detectives stayed at the paint store and tried to call Brenda, who was thought to still be in her house.

As Olson and Thurston made their way to the sniper, SWAT officers parked their white converted RV command post in front of the white house at 6344 Lake Atlin, right next door to the shooter but out of her line of sight. Police had already evacuated the neighbour's house and negotiators entered and took control of the property.

Just after 11am, Olson stood at the back of the parked SWAT van next door to the Spencers' house as Brenda's father was marched up the road from the traffic checkpoint 500 yards away.

The trip past his neighbours' houses surely would have been a walk of shame for Wally Spencer. He was a fairly normal guy of 5ft 7in, wearing a plaid shirt with jeans and a thick leather belt. At 49, he wore reading glasses and had a quiet disposition. Wally was slightly overweight with a full head of ginger hair roughly parted to one side.

Earlier, Det. Olson observed that a shaken Wally was incoherent in not being able to give much information about what may have happened that morning, other than small details of the rooms in the Spencer house.

During their short interview, Wally told Olson his daughter stayed home from school because of stomach cramps. He said she told him she might vomit and was in no condition to leave the house. He knew the signs, as Brenda often struggled with her periods and would take long baths when it was her time of the month. Wally said he just assumed it was just another one of those days.

He said nothing out of the ordinary happened over the weekend, and he was unaware of anything that could have tipped Brenda over the edge. Wally also told Det. Olson that the last six months had actually been pretty good and that he and Brenda had a good relationship. Believing he was getting little out of Wally Spencer, Olson decided to cut it short.

He told Wally there would be a longer interview at some point and certainly once police made contact with Brenda.

Olson handed Wally over to Sgt. Bob Corey, who held him at the seized house next door for a short while. Later he was escorted back behind the traffic cordon down Lake Atlin.

Chet Thurston, designated as the first primary negotiator, immediately began to attempt contact with Brenda. He set up shop in the bathroom of the seized neighbours' house, which had a small window directly facing the side of the Spencer home.

By using his bullhorn megaphone repeatedly, Thurston began to get her attention and tried to coax her to the phone. At the same time, Olson contacted the Pacific Bell telephone company to have the phone lines isolated so outsiders could not call Brenda and she could not call anyone but the officers. It took about 30 minutes, but the direct house-to-house line was established, and Olson was ready for business. He later said, "She had apparently spoken to a reporter before any of us did."

The police and supervisor Palm had been calling the house repeatedly for almost an hour, receiving only a busy signal, as if the phone was off the hook. The Tribune reporters had long since stopped their calls.

Because the shooting had stopped, it was possible the sniper had fled out the back door and over the fence, into the neighbours at the rear, and then on to Lake Ariana Ave. to freedom. It also was possible she had committed suicide. This was to become the most likely scenario in future American school shootings. But police and the SWAT team were assuming Brenda was still alive and in her home.

All sides of the house were still completely clear of police obstruction. The only thing that looked different from Brenda's perspective would be the garbage truck parked over the kerb in front of the school. For whatever reason, Brenda did not try to run. She remained in the house, possibly talking on the phone or with it off the hook. It is unclear what she was doing. It had now been more than two hours since she last discharged her weapon.

The school had been completely locked down since about 9:30am, and now all school buses were given an all clear to begin leaving.

SWAT teams were fully in place, and the suspect's house had been isolated without aggressive activity for more than two hours. At about 11:35am, SWAT told police sergeants to begin evacuating students to Pershing Junior High, as planned. The SWAT gas team assembled in the neighbour's driveway next to the SWAT van. If necessary, they were ready to unleash disabling gas on the Spencer house and its occupant.

With the help of all the officers present, the children were lined up single file and marched across the school playground and onto big yellow school buses. Parents had already been given instructions to assemble at the junior high and await their kids.

Newspapers and TV media outlets were ready and waiting too. The children were quiet as they boarded for the short five-minute journey from Lake Angela Drive.

"They were terrific, incredible. I am just enormously proud of the students and staff," said teacher Barnes.

Eight-year-old Mary Clarke quietly made her way on the bus with everyone else. She had been nursing her abdomen wound since she was shot hours before. Mary said nothing to anyone.

By noon, all the children had arrived at Pershing Junior High and Cleveland Elementary was fully evacuated.

At exactly 12:06pm, Brenda Spencer answered her phone. It was Detective Olson calling from the house next door.

As primary negotiator, Olson was to give it the first try at building a rapport with the suspect. He asked if she was OK and if she needed anything right away? Olson says she asked for a Burger King Whopper sandwich, and he agreed to get her one but only after she surrendered.

"Why do you think you are in this predicament?" Olson asked her.

"Everybody's got problems. It isn't me," Brenda replied.

Olson asked what types of weapons were in the house. She did not answer directly but did say, "The scope on my rifle had been knocked out of place once when I was out hunting. That's why it didn't shoot straight."

Before Olson responded, she continued, "Hey, do you think I can have some lunch?"

He then told her that he was interested only in caring for her safety and the safety of anyone in the area. It was best to resolve the incident as soon as possible, and then you will be able to eat, he said.

In a low monotone voice, Brenda told him she didn't have anything to do and could possibly be bored. When asked about surrendering, she said she was at home and was perfectly satisfied with where she was. "I'm having a lot of fun."

About 10 minutes into the talk, Brenda said, "You need new batteries in your bullhorn."

She said she could hear noises outside her house and could see SWAT officers around the outside of her house and across the road at the school.

"If I had wanted to, I could have shot several of them. Tell them to back off. They are pissing me off."

Olson repeated her demand to Thurston, who informed the SWAT team they weren't helping at that moment. The team moved back from their positions and out of sight. Olson would later say, "She was, let's say, 'irritated' but not raving mad. She settled down after the SWAT officers moved out of sight."

Olson asked her again what weapons she had.

"I have a pellet rifle, and I am a crack shot," she replied. "I used to shoot it a lot in my backyard. I have shot rabbits in the back of the head at 25 yards. They would feel no pain. I'm also a good shot with my .22 rifle."

"Why don't you throw your rifle out the front door through the broken window?" Olson asked.

"No way!" Brenda cried. "I don't want to injure it."

As the discussion continued, Brenda made multiple statements about her rifle and how protective she was. She didn't want anything to happen to it.

Brenda said, "It is my security blanket. As long as I have it, there is no way you will come into my house."

"What reason do you have for the shootings, Brenda?" Olson said.

"I have no reason. I just thought of doing it at the spur of the moment. I'm gonna stay here awhile. I want to have some more fun. It was fun seeing kids being shot in a group," Brenda responded.

She tried to explain that while some kids stood around looking at the victims, she would shoot the onlookers too.

"It looked like a herd of cows standing around the one that was shot. It was really easy pickings." Brenda was revelling in shooting the children.

"It was fun to watch the kids that had red or blue ski jackets. They made the best targets. It was like shooting ducks in a pond, it was so easy. I enjoyed watching them squirm around after they had been shot."

She expressed anger at Mike Suchar, the school janitor. Brenda would have known Mr Mike because she attended Cleveland Elementary about five years earlier.

She said she shot him because he was trying to get everybody off the school grounds and out of the way. She also indicated she knew exactly who he was by saying, "He was always out there ordering the kids around. I didn't think this was a good thing. I wanted to make sure I took care of him."

She said, "Also, I know I shot a pig." She told Olson she hoped to have shot other "pigs," especially the one who drove the trash truck. She said she was angry that cops had blocked her view.

Throughout the full conversation she repeated that she was "really having a lot of fun". It was especially funny for her to see the children falling after being shot, she said. Another source of humour for her was to see the SWAT team members crawling up to her residence from all directions, she said.

When Olson asked her if anything had happened that day or over the weekend that made her upset enough to shoot people, Brenda replied: "Everybody swears at me all the time. My father swears at me. I swear a lot. I grew up hating people all my life. At school, my friends. I hate everybody."

Olson asked why she hated people, and she replied again with "Everybody's got problems. I don't have any problems, but everybody else has got problems. I just grew up hating people all my life because they were mean."

When he asked again her reason for the shooting, she said, "I have no reason for doing anything. I just thought of it this morning."

At the Navajo Shopping Center command post, Bill Robinson, the San Diego Police information officer, gave a statement to assembled media.

"Good news!" he said. "We've initiated telephone contact, and our hostage negotiators are talking to her now. The only ground rule is we'll do anything to try and save her life. We are talking to the father and trying to find out why it happened."

8

SURRENDER

TWO YOUTH COUNSELLORS who said they knew Brenda arrived at a police barricade to see if they could help in any way.

A year earlier, police had arrested Brenda and a young neighbour boy for vandalising Cleveland Elementary. Officers said they broke windows and trashed classrooms.

Authorities assigned youth counsellors to work with Brenda. One of them was Noreen Harmon who met with Brenda often. In her report, Harmon suggested Brenda could be suicidal. A week later, her father Wally and brother Scott collaborated to buy her the .22 rifle and trigger lock for Christmas. Five weeks later she opened fire on the same school.

At Pershing Junior High School, students were reunited with their families. Kindergarteners to sixth graders told stories to parents and media. Parents were just happy to see their kids safe and were allowed to rush forward onto the campus.

Children without waiting parents were led from the buses into the school's auditorium. Mary Clark made her way off the bus and into the auditorium. She was hoping to see her teacher, Mrs Miyashita, and tell her all about her injury. But, when the teacher could not be found, Mary made it clear to school officials that she was bleeding.

Officer Doyle Wheeler and his partner raced for a gurney from his police van and started treatment on the little girl. She was transported to Alvarado Hospital, which was, by now, clear and ready to receive the last victim.

Wheeler said, "She went back to class and was afraid to tell anyone she had been shot." Mary did not arrive at the hospital until about 1pm.

Reporters were at the Pershing Jr. High to get the quotes.

"Me and my friend, James, were coming up the main gate when we heard these pops. It sounded like cap guns," said Paul Carr, 11.

"I thought it was all a joke, but when we saw a girl lying on the floor, James rolled her over, and she had a hole in her leg. We saw people lying there, including our principal. Mr Wragg was sitting there wheezing, trying to get his breath."

Rebecca Wexler, also 11, told the Tribune that after the shooting she was taken into an office where staff were treating one of the child victims.

Teacher Roberta Perry said, "I just can't believe it, I'm in a state of shock."

Judy Tenorio was one of the hundreds of parents waiting to spot their children through the bus windows as the vehicle pulled up.

She told reporters, "I drove five kids to that school this morning. They got out of the car just as the bullets started flying. Someone yelled at them to start running and told me to get out of there. I haven't seen them since, and I don't know where they are!"

She was soon reunited with her two youngsters. None of the kids she dropped off were injured.

The roadblock at the condominium complex near Cleveland Elementary was now crowded with a rowdy youthful group. The temperature had started to warm up, and rumours ran around the area that this was the best site for action. With all other traffic stops beginning to empty as parents raced off to collect their kids, this was the party barricade. Ex SWAT member Sgt. Kelly was moved to the western barricade to assist the SWAT team as officers were trying their best to control the area.

As about a half-dozen SWAT members moved down the road toward the Spencer house, one of the crowd yelled, "Shoot her!" The crowd was definitely up for a big TV-style show from the SWAT team. Every time a SWAT officer neared the house the crowd volume rose with many hoping they would deploy tear gas and force the assailant out of the house.

Many appeared to believe this would end in gunfire, and they were not going to miss it: This kind of stuff just did not happen in San Carlos. But the jumpy audience would not know that the San Diego SWAT team proudly boasted it never had shot a suspect. This day was not going to sully that record.

At 12:26pm, authorities cut off the electricity to the Spencer residence, but Brenda did not appear to notice. For the next 20 minutes or so, Olson started to ask about her relationship with her family and if she was upset with her father. Brenda had continually refused to discuss her father until Olson asked her if she had any message for him.

"Yes, I do. Tell my dad to go get screwed," she said, adding, "I grew up hating people, and I will never change my mind."

Over the next half-hour Brenda stayed on the line but was not very responsive. Olson found himself doing most of the talking and struggling to engage her. A little after 1pm and without being prompted, Brenda started to offer details about her mental state, "Oh, I've seen a shrink. I gave him three pages of notes, but that's all."

Then she began to share her drug history as if she was chatting.

"I use dope. I even fight my friends over dope deals. My father gives me $5 a week allowance. He has been supporting my dope habit for about five years."

When Olson asked her what kind of dope she used, Brenda said,

"I use any dope that I can get my hands on. Today I took some downers, smoked some pot, and drank some beer and whiskey."

She paused for a second and then curiously said, "Let me give you some advice. Don't chew bubble gum and drink whiskey at the same time. It ruins the bubble gum, and you have to throw it away. Also, M&Ms and beer are a bad combination. It'll make you sick." Brenda began to roar with laughter.

Olson wanted to let her speak freely but decided to change the subject and ask a few reasonable questions.

"What did you do over the weekend?"

"I stayed at home all weekend. A friend of mine by the name of M&M visited me. He is 13 years old and lives in Santee," said Brenda. Santee is a further eastern suburban area in San Diego County.

Olson was not sure who M&M was or if he mattered, but he did not interrupt Brenda, and she continued to say, "I like to fight. Whenever I fight, I fight dirty. I had a fight with a friend over a dope deal. He had ripped me off. I had to split his head wide open. It was a gaping wound that needed stitches. I also gave him a concussion."

She was on a roll and finished the story.

"Whenever I leave my house, I always carry a hunting knife, and at night I always carry a knife up my sleeve or a fishing knife in my pocket. That way the pigs won't be able to find it. I'm very good with a knife. At all times I carry one."

She started to brag about shoplifting ammunition from different stores in the area. She said she sometimes does it for her friends, "and from time to time I have stolen ammunition from my father's van. I totally ripped him off. He never even knew. Of course, he's never home to find out anything anyway."

This was largely bragging from the 16-year-old who had only just received her weapon about a month before. Perhaps she was talking about stealing ammunition for her pellet rifle. These small containers would be easy to smuggle from the shelves of a sporting goods shop.

As the negotiation carried on past 1:30pm, Olson asked how many phones were in the house. He wanted to find out which one she was using so he could get her location in the home. The Tribune's Wiegand and Stevens already had concluded that Brenda could see out of the front of the house on the phone she used to speak to them.

She told Olson there were two phones, but she refused to tell him which she was using. Olson could now tell that Brenda was getting bored or tired from the suspected drugs and drink. During this period, she told him, "I'm reloading my rifle. I have plenty of ammunition."

She now complained she was tired and her ears were hurting because of all the time she had been talking on the phone. At 1:40pm, Olson lost contact with her, and it is assumed that she just got bored and hung up.

At 1:48pm, Brenda answered the phone again, and Olson asked her what she had been doing. She sounded angry and said, "I heard noises in the front yard. If they don't stop, I'm going to do something else."

Olson asked fellow negotiator Thurston to speak to SWAT leader Sgt. McFadden again to have his officers stay back and turn their radios down so that Brenda could not see or hear them. He said she needed to calm down again.

A few minutes later at 1:55pm, Brenda told Olson she had boxes of ammunition for her .22 calibre semi-automatic rifle. "I have more than half of the ammunition left."

Brenda's father had told police his daughter might have as much as 600 rounds of ammo available. Brenda made it clear that she had a large amount and could be there all day if she wanted to.

At 2:10pm, Olson suggested that she should surrender, and Brenda said she would think about it. Olson then suggested that they hang up for a bit and let her think about things. He told her he would call her back in 20 minutes. Brenda said she didn't have a good memory and would probably forget their discussion about her surrendering before he called back.

Twenty minutes later, Olson called back after discussing the best way to end this siege with fellow detectives. Brenda immediately picked up. He started by suggesting she leave the house and lie face down on the sidewalk with her hands above her head.

Brenda refused but began to ask questions regarding her eventual arrest.

"Am I going to juvie or the police station? Am I going to be handcuffed?"

Olson understood that she wanted to be taken from the scene in handcuffs. But Brenda said she was prepared to stay awhile, rolling the conversation back about an hour. Olson told her the electricity had been turned off but thinking to himself that she should know this.

Brenda said, "I don't believe you,"

"Go check it out," Olson told her.

"Okay, I will." After a few moments she said, "I didn't think you would do something like that. Everything is going down just like on television."

Brenda told Olson she liked to watch SWAT shows. She also asked if she would be given a lawyer and what the charges against her would be. Olson said the charges would not be up to him, but that if she requested a lawyer, one would be given to her once she was in custody.

Olson also reminded her that the Whopper from Burger King she had asked for in the initial conversation would be hers once she was in the police vehicle.

Switching topics, Brenda said, "Bugs Bunny will be coming on at three o'clock. Let me tell you, watching Bugs Bunny and listening to the stereo is really something."

Then Brenda said, "If I shoot at the police, they will shoot back."

"That's not a good idea, Brenda. You don't really want to do that," Olson responded. "If you have been watching the SWAT movies, you know if a police sniper is assigned to do his job, it will end in tragedy."

Brenda became increasingly agitated again, and the negotiators believed she was considering another attack.

"If you do that, Brenda, I can't control the SWAT officers," Olson said.

Searching for something she could identify with, he added, "They will probably lob gas into your house, and your animals will probably die from the fumes." Brenda had spoken about animals, assumed to be a rat, gopher snake, and dog but she did not give in.

"Well, if that is what has to be done, that's what has to be done. They have to take care of themselves," she said.

Probably after earlier seeing the media vans arrive on Lake Ashmere and within her line of fire, she asked if she was on television.

Olson did not know the extent of the TV coverage but did agree that there was media interest in the area.

"That's great!" she said. Then she told him she would have to sit back and think about things.

"Keep talking to me. You're making progress," Olson replied.

They continued to speak, and Brenda relaxed her position and finally agreed to leave her house and place her rifles on the ground. She agreed to then re-enter the house and bring out the ammunition. Olson told McFadden's SWAT teams to stay out of sight.

Brenda asked, "Should I leave the rifle unloaded or loaded?"

Olson suggested she unload it.

A few minutes later, 16-year-old Brenda Spencer casually left her house and walked about 15ft into the middle of the driveway. She was carrying her brand-new .22 rifle and her pellet gun covered in a dark grey sweatshirt.

She unwrapped the guns and slowly laid them next to each other on the concrete. She then turned and calmly wandered back into the house, dropping the sweatshirt to her right. She got back on the phone as instructed.

To Det. Olson, she was eager and cooperative, so he asked her to pick up all the ammunition and place it outside. He suggested she not put it "too close" to the weapons. "It'll take me a while. There's ammunition all over the house," she replied.

About five minutes later she got back on the phone and said, "Okay, I've got it."

Brenda exited her house for the final time with an arm full of .22 ammunition. The front door was still wide open. She walked down to the end of the driveway, stepping around the two rifles and almost to the sidewalk. She lowered the armful of ammunition boxes to the concrete and looked to her right. Two SWAT team members with shotguns had sneaked their way in front of the garage window and into her view. A few other SWAT officers raced towards her from her left. Brenda did not resist but was startled as she rose slowly to her feet. She was apprehended at 3:06pm.

Brenda was standing directly behind her brother's old green pick-up truck, her hands handcuffed behind her back. Two SWAT officers who came from her right escorted her across the street with another three storming the house to secure the area.

Brenda Spencer stood only 5ft1in and weighed about 90 pounds. She chose to dress in boys' clothes and even though she was 16, turning 17 in April, she looked a few years younger. Brenda was painfully skinny and slight with very little female development; if she had short hair, people might have taken her for a 14-year-old boy.

Brenda also wore wire-rimmed aviator glasses with long, orange hair reaching all the way down to the middle of her back. She wore it straight with a parting down the middle. Even as a child she'd often look as if she had never seen a comb; perhaps this was because she did not live with her mother and did not have a close relationship with her older sister.

She was taken through the school parking lot, out to the back of the school and put into the back of Ted Kasinak's patrol car. Kasinak and patrolwoman Patti Berneathy were selected to bring her downtown to SDPD homicide division for a formal arrest.

"I directed the SWAT officers with Brenda Spencer to my police vehicle, where she was placed in the rear seat," Kasinak said.

Many assumed that Kasinak should be the person who got the "collar" for his heroics earlier in the day. Without his idea to block the view of the shooter by maneuvering the garbage truck into place, many more could have been killed.

My guess is that Officer Berneathy was chosen to ride along because of her sex and age. Patti Berneathy was the youngest female officer at the scene, and it may have made sense for Brenda to have someone she might identify with. They drove out of the school playground and made their way southwest to downtown.

"I looked at my rear-view mirror and could see Brenda Spencer staring straight ahead and motionless. At no time did Officer Berneathy or I speak to Brenda Spencer, and she did not make any statements to us," Kasinak recalled.

They dropped Brenda off and began their reports for the day. Just like any other day for the police, Kasinak said, "We turned in our reports at the homicide division and ended our shift for the day."

Police spokesman Bill Robinson told reporters that no charges were immediately filed, but possible charges would include murder and assault with intent to commit murder.

Later that afternoon, Olson would tell the *Los Angeles Times*,

"You're kind of lost for words at first… the longer you talk, the better the rapport."

He said his major problem in discussions with Brenda was that "she didn't trust me. You just don't know at first what the person wants or what is bothering them; after a while, it's just like you were sitting there talking to them".

Sgt Manny Lopez told the same reporter that Olson "talked to her and finally convinced her to come out."

The dwindling crowd of people at the condo complex eventually was disappointed by the surrender. They were even more disappointed when most people from their vantage point could not actually see the action itself. The moment was captured by TV news crews with cameras high above their vans. Brenda had left her house with small gasps from the crowd on Lake Ashmere Drive. The *Los Angeles Times* reported that a boy yelled to a friend moments after Brenda surrendered, "I don't want to see her. Let's go to the schoolyard and see if we can see the blood."

About 20 minutes after the surrender, a young man was quizzing a reporter about what happened. Told that Spencer had already given up and had been driven away, he replied, "Then what the hell is everybody standing around here for?"

9

INTERROGATION

WALLY SPENCER HAD already arrived at the police station by the time his daughter surrendered. He was escorted to an interview room and was about to be interviewed by Detective Fred Dreis of Homicide Team II.

Once Brenda had agreed to exit the house and had told her dad "to go get screwed," the SDPD thought it was best to get Wally far away from the area. They did not want to take the risk of Brenda seeing her father behind a barricade as she was marched across the campus to Kasinak's car. Wally gave detectives a signed consent form allowing them to enter the house, so a warrant would not be needed.

Wally was kept waiting at the police station for reasons he would not have known. At this stage he was confused and glassy eyed after spending hours at a police barricade deflecting reporters' questions. At about 3:15pm in a homicide division interrogation room, he sat facing Dreis. He was a tough and experienced homicide cop who later went on to the missing persons unit. Most of Det. Dreis's colleagues and friends were investigating at the scene, hoping to capture as much as they could before darkness set in.

Dreis would have settled Wally with a cup of coffee or water and probably started with something welcoming. He was then asked about who lived in the home and what happened recently to make Brenda so angry.

"Brenda lives with me and my son, Scott, at 6356 Lake Atlin Ave. Scott has been gone, so it's just Brenda and I staying at the house," Wally said.

"I came home Friday night about 6:30pm, and Brenda wasn't home. I went to the supermarket and was gone for about one hour while Brenda arrived home. We spent the rest of the evening home together. She went to bed about 8 or 8:30pm, and I stayed up watching TV. There had been no problems, and she seemed to be in very good spirits," he continued.

"We were both up about 9am on Saturday morning and had breakfast. I was out working on the van and one of Brenda's friends came over to visit.

"I was gone between 12 and 1pm, and when I returned home Brenda and Brant were gone. I left about 2 or 2:30pm as they were coming home. I was gone for about a half hour and they were still home when I got back. About 3 or 3:30pm, after Brant left, I watched TV, and Brenda was in her room listening to the hi-fi. We had dinner and watched TV together before going to bed around 9 or 9:30pm." Wally had actually spent almost no time with Brenda over the weekend.

"Still there had been no problems, and everything seemed normal. Before we went to bed, she asked me if the van was locked and I said, 'no,' so I gave her the key and asked her to lock the van. She came back in the house with her sweatshirt, thermal pants, and another shirt wadded up in her hands. She gave me the key back and went to bed. Everything seemed normal," he said.

For whatever reason, Wally gave no account of Sunday and detectives did not push him to discuss it. He obviously thought Brenda's journey out to the van was relevant.

"I got up this morning about 5:30am to get ready for work, and I woke Brenda up about 6:30am for school. She came in and asked if she could stay home from school because she didn't feel well. She said she felt nauseous and was going to throw up. I told her she could stay home, and I left for work about 7am. She said her normal goodbye and was dressed when I left. She had on a thermal shirt with a white T-shirt over it, her pants, and socks, but no shoes."

Brenda had told her father that she was on her period, and that probably was something Wally was squeamish about sharing.

"She must have gotten the ammunition out of the van because we had been shooting last weekend, and that's where the ammunition was. At most, it couldn't have been more than 10 rounds in the house from the clip. She had about 600 to 700 rounds of .22 ammunition left. For Christmas, she got two boxes, 500 rounds each, and I think they were Federal brand individually packaged in green boxes. She got the rifle for Christmas, and, I guess, there's been a total of 200 or 300 rounds fired through it."

He was recounting the amount of ammo that Brenda had readily available. He was obviously unaware that after the siege, Brenda placed 13 boxes of ammo totaling 700 rounds on the drive before being arrested. None of these boxes were green or in 500 round containers.

"After we had been out shooting last weekend, she had cleaned the rifle and put it on the couch. I told her to put it away after a couple of days. She kept the rifle, the pump pellet rifle, and one of the CO2 pistols in her bedroom. The other CO2 pistol is kept in my room, and it's broken. The CO2 rifle is in Scott's room. These are the only types of weapons we have in the house. I don't know if the .22 ammunition is still in the van or not."

Wally either was unaware of her knives or did not see them as weapons. In all the confusion, he may have thought the police were interested only in the guns.

Asked why Brenda would be so upset, Wally Spencer replied, "She is a little disturbed about her mother and I being divorced, but it's been eight years. She is dissatisfied about the world we live in and likes the open spaces in the mountains. Saturdays we usually go to the mountains, but she didn't want to go this last Saturday. I don't understand what happened. It's beyond me why she would do something like this. She's been doing well in school and has brought her grades up. As far as I know, she is not involved in any narcotics or alcohol other than a beer once in a while. I just don't know what could have triggered this."

This was a dead loss to the detectives and would probably not help them with the investigation. Wally seemed disconnected from his daughter and did not appear to spot any real worries in her life. The officers were looking for details to support the criminal case against her and did not drill him on past events.

Even during the hours Wally wandered back and forth at the traffic stop, he never asked if it was his daughter doing this. He never asked if she was acting with someone or on her own. As imaginable as this shooting was he knew she was capable. A work colleague of his would later tell reporters that Wally seemed overwhelmed with raising children on his own, saying, "He used to say it was tough to take care of them. He is quiet, shy, and very soft spoken. He never had much to say. He sometimes comes to work very depressed."

After examining the police reports and speaking with detectives, I felt it necessary to reach out to Brenda and ask her thoughts. I wrote to her directly and to my surprise she responded very politely. She and I have been corresponding ever since.

Brenda told me she was on a lot of drugs and has absolutely no memory of the morning of the shooting. She also said she does not remember speaking with newspaper reporters or riding in the patrol car to the police station. But she did remember what she had to eat that day.

She also told me, "I never asked for a Whopper. I had food in the house. That's a myth." She claims she eventually had Kentucky

Fried Chicken on the day of her offence and the Whopper was never on offer.

I went back to Detective Olson to confirm the details. He said he definitely discussed the Whopper with Brenda over the phone but has no idea what she actually received once she was apprehended.

10

CRIME SCENE

THE SAN DIEGO Police forensic team started their work from the back of the school before Brenda had reached Kasinak's police car. Lab technician Kevin Brown almost bumped shoulders with Brenda and the SWAT officers when he walked down the up ramp with his forensic test cases. Detectives and techs split duties between the school and the house.

Homicide Team III detectives Ron Newman and Gene Back met lab tech Al Start and immediately began processing the scene at the school. Det. Newman began taking notes as Start took photos and began tests on the bloodied walkway. Det. Back began cataloguing the wider area.

At the house across the road, Homicide Team II began their investigation with the driveway and entrance to the house. Lab tech Brown immediately went to the two weapons in the middle of the drive. The Ruger .22 and pump pellet rifle were tagged and processed while the media captured it all with long-range lenses.

Sgt. John Kennedy was photographed standing in the doorway with his hands through the two broken windowpanes. In his light blue three-piece suit, Kennedy stood frowning behind the white door and broken glass. The *San Diego Union* ran the photo next morning.

Brown stood just long enough with both weapons in his hands to be photographed from a few angles. The pellet gun looked remarkably like a dangerous weapon although it may not have been shot that day. It certainly would not have seriously hurt anyone across the street. Kennedy oversaw the area while Brown tagged and removed the rifles and ammunition at the end of the drive.

Reported as "unexpended long shelled .22s were in numerous cardboard boxes and one plastic container" the ammunition was actually: 700 rounds of ammo in 12 boxes of Federal Brand Hi Velocity Power-Flight .22 Long Rifle Rim Fire Cartridges x 50 rounds and one clear plastic box of undetermined manufacture x100 rounds.

This rifle load was introduced in 1970 as part of Federal Brand's discount range. They came from the Minneapolis factory and were made of a lead bullet loaded in a brass case. The box was gold and white with a squirrel on the front and a rabbit on the back panel. The end flaps said, "Extreme Range 1 ½ Mile" and on the front said, "WARNING: Keep out of reach of children." It was never revealed who made the large plastic box of unexpended bullets.

The detectives photographed the green pick-up truck in the driveway but did not search it as it was not part of the crime scene. It was also photographed by the media revealing a bullet hole in the back windshield. This did not happen during the siege and fixing it was something Brenda's brother, Scott had on his to do list.

Lab tech Brown was one of the first to enter the house and start processing the entrance way.

Brown faced controversy and a tragic end after he retired from the police in 2002.

In 2012, he was implicated as a suspect in the unsolved murder of a 14-year-old girl whose body had been found on a beach at San Diego's Torrey Pines State Beach in 1984. Unaware the victim was 14, Brown said he had relations with many people in the 80s and couldn't be sure if he knew her. His DNA was found on the girl's body, but he brushed it off as contamination as he worked in the same lab where it was tested.

Brown passed an independent polygraph test but took his own life 16 months later. His wife says police hounded him for over a year and he had a nervous breakdown. His suicide drew attention to other cold cases with possible contaminated evidence.

The Spencer house was documented as a single-family dwelling of light brown stucco with white wood trim and a dark brown garage door. Detectives Dick Thwing and Jim Shively oversaw the operation in the house and focused most of their attention on the entranceway. The detectives would photo document the entire house, but the crime scene was only the front entrance.

Det. Thwing, who had joined the force 10 years earlier, was a big man known as the life of the party with a huge laugh. Det. Shively was the longest serving member of the homicide teams and prided himself on not getting emotional, no matter how gruesome the evidence.

"We didn't have extensive work to do," Thwing said. "By the time I got there, she was already on the phone telling people what she did. You don't have to be as careful with your investigation when you already had a confession."

The SWAT team had been through the house to make sure it was clear of danger and left the front door wide open. Homicide Team II arrived just as the SWAT team had finished their sweep and were leaving.

"Once they were done, then we went to work," Thwing said proudly. He lived nearby and was familiar with the area.

Just inside the door on the entrance tiles were scattered cartridge casings and little else. The police report listed them as 36 empty cartridge casings and two live rounds in an area about 7x6ft.

"Entranceway was slightly wider than it was deep and was a beige colour tile," said Det. Thwing. Just outside of the entryway were the white folding knife and hunting knife sitting next to a small bottle of Southern Comfort.

To detectives, the folding knife looked to be for filleting or gutting fish, and the hunting knife was dark with a brown leather handle. The pint-sized bottle was listed as a quarter full without its cap. There were no indications the alcohol spilled as the floor was dry and clean. Thwing said he saw no drug remnants or paraphernalia anywhere in the house, and the house did not have any other alcohol bottles despite that being reported in the media.

On the left was about an 8ft hallway to the bedrooms but "I can't really call it a hallway," said Thwing. In the hall was a rotary telephone with a cord long enough that it could have been transported anywhere throughout the house. Detectives saw no second phone and concluded this must have been the phone Brenda used to communicate with reporters and police.

The first bedroom was Brenda's with two corner windows facing the driveway. It was small, untidy, and cluttered with a few magazines and clothes. A single bed was against the wall with sage-coloured shag carpet. On the bed was a brown and white imitation leather gun case that detectives took into evidence. Next to the bed was a night table covered with random electronics and a small lamp.

On top of the chest of drawers was a small stereo with a couple of speakers. "It looked like a tape player in the room, which could have possibly been an 8-track player," said Thwing. He also thought that it might also have been TV parts. Brenda's room had no posters or pictures and only an old clock hung on the front wall. The police photographed this room and moved on.

Brother Scott's bedroom was in just as much disorder as his sister's. He had bunk beds and camping gear scattered around. His room was clearly a storage area and was full of red coolers and camping gear like sleeping bags. In the far corner was the CO2 air rifle Wally had described. Police listed this room as a bedroom in disarray, although that could have described the entire home.

Wally's room was much the same as the others with clothes, food bowls, fizzy drink cans, and papers on the floor. A large mattress sat directly on the floor in the corner. The table across from the unmade bed was built out of cinder blocks and wooden boards. On it were stacks of magazines and a TV in pieces.

Thwing described Wally's room as "less cluttered than the other rooms" although pictures disagree with that assessment. There were also no alcohol bottles or any suggestion Wally was a drinker (news outlets had incorrectly described him as an alcoholic) or that the house was scattered with empty bottles.

In the police photographs, Wally had what looked like a dollhouse at the foot of his bed against the back wall. It sat on the floor directly across from the door and is the first thing you see in the room prior to entering. The police made no mention of the dollhouse in any of their reports, and it struck me as a very interesting thing to leave out of a report. Why would a grown man have a dollhouse next to his bed?

I asked Brenda about this directly. She said, "Yeah, my dad had a doll house in his bedroom, it belonged to my sister, she outgrew playing with it and it just kind of landed there. I guess it was for me to play with or something. I never played with it. I was too into Hot Wheels."

The garage had a big window facing the school, and Thwing believes it was converted into Wally's bedroom. The floor plan of the house shows the only entrance is the large wooden lift up double door. I thought this was an odd way to enter a bedroom and double checked this detail.

A neighbour of Brenda's told me it was a functioning garage, and inside was a kind of fort built with old pallets and used carpet. She said they had to climb over oil cans and greasy car parts to get to the fort. The space inside was only big enough for kids and was not safe if a fire ever broke out. She also told me the fort held a lot of Brenda's drug paraphernalia.

The police report made no mention of the fort or the CO2 pistols that Wally said were in his room. These spaces were not extensively searched, and detectives photographed them and moved on.

I asked Brenda about the converted room. She said, "the garage was just a garage" and made no mention of the fort. But I think this is relevant because the garage's large window is easily the best vantage point for the school across the street. The inconvenience of having to lift the garage door may have been the reason she chose not to mount her weapons there.

The living room, just off the entranceway, was covered in unvacuumed light brown shag carpet. Police reports listed it as having a large double lounger and small couches but not much else. The furniture's white fabric was ripped, exposing foam, and they were used to dry clothing. The floor had a small collection of oil lamps and a small TV facing the couch.

The report describes a homemade TV set as being the only thing out of the ordinary. It was placed on a table but covered in clutter. To Thwing, it looked more like a television made from spare parts and was not a known brand.

Brenda told me, "The TV was a home built one. My dad was an electronic technician, so he could build anything. It was a kit he had gotten."

Wally did work as an audio-visual tech, and Thwing assumed he probably built this himself from other broken TVs. This was the only one listed in the police report or remembered by detectives. But pictures would reveal there were others.

Behind the front living room was the kitchen and dining area. It was covered with pale yellow linoleum described as "filthy but slightly cleaner where people travelled" by Det Thwing.

The official police report called this area extremely messy and cluttered with various foodstuffs. The dining table was covered in pre-packaged snacks and various bottles.

"It was like they did not have a condiment shelf," said Thwing. "It was really sad. You don't realise people live that way until you have to encounter it."

Detectives never opened the back door or went into the backyard. The SWAT teams and Astrea helicopter surveillance was present for the past six hours, so this may have played a role in that. Though Brenda had spoken of pets, the officers saw no sign of any animals while they were in the house. Thwing jokingly said, "I didn't have any animals to deal with."

The official report was not time-stamped, and it is unknown exactly how long the detectives searched the house. We know the detectives arrived just after the surrender at 3:06pm, and Thwing said the search was over in about two hours. Detectives say they left just before it got dark and removed the police tape from around the scene.

Sunset was recorded as 5:18pm, and the clock photographed in the living room listed the time as 5:20pm, but it is very possible the clock's batteries were dead and showed an incorrect time.

"We had people staring at us. I remember when we left there were people still there," Thwing recalled. "When we were taking down the tape they were still hanging around. There were eyes everywhere. It was an event."

Dick Thwing passed away in 2020, shortly after our last conversation. Dick, a highly respected detective, moved to the Nevada city of Reno after he retired from the SDPD.

At the school, Dets. Ron Newman and Gene Back, with lab technician Al Start, were joined by San Diego Unified School District officials. More than six investigators were photographed at the scene and neighbours recall a tremendous clean-up operation.

Detectives plucked bullets from walls, and school officials started generally tidying up. Although none of the activity was officially documented, it probably went on into the night. Michael Guerrero, the assistant janitor, remembers trying to start work the day of the shooting.

"When I arrived at the site, the police had cordoned off the school, and I was not allowed in," he said. "Since I was part time, I was not involved with getting the site ready for reopening. During the time repairs were made, and I don't recall seeing any bullet holes." Guerrero returned to work the following afternoon and continued his normal routine.

Brenda was processed in the police homicide division at the same time her father was interviewed.

Police took her clothes into evidence, allowed her to keep her glasses, and gave her an orange prisoner jumpsuit to wear as she left the station. The legs and arms had to be rolled up to fit her small frame.

Det. Chet Thurston, the man who irritated her for hours with the bullhorn, and Det. David Ayers conducted the "perp walk" across the parking lot. Walking the perpetrator is an American phenomenon in which police parade a suspect past waiting media. Local TV crews had already captured Brenda's arrest and transport from the school, but this was the first chance for the public to see the killer up close. It was now evening, and news cameras and lights were just inches from her face as she made her way. Brenda looked tiny next to the two detectives as they escorted her to the back of a blue unmarked sedan.

At the end of the business day a spokesman for the district attorney's office, which would handle the court case against Brenda, said, "She will have a full hearing before the juvenile court within the next few days. The court will decide, during the closed hearings, whether she will be tried as an adult or juvenile."

In 1979, California legal guidelines suggested that if a crime was deemed to be a result of adult thinking, an underage suspect could be tried as an adult. But if a judge decided it resulted from adolescent thoughts, the suspect would be tried as a juvenile. If tried and convicted as an adult, 16-year-old Brenda Spencer could be sentenced to life in prison without possibility of parole. But, were she to be tried as a juvenile, a court would retain jurisdiction, and she would have to be released by her 23rd birthday. Brenda was to be held in the female section of San Diego County's juvenile hall detention centre, pending a judge's decision on her status.

The question of the death penalty had long been a tangled one at the time in California, which had put many killers to death in years past. The state had executed no one since 1967, and the California Supreme Court ruled in 1972 that the death penalty was unconstitutional. That controversial decision spared the lives of 105 death-row inmates, including serial killer Charles Manson and Sirhan Sirhan, assassin of presidential candidate Robert F. Kennedy.

But a few months later, California voters, outraged by the court's ruling, used the state's ballot proposition procedure to reinstate executions of killers. Voters have since defeated two ballot propositions to repeal the death penalty in the Golden State.

Hundreds have been sentenced to death in the years since, but it has been carried out for relatively few because of continued legal wrangling.

The first person executed in California since 1967 was Brenda's fellow San Diegan, Robert Alson Harris, who died in the gas chamber of San Quentin State Prison on April 21, 1992. Harris, who already had served a prison sentence for beating a man to death, was convicted of stealing a car from two teenagers, shooting them to death, then using the vehicle to rob a bank. The crime occurred in July 1978, six months before the Cleveland Elementary shootings.

11

MEDIA FRENZY

BY 5PM THAT evening, all local television channels were broadcasting live from Cleveland Elementary. Any and everyone came out of the woodwork to tell a story about the shooter and get on TV.

Michael Tuck, the newly acquired anchorman for KFMB News 8 (the CBS affiliate), was interviewing almost anyone who walked up near Lake Atlin Ave. The ratings went through the roof, and News 8 would become San Diego's number one news station for the next five years.

At the time, KGTV – The News 10 (ABC affiliate) with Jack White – was the city's most watched evening news. White was a local who had covered every story that hit San Diego since 1968, and he wasn't going to miss this. He was known to emcee beauty pageants, cover restaurant reviews and work on local radio. The makers of the Will Ferrell film "Anchorman: The Legend of Ron Burgundy" selected White as their San Diego consultant. There was nothing he couldn't cover.

National newspapers and weekly magazines sent their stringers out to get the story. Good Housekeeping and Reader's Digest, which were not famous for true crime stories, published detailed accounts of the event. By next morning this was an international story with many of the quotes and sound bites taken from the local news sources. They interviewed neighbours, parents of Cleveland children, and as many of Brenda's peers as possible. At times teenagers lined up to speak with the media to get on TV or get their names in the newspapers.

Gail Dinkel from KCST Channel 39 (NBC affiliate) parked herself at the scene and grabbed anyone who said they knew the shooter. As the teenagers returned from school and walked up to the news cameras, she interviewed 15-year-old Colleen O'Connell.

The O'Connell family lived at 6333 Lake Ariana Ave and shared a back fence, right behind the Spencers. For most of the day, SWAT officers had been posted on their roof.

Colleen was a freshman at Patrick Henry and heard from a teacher that there was a shooting near her house. She asked to be excused and called home from the school payphone but got no answer.

She told me, "I then called my dad at work. He told me they were evacuated to the house across the street. My mom, brother, and grandparents were home when the shooting started."

As soon as school was over, Colleen's brother Patrick met her at the corner. They hopped fences to get around the police blockade, and her brother took her to where the family had moved temporarily.

They listened to a neighbour's police scanner and heard that SWAT was going to go in if Brenda did not surrender soon. Colleen and her brother went around to the best vantage point on the east side of Lake Atlin Ave.

They stood there with a 15-year-old schoolmate and neighbour named Andy Kygar while Patrick took photos. Colleen said Andy told her, "She [Brenda] should just kill herself after shooting those people."

Less than three years later, Kygar shot and killed his ex-girlfriend, Becky Reynolds, 17, in her car and then drove around with her body for more than an hour. Finally, he parked on a residential street in the San Diego suburb of El Cajon and took his own life with the same gun. The family, which gave him no funeral, still live near the O'Connells.

Later that evening, Colleen was on a KCST broadcast, "I was in the house next door, and I heard her [Brenda] say that she was going to go out and break the law so the police would come up to her car, so she could blow his head off."

The reporter asked Colleen if she thought Brenda was serious and she replied, "Yeah."

Producer Heidi Schulman sent out this third hand account of someone overhearing Brenda's bizarre story about shooting cops from her car to all national NBC affiliates as part of a 90-second reel.

Colleen repeated her story to the *Los Angeles Times* saying she had talked with Brenda several weeks ago and been told she wanted to "blow a police officer's head off".

The O'Connell family appears to have spoken to every reporter on the job. Colleen's sister, Kathy, 18, said the Brenda Spencer she knew was "kind of strange. She was a quiet girl, but she could be aggressive when she talked."

In 2020, Colleen remembered Brenda, "She was a year ahead of me, and it's not like we had a lot of interaction. I just think that she is a weirdo and that's why she did it. I don't think there was any more thought into it."

The O'Connell's have the rare distinction of living very near to two murderers. This strange fact was not lost on Colleen when we both nervously giggled about it during the phone interview.

Union reporters went to Garfield alternative high school but failed to find anyone who remembered her.

In 1977 and early 78, Brenda's attendance and grades had slipped so badly, she was forced to leave her local high school and attend an alternative school close to downtown San Diego. This blip in

Brenda's education must have been a complete hassle for Wally. To ensure she attended Garfield, he would have had to make the 40-minute round trip to the school each day.

Garfield High School was purpose built to help benefit wayward students who didn't fit in with normal education. It was not unusual for students to attend for six months, buckle down, and show they wanted to get back to normal high school. Brenda attended for a semester and returned to Patrick Henry in September 1978.

Reporters quoted schoolmates saying Brenda Spencer loved animals and was affectionate to neighbourhood kids. But they also said she was a drug addict who had used a knife to torment people who did not understand her.

One friend said she loved animals and talked about nothing else. Another said she was seen crossing the road into the schoolyard with lighter fluid. Schoolmates claimed she would watch cop shows and cheer when one was shot; but others simply called her an average student, who was quiet and usually stoned.

A schoolmate, not identified as a friend, said Spencer was artistic and intrigued with images. They said her favourite class was photography and that she had once won a television set as a prize in a photograph contest.

Neil Heinberg, Patrick Henry High's industrial arts instructor, who was Spencer's photography teacher, said she did not stand out from his other students.

"She entered my class a few weeks late last semester. She was very introverted, but she seemed to get along well and got into the swing of things after a few weeks. She has that eye to take more than the usual snapshots, but she was a completely average student. In fact, the only thing that set her off from other students was her bright red hair."

Heinberg was a popular teacher and usually clad in checked

shirts and jeans. He wore sandals and a hip beard with a habitual big smile. Brenda liked him.

An anonymous female friend was quoted with a list of damning statements saying Brenda was "crazy about guns. She liked to kill. She used to say she's gonna make her living being a sniper. She hates cops. She's always saying she wants to kill cops, wants to blow one away. I thought she was crazy. I thought she was just talking. I didn't think she'd really shoot somebody."

The same girl said Brenda had been caught stealing ammunition from a local store and was in trouble with police "and that's why she disliked police so much".

Dawn White, 16, was one of Brenda's only close friends to speak with reporters.

"She was a good shot," said Dawn. "I went into the desert with her last year to go target shooting and she killed a lot of lizards and squirrels. She almost never missed."

Dawn was referring to the property Wally Spencer owned in Potrero, about an hour southeast near the Mexican border. Brenda would often bring her friends with her when they went in Wally's old van.

One girl claiming to be Brenda's friend was 16-year-old Tracy Mills. She said, "she always talked about getting wasted on drugs… and about shoplifting all the time. She seemed proud of the fact that she was a good shoplifter, but maybe that attitude is why she really didn't have any real close friends. She ditches school a lot."

And finally, she said, "She always seemed like a radical."

That quote was later misattributed in various publications.

The Union reported that Brenda was already being counselled through Youth Services. The police said there was a representative known to Brenda at the scene for most of the day.

Noreen Harmon was appointed as Brenda's juvenile probation

officer/counsellor after her previous run-ins with the law. SDPD never officially spoke with Harmon while she was at the scene and Det. Olson was never made aware of her presence.

The New York Times reported that Brenda shoplifted gloves, flashlights, and film from local shops but had only boasted of stealing ammunition. It also quoted neighbour kids saying, "she was mostly crazy when she was stoned" and "that was when she got wild ideas about killing cops. But we just thought she was showing off."

The *Los Angeles Times* reported Brenda was "kind of quiet" and "kind of weird". A senior at her school, Terry Sizemore, said, "she was just this very weird girl. She'd shoot birds and cans. She got in trouble a lot for being truant and not doing her work. She was different, that's for sure. But she never really bothered anyone." Stuart Heising, 16, told the *Los Angeles Times* he was in Mr. Bassett's English class at Patrick Henry High with Brenda before she was suspended in early 1978.

"She sat in front of me in English last year. She was always talking about guns, bragging about the guns her father had. She failed out of school last year and then came back this year. I didn't know her really well. I guess no one did," he said.

Stuart also told the paper that Brenda once threatened a fellow student who had teased her on the telephone that she "would blow his brains out with a gun".

Maryann Stevenson said she knew Brenda since the 7th grade but had not spoken to her at high school.

"She was super quiet and kind of a loner. I used to jog by her house and talk with her dad and he was real friendly. She used to dress like a guy and be like a guy. Living with her brother and dad, maybe that was why."

Neighbour Eric Holt, a university student, who lived four doors down from the Spencers and knew Brenda's brother Scott, said of her, "she has always been different from other kids."

Donna L. Point, a 17-year-old classmate of Brenda's, told multiple reporters, "I never thought she'd do something like that, but maybe she just kept her problems to herself."

Another classmate, Jolene Davis, said, "you'd always see her walking around by herself at school. I don't think she had any friends. But it wasn't like she was real sad or anything. You'd see her smiling and laughing sometimes. She just had this thing about guns."

It seemed as though everyone at her school or in the neighbourhood had an opinion about Brenda even if they did not know her.

The *Los Angeles Times* reported that Brenda had previously "got into trouble" when she used a BB gun to shoot out the windows of Cleveland Elementary earlier but there is no evidence that she used a weapon when she vandalised the school the previous summer. It was also reported that, "despite the talk about guns, students who knew her said that they were never afraid of her or thought she would harm anyone."

The wire service United Press International sent out a similar story that included the O'Connell quotes and reports of BB gun vandalism. The story said Brenda had an arsenal in her father's garage and liked to watch violent scenes on television. She was incorrectly described as a 16-year-old blonde, honour student with a history of petty theft and drug abuse who fired into the school yard.

UPI also reported she had barricaded herself into the house and had dug a tunnel in the backyard so she could hide. This story was published in a number of major newspapers in the United States and across the globe.

Tribune reporter Steve Wiegand told me, "The cops never contacted me during the shooting or even after. That evening, I went down to the police headquarters for some follow up." He was pointed out by the police chief and was interviewed by several local TV stations.

The morning after the shooting, press reported that two high-ranking officials in the district attorney's office confirmed prosecutors would urge that 16-year-old Brenda be tried as an adult. But a petition was filed in juvenile court charging her with two counts of murder and 10 other criminal charges. Murder lying in wait and multiple murder were two extra sets of special circumstances added to the charges.

Over the next few days and weeks, stories about the angry teenager with a gun would dominate the media. Brenda Spencer would soon become an international figure based on information provided by kids and parents at the scene.

The Brenda Spencer case became a trial by media long before it reached a court to determine if she would be charged as a juvenile or an adult. Psychologists read these stories, formed early opinions, and offered them to anyone who would listen.

12

AFTERMATH

EDUCATION AUTHORITIES ORDERED all public schools in San Diego County to fly flags at half-mast the following morning in honour of Wragg and Suchar.

"Our concerns and sympathies are extended to the two families and to the parents of those children who were injured in this senseless attack. We are fortunate that their young lives were spared," said Schools Superintendent Thomas Goodman.

The school district agreed to reopen Cleveland Elementary the following day in a show of strength, but it moved the regularly scheduled board of education meeting from Tuesday to Thursday. No extra police or security was ordered, and the school started its day.

A school janitor gave the sidewalk one more scrub to remove lingering blood stains. Of the school's 319 children, only 69 stayed away or were kept home by parents.

The front of the school was more crowded than usual as parents congregated to talk and share grief. Before school started, a few children stopped to look for bullets in the trees and bushes, and a couple went over to the Spencer house to snoop around.

Reporters were back on the scene and just after the school bell rang, they hopped across the road and knocked on the Spencers' door. Wally did not respond to some but told others to go away and leave him alone. He could be seen easily through a window in the door, sitting in his lounge, staring straight ahead, seemingly ignoring the situation.

Wally never answered and soon placed a handwritten note on the front door. It said:

> *To the news media:*
>
> *Mr. Spencer is in shock and agony over the events of yesterday – the deaths of the principal and custodian, the wounding of the children and policeman, by his daughter Brenda...*
>
> *He cannot, at this time, add to the comments of others who knew her. He will shortly see and speak to her...*

The reporters tried to make contact with Brenda's mother, Dot, but were told she would be out of town for at least a week. They grabbed anyone they could for a quote.

Two doors down at 6332 Lake Atlin, a five-year-old neighbour boy named David Lipe said he liked to play in Wally's old van and with Brenda's pets. He said he still liked Wally but was now afraid of Brenda.

Parent Veronna Rodgers told reporters that her daughter, Tanisha, six, was too frightened to go back to school so soon, but her eight-year-old older sister made it a point to walk herself all the way there. Mrs Rodgers had collected both her children from the junior high school the previous afternoon.

Daryl Barnes had been appointed interim principal of Cleveland Elementary after the emergency. He worked with the Parent-Teachers Association to try to restore normality. School district authorities immediately posted counsellors and psychologists to help.

"The staff got together and decided it would be wisest to get back to class the next day. Each teacher then spent time in their own way trying to explain what had happened and how the healthy students could help those who had been hurt," Barnes told *San Diego Union*.

"Mostly, we just talked it out – in class, in assemblies, in one-to-one counselling for those kids, teachers and parents who needed it. People were told not to be afraid to talk about it, to show emotion. We said time would heal."

Jean Malcolm was a school counsellor assigned to Cleveland Elementary four months before the shooting. She visited weekly to counsel the children and said the incident loomed in the consciousness of children and adults alike. But "on the surface," she said, "the kids are fine. There's no evidence of any problems or residual effects."

Dr. Perry Bach, a child psychiatrist and chief of adolescent and children's services for San Diego County's medical department, brought in six district counsellors to help with the students. He headed the psychiatric team that stayed at the school for the two weeks after the shooting.

In the first few weeks he said some children expressed fear in dreams or verbally, but things swiftly returned to normal.

"I think one of the mistakes would be to expect it to be completely worked through. It will not just go away," Dr. Bach said after students and parents told him things pretty much went back to normal quickly.

Mike Simpson, a representative of the local school board, told the Associated Press, "We called many parents last night asking them to bring their children in today. We've got to break down the shock."

Children peppered teachers and staff with questions about what happened and what would happen next. Many children wrote get-well letters to their eight injured classmates as a project to help deal with the event.

"I had bad dreams and thought the lady would still be here. But my dad said it's all right now," said nine-year old George Johnson.

Teachers Kathy Keith and David Gee also felt the effects of the shooting. A few days before the school finished for the summer, Keith jumped to the floor when she heard firecrackers at a funeral.

Gee told reporters, "time is a great healer. Children's time spans are very short, either forward or backward. Six months from now is like 60 years to them, and I'm sure thinking back is the same way."

That same day the faculty quickly organised an impromptu memorial service at Cleveland Elementary. Students and teachers, past and present, shared anecdotes, and stories about the fallen men. It was a less formal ceremony than the official memorial services to come.

The slain principal's daughter, Penny Wragg, came to the school to collect his things and saw the blood on the sidewalk where he had been shot.

Two days after the shooting, family and close friends gathered at the Erickson-Anderson Mortuary Chapel in La Mesa for principal Burton "Burt" Wragg's funeral service. His daughter gave a moving eulogy. She spoke of her parents' recent 25th anniversary cruise to Panama and said her mother would always cherish the memories.

Wragg, a mentor to the children and war hero, was just 53. He had dedicated his adult life to educating young people. With 30 years of experience in San Diego schools and a military veteran of World War Two, he was a Southern California native and had graduated from San Diego State University with a teaching credential.

The weekend prior to his death he painted a room with his daughter. She had only started college that autumn and was living away. They decided to redecorate her old room together, and mother Kathe was left with cleaning up the mess.

Michael Suchar was given an honorary military service at the Veterans of Foreign Wars Post 3787 that Saturday morning. His wife said she had a bizarre premonition of the shooting and asked him not to be a hero if anything happened. Mr Mike told her there was no way he could be a coward if the kids needed him.

Suchar had been a chief boatswain's mate in the US Navy and served on underwater demolition teams in both World War Two and the Korean War. He was a native of Youngstown, Ohio, and joined the school district in 1968. Mr Mike, who was 56, was survived by his German-born wife, Valentina.

At no time was Brenda Spencer's name mentioned in either service.

Less than 10 days after the shooting, the official faculty changed at the school, and the San Diego school board began to hand out awards for bravery at the scene.

The San Diego School Board, led by Superintendent Thomas Goodman, announced the appointment of another ex-serviceman, Dr. Robert "Bob" Rice as new principal of Cleveland Elementary. He had moved to San Diego from Berkeley, California, after his military service. Daryl Barnes, the fourth-grade teacher named as acting principal in the wake of the shooting, returned to the classroom. He had not yet completed the needed steps to be appointed principal.

The board named Wragg, the fallen principal, and janitor Suchar as recipients of the first bravery awards. It also praised actions by the entire staff.

As the school returned to normal, the new principal, Dr Rice, drew support from the children and the Parent-Teacher Association at Cleveland Elementary.

"I think it's a reaction from all this. I've never been at a school where the kids have been so nice to me," he said. He thought the injured students appeared to have taken the events of that day better than some who were not hurt.

Rice, who was good friends with the fallen former principal, believed the community should reach out to Wally Spencer, also a kind of bereaved parent, to help the healing.

"We probably should build a bridge to a lot of people, including Mr. Spencer," he told Union reporters.

The injured children were recovering either at home or in the hospital, and none of them attended school the following day. All but two victims would return to the school the following month.

The youngest victim, Audrey Stites, returned to school the following week and kept her elbow injury covered.

Crystal Hardy was not able to keep her hand wound covered. She showed the kids her injury and proudly told them all about what happened saying, "It really doesn't bother me anymore."

Fifth-grader Julie Robles said her classmates were "staring at me. I was afraid to come back, but I wanted to see my friends".

Robles told the *San Diego Union* that she and her three sisters no longer walked home alone from school but said, "I don't feel scared anymore." She said a friend asked her, "'Don't you feel like shooting her back?' I said I feel she's getting enough punishment as it is."

That April while fundraising, she visited the Spencer house and sold a box of candy to Brenda's brother. She was still physically recovering from where the bullet had passed through her body. Robles chose not to identify herself that day, and Scott Spencer was unaware of who she was.

Her mother, Patricia, said she had kept all the news clippings of the event to give to Julie when she felt the time was right.

Mary Clark and Greg Verner were considered two of the shyest students and left empty seats in their classroom for two weeks. Their third-grade teacher, Mrs Miyashita, visited the injured students in the hospital and found them in good spirits.

She was so pleased to see them rebound so positively and listened intently as they both recounted their actions that day.

Verner had been in the hospital overnight before returning to school. He told the newspapers upon his return that "it feels good" to be back in his class again. Verner rejoined his lessons with a bullet still lodged near his buttocks.

Mrs Miyashita was especially worried about eight-year-old Mary because she was part of the group herded to the auditorium and then to the awaiting buses. She was too shy to tell anyone she had been shot in her abdomen. She spent a week in the hospital before returning to school.

Three were not released as quickly as the others from the hospital.

Nine-year-old old victim Cam Miller eventually returned to his fourth-grade class after being shot in the back. He felt he was treated as a celebrity for the first few days. "I can't play team-ball and stuff like that. I'm waiting for the doctor to say OK," he told reporters.

Miller had the horrific experience of being transported to the hospital in the same vehicle as Mr. Mike, the fatally shot janitor.

He said he dreamed that Brenda visited him in his sleep. His mother, DeLois Miller, told the *Los Angeles Times*, "She came to apologise." After the shooting, Cam usually carried a flashlight with him when he visited the bathroom late at night.

He was not sympathetic to Brenda.

"I don't want to forgive her," he said. Having spent the first few weeks ignoring the news, Cam later followed the case with interest, even though she "gives me the creeps".

Nine-year-old Christy Buell spent three weeks in the hospital after the shooting. Christy's father, Norm Buell, picked up his daughter from nearby Alvarado Hospital on Feb. 16.

Christy was shot twice, with one bullet going through her kidney, severing intestines, and bouncing off a bone and the colon. This bullet damaged a nerve to her right foot and left it partially paralysed.

While in the hospital, Christy wrote Valentine's Day cards for all the kids in her class. She was also hard at work with thank you letters to the 30 or so people who sent her cards and gifts.

The Buell family's living room was full of games, stuffed animals, and toys from well-wishers. Bill Kolender, the city's chief of police, graciously visited her once she was at home and gave her a pin shaped like handcuffs.

She had two follow-up operations to her midsection and would be paralysed in her left leg for more than a month. She was forced to wear a brace, which she nicknamed "Clicker" because of the noise it made.

Christy returned to the hospital for more surgeries for months after the shooting, and it would be almost a year before her foot fully healed. In total, she spent 42 days in the hospital and had to wear a colostomy bag until the summer.

Christy remained at home and was tutored while she recuperated, but she would never physically return to Cleveland Elementary, although she did eventually return to full-time education.

Her father felt it best to refuse formal psychologist interventions from the school and keep the healing within the family. They had dealt with the mother passing years before and felt strong enough to deal with this also.

Norm Buell said that even though her daughter did not like school very much, she really wanted to swing by Cleveland to see her classmates. They stayed for about an hour and had a really good look at the house across the street, having never really thought much about it until then.

Norm had not met the Spencers before the shooting, but he telephoned Wally after Brenda's arrest. He wanted to have a chat about the kids. Both were single parents, and Norm felt it could help things.

To Norm's surprise Wally answered but only listened for about 10 minutes before making his excuses. He thought Wally sounded very depressed but was happy that they had made contact.

"I feel very sorry for the man. I've told him I have no animosity towards him," Norm told the *San Diego Union*. "He acted very sorry. He said he wished he could turn the clock back."

"I'm a single parent. I could blow it, too. It could happen to double parents. We're lucky we didn't have any deaths of the children, no paraplegics, no quadriplegics."

Three months after the shooting with his daughter safely at home, Norm decided it was time to finally meet with Wally and speak frankly.

"I went over there, father-to-father, hoping to talk to him," Norm told the *San Diego Union*. He said he knocked at a screen door and could see Wally sitting and watching TV. Norm asked to speak with him, but Wally told him to go away and to leave him alone.

"I wanted to tell him that I was a single father, too, raising four kids alone, and I know it's a hard job and a thankless job, and I know you probably did the best you could, that Christy was going to be okay." Norm and Wally never did have a father-to-father chat.

Norm made a special mention of the financial pressure the medical bills had put upon his family. He told the reporters that it was with reluctance that they may have to take legal action against the Spencers for pain and suffering.

"We're looking at $15,000 in medical bills," Norm said.

The first child to be hit by Brenda's volley of bullets was another nine-year-old, Monica Selvig. She spent more than a week in the hospital after surgery to her side.

While still in the hospital, her parents wasted no time in getting started on a civil case against the Spencers. The school was giving awards to the brave teachers who certainly saved lives that day and the Selvigs were filing court papers in Monica's name.

Lee and Marilyn Selvig's personal injury suit would allege gross negligence and reckless conduct by Brenda's father for furnishing the weapon. The suit claimed Wally knew of prior shooting incidents by his daughter and was aware of her violent, anti-social behaviour. The suit sought $300,000 damages and focused on what it said was Wally's inability to parent.

As a practicing lawyer in San Diego, Lee Selvig was out in front of the issue and wanted to make sure this was dealt with quickly. The other victim's parents would watch his course of action closely and evaluate their own chances for a payout.

Monica's physical injuries healed in time, and she returned to class a month after the shooting. Eventually, she finished the sixth grade at Cleveland Elementary and learned to deal with her over-bearing father.

Officer Robb also spent more than a week in Alvarado Hospital. The bullet had entered his neck and was now resting near his spine. His life would never be the same.

He recalled, "The next morning, I wake up in the ICU, and the doctor comes in and tells me I am a lucky guy. He had thought for sure that he had lost me last night. I had died and my heart had stopped; they weren't sure they were going to get me back.

"Well, I had to go see a cardiology specialist and all kinds of crap for like the next six months after that and do all kinds of tests and everything. They never could find anything wrong with me. They never could find out why that happened."

He eventually returned to active duty but with a bullet lodged near his spine. The bullet-proof vest pushed into his injury, and it made exiting his vehicle quickly very difficult.

"I continued working after getting shot," he said. "I got patched up good enough and talked the doctors into certifying me to go back to duty. I was able to actually go back to the street and work as a patrolman for a few more years after that."

13

BRANT FLEMMING

IN HER TALKS with Det. Olson, Brenda spoke about the best friend and former next-door neighbour she called "M&M." His name was Brant Flemming, and they often got in a bit of trouble together, she said. Brenda and Brant would shoplift and retrieve stuff from garbage cans, a practice known as dumpster diving. They also were stopped a couple of times for trespassing, she said.

Roderick Brant Flemming was born in Los Angeles on Nov. 6, 1965, and preferred to go by his middle name. At just 13, he was three and a half years younger than Brenda. His mother Aleta had borne two children in quick succession when she was very young, and Brant never had a relationship with his biological father.

Neighbours said he purposely behaved from an early age like a fatherless child and resented parental figures. Brant lived next door to the Spencers with his mother and his younger sister Leann until the autumn before the shooting. His stepfather was a police officer named Larry Piech, who had left the family home in early 1978.

Piech worked near the Mexican border in the southern division of the city police department's operating area. He had married Brant's mom in 1972. In his early 20s and without children of his own, he was described as a good person but lacking warmth for children at that stage in his life.

The relationship between Larry and the kids was not as positive as Aleta had hoped and the marriage lasted less than five years. Brant was known to have a distinct dislike for police and shared this view with Brenda. This hatred may have come from his relationship with his stepfather.

Aleta and her children eventually packed up the house and moved about eight miles away to a district called Santee. Aleta would remarry many times over.

Brenda and Brant would spend a lot of time playing on their bikes or in her bedroom listening to music and flipping through magazines. Brenda had subscriptions to Omni, National Geographic, and Smithsonian magazines.

The pair would also spend a lot of time in a makeshift fort in her garage. The only way to access the fort was to navigate around Wally's hoarded car parts and crawl your way in.

A neighbour described the place as a clubhouse of sorts, "not a room, but a cubby that was difficult to get to." Made up of pilfered carpet and plywood, there was barely room for all three of us to sit in there. We crawled in and could not stand.

She had a lot of candles and of course smoking paraphernalia... and it was surrounded by greasy old car parts and buckets of used oil etc. that made walking in the garage impossible, and I recall always worrying that she would catch something on fire and not be able to get out."

It was probably here that Brenda introduced Brant to drugs. She spoke often about Quaaludes, magic mushrooms, and LSD, but most kids in the area were so young and had no idea what she was talking about.

The Flemmings had an above-ground vinyl-lined pool and would invite neighbour kids over to swim. Brenda was a familiar face at these pool parties and known for bragging and an apparent need to surprise people.

On hot summer days, Colleen and Mary O'Connell would hop over the back fence to use the pool.

"She used to say a lot of weird stuff and would hang over the fence and talk. Their [the Spencers'] backyard was just dirt and weeds; the front was like that too," Colleen told me later.

She also remembered it was the first time she was shown drugs. "One day we were all talking, and he [Brant] said that she gave him some pills. I said, 'Why would you take them? you don't know what they are.'"

Colleen maintains she was not friends with Brenda. "I knew her from going swimming at the pool but was *not* friends with her. She was just a third party of something else."

Wally did not like Brant. To him, the kid was the reason Brenda started doing badly in school; he thought his daughter identified with younger kids only because she was so small herself. Brenda's brother, Scott, said Brant was the meanest little kid he had ever met and he hated the police because his stepfather was a cop. Teresa Spencer, Brenda's older sister, said Brant was just mixed up and they were not good influences on each other.

The day after the shooting, police went to speak with Brant at Cajon Park School. Officers first gained permission from the principal and Brant's mother for an interview with him and his sister. They were interviewed separately and without a parent present.

The police did not have high hopes for children so young to help with their investigation.

Brant appeared to revel in the attention from the police, but his interview would be useless in determining any new information about Brenda's behaviour.

BRANT FLEMMING'S POLICE INTERVIEW JAN. 30, 1979:

"I have known Brenda for about four years now. I used to live next door to her. When I lived next door to her, we were friends. I wasn't her boyfriend or anything like that. We were like a 'gang.' Brenda and I got busted once for breaking in [to] the school. That was about two years ago.

"We also got busted two times stealing things out of a store. Brenda and I were always kind of planning things, but we never really carried them out. Brenda used to say that there were three dominations in the world. The first domination was people who planned things. The second domination was the people who did minor things like misdemeanors. Then there was the third type of domination like major things such as sniping or burning or blowing things up. I would say that the third domination would be things that could get you in jail for a good long time. Brenda said that we were like the third type.

"Brenda had a record by the singing group KISS with one of the songs that said, 'Set the world on fire.' We used to play that all the time. She also had a record by 'Alice Cooper' about dead babies and we played that a lot too.

"Brenda would get high once in a while on booze and pills. Lots of times we would plan things like going to kill a cop or blow up a school or mug somebody for their money. Her most favourite thing was to kill a cop.

"She had two plans to kill a cop. The first was that I would take her .22 pellet gun, and she would take her dad's Luger B.B. gun. We would go to the park where the cops did their reports. The plan was that I was to go to the passenger-side window as she walked over to the driver's window if it was up. She would ask the driver to roll the window down. She'd use the pretence of maybe asking what time it was.

"When he did roll the window down, she was going to tell him that if he moved, that I was going to blow his head off. She would say things like I had a hair trigger. I was going to stand there pointing the gun at the officer.

"We later found out that wouldn't work because the .22 would go through him and get her, and we didn't want that. We worked something else out, but after she told him not to move, she would have him put his hands through the steering wheel and take his belt off. When we found out that the bullet would go through him, we changed it then, and we were going to take him into the bathroom and get his .38 and his shotgun. We were going to handcuff him then and shoot him there.

"The second plan to kill a cop was to egg his car or break his window. We planned on running then and have him chase us into the boys' bathroom. We knew that the cop would probably chase us into the bathroom, and when he got in there, she would hit him in the face with an axe. We had a problem with that plan too because we checked and found that there wasn't enough room to swing a good-size axe.

"After I moved from there, Brenda and I were still friends. I'd still visit her once in a while. It would take me about an hour by bike to get over to her place. I went over there last Saturday, and I visited with her. She said that she was going to do something real big Monday.

"We were always saying those kinds of things, but we never did it. I thought she might shoot some windows out with the .22 that her father bought her. When I found out what she had done, I felt kind of happy because I could trust her because she had been telling me the truth. She never told me that she was going to shoot any kids. She just said, 'Wait until Monday and see what I'm going to do. It might even be big enough to make the news.' We always said that we would kill ourselves before we would give up.

"When I heard on the radio about 3 o'clock that she had come out, I thought to myself why did she do that and give up? I saw it on the news, and I saw that she was wearing that hat. She wore it before when she got busted, and I know that hat was really good luck to her."

A few days later, Brant and his mother spoke with the *Los Angeles Times*. Brant revealed elaborate plans to kill cops and details of Brenda's other obsessions. The article included the usual neighbour quotes relating to shooting of cats, drug addictions, and poor school attendance.

Brant described the plan of going to the shopping centre called Parkway Plaza in El Cajon and approaching the window of a police car, "and then she'd reach in and get the guy's belt and pull out the real .38."

Brant said that she had something big planned and "I'll call you Monday night if it doesn't come off. If it does, you'll know about it, because it will be all over TV".

The Saturday before the shooting, Brant said, Brenda showed him .22 calibre bullets all lined up on her bedroom table. He told the reporter that Brenda built a fort in the garage with crossed guns on a sign hung above it like skull and crossbones. She called the sign "The Reaper" and nicknamed her bicycle Jack the Ripper. Brant also said he once went to the mountains with the Spencers to clear brush and shot rabbits but was always under adult supervision.

He said they spoke about going hunting to kill a cat or a cop.

Brant was often chided because he had to go in for dinner at a certain time, but Brenda had none of these responsibilities.

"I can't remember any discipline or her being put on restriction," Brant's mother said.

She said Brenda spoke about death and killing over the time they lived next door. "But we always thought it was to impress the younger kids," she said.

Brant's mother spoke with Wally Spencer about how to discipline the two children, and he told her, "You love them, and you talk to them and try to give them what they want. But when I ask Brenda what she wants, she won't tell me."

Aleta said, "I'm tired of hearing people at work saying what kind of father would give a kid a gun. I know it wasn't a blatant, 'I-don't-care-sort-of-thing.' It was out of love."

When there were problems, she said, Wally would cry and ask Brenda, "Why do you do these things?"

"They used to sit around and talk about what a rotten place the world is and about how everybody hassles you – but nobody hassled them."

Brant's mother said Brenda told her of a major drug episode she was having, and the next day Brenda would be fine. It was like Brenda seemed to relish and enjoy "saying things that just were not true in order to get attention."

She said Brant started to get calls from Brenda the week before the shooting and she started to talk about killing cops and guns again.

Brant never really made much of himself, and in his late teens he struggled with drugs. The family easily could have blamed Brenda or the event for his lack of achievement. After they moved to Santee, he attended Santana High School and enjoyed being part of the speech club. It wasn't to last, and he dropped out in the early 80s before graduating.

Brant bounced from job to job and moved to Phoenix, Arizona, for better prospects in 1990. He got his first career job and joined the Boilermakers Union. To the delight of his family, he was finally getting himself on track. But early on June 1, 1993, on his way to his first day at a new job, he was killed in a car accident.

His vehicle rolled over at speed. No one else was injured in the single-car accident. His sister Leann identified the body. She flew to Phoenix by herself as their mother could not bring herself to make the trip. Roderick Brant Flemming was just 27 when he died.

Brenda undoubtedly introduced Brant to drugs. He was much younger and looked up to his neighbour. She was the dominant personality despite repeated attempts by the Spencers to paint Brant as the leader. His family described him as "a character" but "had a loving, kind, yet wounded heart and soul".

Brenda told me, "I never kept in touch with Brant. Why would I? He used to follow me around all the time 'cause that was the only time he didn't get beat up." I believe Brant was overwhelmed by the bravado of the older girl and never recovered.

14

FAMILY

DOT HOBEL AND Wally Spencer were living in Los Angeles when they married on Dec. 12, 1954, at the Community Congregation Church in Chula Vista, California. It was her parents' local place of worship, just south of San Diego. They obtained the license to marry about two weeks earlier and returned the completed document two days after the wedding. Wally had just turned 26, and she was just 19.

Wallace Edward Spencer was born in White Eagle, Pulaski County, Arkansas, in the autumn of 1929. His father, Claude, was a local truck driver and his mother Edna Maurice was a homemaker, originally from Texas. According to the 1940 census, he was the second of four children, and the family lived just outside Little Rock, the Arkansas state capital city. Once an adult, Wally joined the U.S. Navy and made his way to Southern California and settled in Los Angeles.

Dorothy Nadine Hobel was born in 1935 to James Laverne Hobel and Ruth Nadine Hobel in La Mesa, California, about a 10 minute drive from San Carlos. She was the youngest of three children and the only daughter.

Dot's parents had left the little town of Leigh in Colfax County, Nebraska, and migrated west to get married. They were part of a huge swarm of people moving west at the end of the roaring 20s.

James soon began working at the Rohr Aircraft Corporation in Chula Vista. His brother, Emil, travelled west with his family to join them.

By the time Dot was five, they had moved to the district of Normal Heights in San Diego. Her father became a city councilman representing an area just north of Downtown San Diego. He was imprisoned for embezzlement in 1939 but later pardoned. Despite this, he continued his career at Rohr, where he rose to become vice president of industrial relations.

James then won election to a seat on the suburban Chula Vista city council and eventually became mayor. He served one term in the early 50s, then suffered a knee injury while tobogganing in March 1951 that forced him to make "deals" at his home.

When he was embroiled in a scandal relating to planning permissions and Rohr's financial influence, James was recalled from his political post. Soon after his political career ended, he divorced Ruth and took up with Trudy, who was almost 10 years younger than she.

He died at 82 in 1989 and never made public comments about his granddaughter.

Brenda's grandmother, Ruth, told the *Chula Vista Star News*, "You just can't realise these things. She's sick, definitely ill, and I feel so sorry for the families" in regard to Suchar and Wragg. "She loved animals. When she was a little kid, they had at least five or six animals at a time."

Ruth acknowledged she had little contact with Brenda over the last few years and said, "a person can change. Something went wrong someplace. She was having troubles in her later years. You wish you could bring it back and change it, but you can't. It's hard to figure out. It's tough to raise kids these days. Anybody who does is courageous."

Ruth Hobel would keep more than 60 cats and isolate herself for many years after the divorce. She died in 1980, and her children came and cleaned up the old house.

In the same article, step-grandmother Trudy Hobel said: "It's obvious we didn't know her [Brenda] as well as we should have. But we did know her enough to love her. It's a very trying time for all of us. We feel very devastated by it." Trudy Hobel died in 2005 and is buried with her husband, the former mayor, at Glen Abbey Memorial Park in nearby Bonita.

Brenda's mother Dot graduated from Chula Vista High School and ventured north to Woodbury College in Burbank, in the suburbs of Los Angeles. She studied business and lived in a small, rented apartment in an historical building in Sanford, about half a mile from Wally's place.

Wally was an enlisted serviceman enjoying the Los Angeles nightlife when he met Dot. After the wedding, they settled in San Diego, and Dot started a three-year course in accounting at a local college, often doing night classes after work.

Scott Matthew was born in December 1956, and less than two years later, Teresa Lynn was born in August 1958. The family took a break from baby making to buy a house at 6413 Boulder Lake Ave. in the relatively new area of San Carlos. Brenda arrived on April 3, 1962, and was moved straight into the new home with her brother and sister. She was born in a hospital in National City, a coastal community in southern San Diego County.

A neighbour who lived nearby on Boulder Lake Ave. said Brenda grew into a "spindly tomboy who was no bigger than a bar of soap." In a *Los Angeles Times* interview, she said the girl picked wildflowers and roots and presented them to her mother as bouquets.

The neighbour also said Brenda rode wheelies on her bike and slid down hills on cardboard.

"I'd say to my son, don't let Brenda get hurt, and my son would say, 'Hurt? You can't hurt Brenda. Brenda's all right for a girl.'" The neighbour described Brenda as "normal, normal, normal."

Brenda was a Campfire Blue Bird, a group similar to the Girl

Scouts, played golf with her mom, and was part of the newly formed Bobby Sox softball league for girls in the area. The neighbour remembered Dot "forever hauling the kids around" from one event to another.

Brenda said her father was extremely thrifty and never spent money on anything frivolous like teddy bears or toys. She told me, "I didn't have a favourite stuffed animal. Dad always said they were stupid and a waste of money."

When Brenda was nine, she played in one of San Diego County's top-level junior golf tournaments. Dot and all the kids were more than proficient golfers, her grandmother said. Soccer was another of her favourite sports; her brother Scott went on to play for the high school team.

By late 1971, Dot accused Wally of adultery and filed for divorce. She claimed he was running around with other women and threw him out. She said Wally had asked if he could leave for a year and come back later when it was out of his system. Dot believed he had already rented an apartment somewhere and was ready to go. Dot filed for divorce a few days later. Wally later said the entire story was just a rumour and simply not true.

Wally moved out and eventually bought a three-bedroom house on Lake Atlin Ave. The divorce was finalised in January 1972. Brenda was nine.

The children stayed at the family home on Boulder Lake initially, but this changed during the next year. Scott was first to leave and Teresa followed soon after. Brenda did not want to be alone, so she soon moved in with her siblings.

Brenda told me, "I remember when my parents split up. My dad hit my mom, and she filed on him. They used to argue back and forth all the time. Dad filed for custody of the three of us just to get back at Mom."

In what appeared to be a hard-fought custody dispute, Wally got the kids and had to pay Dot alimony. At the time the San Diego courts took what they thought was the responsible decision and asked the older children what they wanted to do.

Both Scott and Teresa told the court they wanted to stay living with their father, and "the judge didn't want to break up the family," said the grandmother. The children did attend private school but moved to public schools after the divorce.

Dot said Wally convinced the kids to tell the judge they wanted to leave, but it may be that the two teenagers just preferred to live with fewer rules. The new house was less than a mile away and just across the road from Brenda's new school on Lake Atlin Ave.

Dot was given visiting rights with the children, but the kids came and went from her home. Scott said he tried to live with his mother but was kicked out. He said he was wild at the time, and only his father could handle him.

Dot kept the family station wagon, and Wally the old Ford green van. Wally was ordered to pay $200 a month for the next two years and then a nominal $1 a month for the following three years. At the time, Wally was making more than twice the salary of his ex-wife and the home on Boulder Lake still carried a high mortgage. The $200 was about a quarter of Wally's take-home pay at the time and would make their incomes about the same for 24 months.

By late 1973, Wally had fallen into arrears on the alimony and filed documents with the court in May 1974. He unsuccessfully petitioned the court to remove all alimony payments and for Dot to pay him $150 a month for child support.

Wally always complained about money, hoarding as much as he could. Brenda said, "If I had a dollar for every time he said, 'If it wasn't for you kids, I'd have some money.' I'd be a billionaire."

Dot's neighbours said Brenda would visit after school. She would climb the back fence and play with the dogs while waiting for her mum to get home.

"I'd see her maybe once a week, and then she'd come over and spend part of the weekend with me," Dot said. Brenda would sometimes be waiting at the door when her mom came home from work.

Her grandmother said Brenda would be tearful when it was time for her to return to her dad's house. A former next-door neighbour told the *Los Angeles Times*, "I can still see her now sitting out on the windowsill for hours so tiny and alone, looking out toward the school with her arm around the dog."

She remembered Brenda climbing trees and sitting in their tree house but that she was also quiet and appeared to be a lonely girl. They moved away in 1974 and told the new tenants that they "were going to have a wonderful little girl next door."

Brenda was well known on the street, and many different neighbours remembered her as a girl who would pop by to show them new animals she was caring for.

Dot later said, "She [Brenda] was very active, and she was always happy and a good child, well-behaved, and never had any problems in school." Brenda's mother maintains she was a perfect child while she lived with her.

15

ARKANSAS

THE SPENCERS VISITED Wally's family in Arkansas during the summers while Brenda was growing up.

I wrote to Brenda to ask her specifically about this time.

"Things would have definitely turned out different if I had stayed in Arkansas," she told me. "Arkansas was cool for me because there wasn't any stress or pressure there. I could just be a kid. Not a kid raising myself, just a kid."

Her grandparents were always pleased to see her when she came.

"My Ma-maw was a Christian witch, and my Pa-paw taught me everything I know about plants and herbs. A lot of which I've forgotten over the years," she said.

Brenda said her "Uncle Bill and Aunt Jane also lived just outside Little Rock".

"At the time they lived out in the country, but the city has since grown around them. I lived in a little town on the outskirts of Little Rock, Arkansas. Had lots of fun there. The city of Little Rock has expanded since I was there last. We now have a street address there. The city is building up around my little neck of the woods."

Brenda was taken hunting and taught how to handle a weapon from an early age. At 12, she had her own pellet gun and handled her uncle's larger rifles quite often.

"We hunted all the time when I went to Arkansas with our family," Brenda would tell the parole board years later.

In the summer of 1974, when Brenda and the family went to Arkansas to visit Wally's parents and siblings, a major crime in the area was big news on local television – involving a woman coincidentally also named Brenda Spencer, who shot and killed a police officer in a small town just outside Little Rock, not far from her uncle's home.

In April 1974, the *other* Brenda, 23, and two female accomplices broke out of a Kentucky prison and crossed the border into Arkansas. They wrangled some weapons and a car and robbed a grocery store. The three fugitives fired at pursuing police, killing Officer Morris Greenwalt, 51.

Eventually, they took refuge in a large family home just north of Hazen, Arkansas. Two families were held at gunpoint, and the police surrounded the house. A short fruitless negotiation with the police began with Spencer falsely claiming they had already killed people inside. But about an hour later, the fugitives raced from the home with three hostages.

Unfamiliar with the area, they drove into a closed high school parking lot. Police surrounded them once again and began to talk them out. The hostages were released unharmed, and the women slowly gave themselves up. All three were sentenced to life in prison for murder, burglary, and kidnapping.

Brenda was 12 the summer the women were convicted. She watched the verdict announced on KATV Channel 7 while on vacation in Arkansas and saw the three as they were led across the road from the courthouse to the jail.

The crime was huge news in rural Little Rock and is still talked about in cafés and bars in the area. Like the "other" Brenda Spencer, teenage Brenda Spencer had made numerous threats and false claims during her stand-off.

Wally was a small-town Arkansas boy with a humble upbringing, who was hard work to speak to. Almost all of Brenda's friends say they tried to communicate with him without success. By the mid-70s, Wally was still working at San Diego State University in the audio-visual department as an equipment technician. He was known to be quiet and a soft-spoken homebody.

Wally's sister, Jane Sutton, spoke to the *Los Angeles Times* by telephone, saying he was "just like everybody else – a man who likes apple pie and mom, and everything like that."

Co-workers described him as a guy with no small talk and said he stuck to business most of the time. He was known to the neighbours as someone to say hi to, but that was about it.

An acquaintance of Wally told me, "He was an exceptional hoarder. The garage was piled high with stuff he couldn't seem to bear getting rid of, but it was either super out of date or worthless. He'd go to Big Lots and buy weird shit thinking he got a good deal, but it was stuff he'd never use."

On the other hand, Dot, the San Diego native, was known as popular and outgoing. She was still the bookkeeper for the Andy Williams Golf Tournament during half of the year and retained full-time clients such as the University of San Diego and local church and community bookstores from her home office on Boulder Lake.

By 1975, the Spencer kids had all moved from private school into the local public system. Scott had graduated from Patrick Henry High School, and Teresa was at the same school and had just finished her sophomore year. Brenda was attending Pershing Junior High School and was just 13 when she and Brant were arrested for petty theft.

The local schools had just finished for the summer, and on June 22, they were picked up by police in the nearby community of El Cajon. Shop staff said they saw nine-year-old Brant go behind the gun counter at the PayLess Drug Store and take a small 20-round box of .45 calibre bullets.

Witnesses said they saw Brenda instructing the smaller boy on what to do. Brant then grabbed two cans of Coke and put them in the same paper bag. When confronted by security, Brenda made a run for it. Brant stayed and told the guard that he did take the items but was told what to take by an older girl.

The cops took Brant home to his mother and then went next door to speak with Wally. The El Cajon police counselled both parents and closed the case.

Brant was confronted by his police officer stepfather and almost no action was taken against Brenda. Years later, she told investigators they took the bullets because she thought they could sell or trade them for drugs.

When Brenda was 14, she had had a bike accident while riding with a friend. She blacked out after hitting a street signpost. She managed to get back home and either did not tell her father, or he did not understand the urgency.

At her mother's house that evening she felt sleepy, and Dot thought she might have a concussion. Dot did not take her to hospital and thought Wally should handle it. She suggested Brenda tell her dad to take her to a doctor if she did not feel better.

The following day Brenda struggled to remember the incident, and her sister Teresa took her to a hospital. Brenda was treated and released but did complain of headaches more often.

Brenda's brother Scott was 19 with long reddish, sun-bleached hair and often wore a headband to keep it under control. He had just moved out of the house to live in El Cajon with friends.

Scott and Brenda were close and were known to smoke marijuana together. Scott said Brenda idolised him and they liked to go places together. She was like a little brother, he said, because she was a tomboy, and they shared the same outdoor interests.

Scott was outgoing, unlike his father. He moved to Victorville in the California desert and then back again before the shooting.

Teresa turned 18 in the summer of 1976 and was only slightly taller than Brenda at 5'3". She was just graduating from Patrick Henry High and was far more worried about appearances than the rest of the family. She started at San Diego State University the following autumn to study commercial art. To save money during college she remained living at the house for the first few semesters.

Teresa was not as close to Brenda as her brother and did not love the outdoors like the rest of the family. Teresa was more introverted like her father, but that may have been the only thing they shared. She was the only person who did any chores around the house and would often untangle Brenda's hair and do the laundry.

Brenda said she wanted to be a veterinarian and gave books about animals to the neighbour kids. But when her mother told her that her school grades were not good enough to become a vet, she responded, "Ugggh."

Brenda kept many animals, and the house was like a zoo. She gave her pets interesting names like Nakia, Daddles, Calab, Socrates, and named her rabbit Fox. She was most fond of a female cat named Tanahie, which she assured me means "demon" in the Native American Seminole language. But I could never find proof of that.

Tanahie would "get that gleam in her eye, and you just knew she was up to something. She used to attack my sister all the time," Brenda told me. "My sister would tease her… my sister was sitting on the couch watching TV when all of a sudden Tanahie flew up from behind the couch, grabbed my sister, claws out by her forehead, and bit her on the nose. I told her that's what you get for teasing her. So, I named her right."

"I had cats, rats, dogs, a squirrel, and a rabbit growing up. Plus, kids in the neighbourhood would bring me all the injured birds they found, and I would take care of them and set them free when they were healed…

"Oh, and I had snakes. I almost forgot them. I had a ring-necked snake, full grown. It's about 10 or 11 inches long and big around as a pencil. Then I had a five-foot long bull snake; it's also called a gopher snake."

At some point in late 1976, Wally bought land in Potrero, California, to use on weekends for camping, hiking, and shooting. Potrero is a small town in an area known as the Mountain Empire in southeastern San Diego County near a Mexican border crossing. This would be considered the outback of the county but sits only about a 45-minute drive from the house.

Wally took his van down the dirt roads to the plot on Coyote Holler Road. They would always refer to this land as the mountains and spend every Saturday or Sunday there. The land had no structure and was used for day trips in the early days.

Brenda brought friends to the mountains to shoot her pellet gun or her dad's CO2 pistol. She would mostly shoot cans and targets but was known to sometimes shoot gophers and other pests that came onto the land. Wally said she once shot a couple of rabbits with her pellet rifle because she wanted to know how they tasted.

Wally and Brenda made friends with another family in Potrero and spent a lot of time with them. Tom and Jan Minor owned a plot near them on Coyote Holler Road, and Wally had to virtually drive through their land to get to his plot.

They met when Wally was clearing brush on the edge of his land, and he and Tom got to talking. The Spencers rarely spent the night because there was no shelter on the property, but they had plans to build.

The Minors were finishing building their own homestead. Tom was ex-military but chose to live off the grid and grow pot under his house. Brenda was handy for the Minors because she could fit in the crawl spaces and fix things. She also showed the Minors her new rifle and how she could take it apart and put it back together again with her eyes shut.

Jan and Brenda were friendly with each other, and the neighbour girl was also good with Eric, the Minors' five-year-old son. Eric grew up to be an award-winning cannabis grower and breeder in central California. He specializes in CBD-rich genetics for medicinal purposes and advertises that he is a second-generation cannabis farmer.

Brenda spent a lot of time on their land, hiking with their dogs. She had great admiration for the Minors and would also bring her friends to meet them. Her friends Susie, Dawn, Shari, and Brant Flemming were just a few of those who visited the mountains with her.

Back at home, Brenda would shoot birds from her back yard and sometimes have to climb into the neighbour's property to collect her kills. One neighbour said she would cut off the wings and pin them to a board to dry. Brenda would study small animals and make remarkably intricate drawings.

The neighbour remembered her frog drawings best. "When she showed me her drawings, I was blown away at her talent. She drew animals (I remember the frogs the most) with incredible detail."

They also said Brenda surprised her in many ways.

"I had a beloved cat that would come when I called. I called him from my front door one afternoon; he was evidently across the street at the school. I did not think to look for cars, and he got hit. He was jerking and flopping, and I could not go out to him, but somehow Brenda knew it had happened and went to him to comfort him. The driver took the cat to the vet, and my mom took me to a doctor's appointment. When I got home, Brenda came over to give me his collar. She thought to keep it for me. The cat did not make it, so I appreciated having that."

In the summer of 1977, the Spencer family's neighbours, the O'Connells, came around to ask Wally to tell Brenda to stop firing her pellet gun in the backyard. They shared the back fence and said that Brenda was firing randomly for hours, and it caused them concern. They knew everyone on the block, and the Spencer house was known as "the weird house, just like on the movies" as Colleen O'Connell put it.

In September 1977, like her brother and sister before her, Brenda started at Patrick Henry High School. But when she was expelled for truancy in her first year, she was moved to Garfield High, the alternative school for teenagers who needed help, for a year before returning to Patrick Henry.

During this stage, Dot didn't see Brenda for months at a time, then she appeared, out of the blue, and would stay for a few nights in a row. Dot has always said that Brenda was the perfect daughter before the divorce. Trouble began, she insisted, as soon as she moved out of the house.

On Jan. 16, 1978, a year before the shooting, Brenda, 15, and Brant Flemming, 12, were arrested for vandalising the school, smashing a window, writing on blackboards and spraying the fire extinguishers. A neighbourhood girl named Cassandra Freese told the police that Brenda and Brant were the culprits.

Because they had removed items, San Diego police arrested the pair for burglary. Brenda said she and Brant were drunk and knew their way around the school because they had attended there.

This was the first time she was in real trouble. Brenda had only been in mild trouble for shoplifting years before and with a different police force who did not keep records. Police again took her home, not seeing her as a huge risk. Brenda told her brother it was all Brant's idea and said he had broken into the school and then found her to show her what was inside. Brant was the far younger participant and the likelihood of him directing the older girl's actions is far-fetched.

Cassandra Freese was a Pershing Jr. High School student whose grandmother lived on the same block as Brenda. In the middle of the day of the break in, she and a friend were riding bikes past Cleveland Elementary when she heard breaking glass. They rode into the school to check it out.

Cassie and her friend could clearly see Brenda and Brant in the classroom breaking things. Cassie kept watch while her friend rode home to tell her parents.

"I stayed there keeping an eye on Brenda till the police came. She had taken off before the police came, and my girlfriend and I rode around with the police to find her," Cassie remembers. "We found her and the other kid on their bikes in the parking lot of an apartment complex on the corner. . . She saw us in the cop car."

Police arrested Brenda and Brant and released them to their parents with a referral to counsellors at San Diego's Youth Services. That summer, Brant Flemming's family relocated to Santee, where he continued counselling at Cajon Park School.

As instructed by police, Wally took Brenda to see the counsellors in San Diego. He initially sat in with her for the first three visits, and then Brenda attended alone. Counsellor Noreen Harmon was assigned to work with Brenda for regular sessions after school.

Harmon noted that she tended to put up barriers and resisted probing questions about her family. Brenda resented the lack of closeness in her family and was pleased with the family outings to the mountain property. She showed no indication of significant violence but did say she wanted a rifle for Christmas.

She was evaluated as a tomboy without female influences and role models but having no outstanding problems that required a referral to other agencies. Brenda continued seeing Harmon, on and off, for the next 11 months. Their sessions became more sporadic after the summer, but they did meet before Christmas and then finally in juvenile hall.

Brenda reportedly liked Harmon and shared intimate details with her. SD Youth Services allegedly submitted reports to Patrick Henry school and to Wally. These reports have never surfaced, and Wally says he knew nothing about them.

When Harmon was interviewed later for a probation officer's report, she gave a more candid assessment of her young charge. She said Brenda had a fascination with drugs and guns and it was all she would talk about.

The burglary case had been officially closed when Cassie Freese started as a freshman at Patrick Henry High. Soon, Brenda began to follow Cassie and her friend home from school and harass them.

"Brenda would stand in the middle of the street outside of our houses yelling that she was going to get even with us for what we did, turning her into the police. Our parents started picking us up from school to keep us safe," Cassie told me.

None of the family had liked Brant, but he and Brenda were inseparable for years.

Wally said he never knew where Brenda was most of the time and she was hard to control. But once Brant moved away it was a different story and Brenda spent time with girlfriends.

Brenda turned 16 in April 1978, while still attending Garfield High. Wally bought Brenda a camera and began to take her on photography trips up the coast to Morrow Bay. Photography was Wally's hobby, and it was something, he thought, the two of them could share.

He was taking a photography class at night and for a project he took Brenda to the San Diego Zoo to take pictures. But Wally said she did not like seeing animals confined and was more interested in the training of hawks.

Brenda said, "The Humane Society was doing a photo contest, and we got extra credit in my high school photography class if we entered it." Months later, she would use Wally's 35mm Canon to snap a man leading his dog through an obedience course. This photo won first prize in a major San Diego competition.

Brenda is still clearly proud of the achievement, telling me, "I actually won the grand prize and two first places. They had more than one category. The grand prize was a TV, and the two first places was two 16 packs of colour film. The photo that won the TV was in the working dogs category. It was the police dogs working called 'Going Through the Motions.' One of the other photos was in the farm animals' category. It was a baby goat staring off into the distance called 'California Dreaming.'"

16

THE LEAD UP TO MONDAY

THE SUMMER OF 1978, Scott was living a few miles away in El Cajon. He was arrested for cultivating marijuana but was released pending further investigation and moved back into his old bedroom to await his fate. The drug offence was eventually dismissed for lack of evidence. Scott was able to save so much money on rent that he planned a couple trips away for later in the year and in January.

Conveniently, Teresa had a friend looking for a roommate at the same time as Scott's return. She packed up all her things and left in her Subaru. She said she moved out of the house to live closer to her university classes. But it is more likely she did not want to live with Scott again and gave him back his room. Teresa was known to be the only person to clean up the house and take care of the day-to-day routine. Once she left, the house fell into complete disarray.

Wally was still taking evening classes for various things such as photography and pottery. He would get home from work and go straight out, three nights a week. Brenda was usually in bed when he got home, and she spent a lot of time alone that autumn and early winter. Dot said Brenda was self-sufficient and could lock herself in a room alone for hours and entertain herself.

Scott said Wally and Brenda had a big argument about her having to go back to school at the end of the summer. Brenda said school was boring; Wally insisted she go.

So, she started back at Patrick Henry that September, attending classes sporadically and still meeting with counsellor Harmon. Just before the Christmas break, Brenda saw a psychologist on Harmon's recommendation, but Wally said he never received a report or diagnosis from anyone. That Christmas, Scott and Wally bought her the rifle and rifle lock for Christmas and were excited to give it to her. She had been asking for one for months.

At Christmas, Uncle Vern came down from Van Nuys with his wife Barbara and their two kids, Chris and Marianne.

"My Aunt Barbara was nice," Brenda told me. "We always went up to their place for Thanksgiving. Christmas was at our house, but I do have some good memories of it."

Her grandmother told reporters Brenda helped to cook a huge meal for visiting family and had a keen interest in cooking. When I asked Brenda about this she disagreed.

"I didn't cook when I was a kid; just opened a can and heated it up."

Christmas morning, she received the Ruger .22 rifle with a mounted scope from under the tree. While her relatives looked on, she also unwrapped a trigger lock from her brother Scott. She also got a stack of books about animals and 500 rounds of ammo to go with the gun.

Her brother and father had clearly discussed the matter and felt she was in a reasonable state of mind to receive such a gift. With or without a report from SD Youth Services, Wally thought the rifle would make his daughter happy. In his mind, he was being a good father.

Brenda's Arkansas relatives did not think there was anything odd about giving a 16-year-old a starter rifle. Anyway, she was back in her normal school, and things were on the up.

"I bought a rifle for her Christmas because I thought she was ready for that, and we used to go up in the mountains, and she used to target shoot up there," Wally said in an interview years later.

Dot said she was furious Wally bought Brenda a rifle even though she knew the girl had wanted it. Teresa agreed with her mother but did not intervene. Brenda had been responsible with her pellet rifle over the years and promised her mother she would use the new weapon only in the mountains.

Brenda had begun to call Brant on the phone but had not seen him since he moved away in the summer. She bragged about getting the new rifle and wanted to make plans to show it to him. Brant was interested in seeing a real rifle, but he lived so far away, and his mom was not willing to drive him over.

In the middle of January 1979, Scott left for Philadelphia with a friend. He had planned to travel for a bit and return sometime in February. Brenda made her last trip to the Potrero mountains; she and Wally went down for a weekend and met with the Minors.

Wally believes she shot about 200-300 rounds through the new rifle since Christmas, and she still had a great amount of the Federal brand ammo left for future trips. He said she shot only at targets and tin cans, may have fired at a few squirrels, but never killed animals.

The week before the attack on the school, Brenda and her sister went hiking with the pellet gun and shot at cans. On that Wednesday, they went with Teresa's friends to the Torrey Pines golf course on the cliffs overlooking the Pacific Ocean to watch the golf pros' practice day.

Dot invited them to see all the celebrities and said Brenda was happily running around the complex looking at famous people.

That weekend Brant rode his bike more than an hour to see Brenda. Wally came and went that day running errands, and he saw the pair of them listening to music in Brenda's room.

Brenda and Brant decided to ride their bikes around the corner to Cassie's house on Lake Aral. Brenda had not stopped harassing her for getting her busted. They planted themselves across the street and stared towards the house. Neighbours told police they started to yell obscenities, something Cassie disputes.

"Brenda spent an entire day sitting across the street from my house staring at my stepdad while he replaced the brakes on our car in the carport. My mom was really freaked out and didn't want to even leave the house or let us kids leave the house. Brenda looked and acted absolutely EVIL," she said.

What Brenda did not know was that both witnesses to their crime, Cassie and Theresa, lived across the street from each other. Both families were frightened to come out. The Freese family held tight and eventually Brenda and Brant rode away without further incident.

By the time Wally returned home, Brenda and Brant were watching TV as if nothing had happened. Wally had no idea that any intimidation had taken place or that the pair had even left the house.

Brenda popped out to Wally's van and retrieved multiple boxes of .22 ammo at some point over the weekend. Wally kept his van unlocked and in such an unkempt state that it would have been easy to remove something without him knowing.

Wally woke about 5:30am on the morning of the shooting and got himself ready for work as on any normal weekday. About an hour later, he went to wake Brenda for school. He opened her door to find she was already awake and getting dressed. She was wearing light brown corduroy pants and a white shirt over a grey thermal undershirt for warmth.

Both his other children were good students and had graduated from high school without problems years before. Brenda didn't care for school and often made up several excuses not to go. She was a latchkey kid and could easily leave the house with the intention of arriving at school, only to turn around, go home, and sleep the day away. Her father was at work, and her siblings were out of the house most of the time.

On this Monday morning, Brenda told her father she was not feeling well and said period pains were extreme so she wanted to spend the day in the bath or bed. He allowed her to stay home, although she had only recently been accepted back into her normal high school.

Wally left for work as normal just after 7am in his cluttered van, leaving his son's old green pick-up truck on the driveway. Exactly what Brenda did over the next 90 minutes is only speculation, but it is assumed that she finished getting dressed and did not eat breakfast.

Once alone, Brenda unzipped her new rifle from its case and removed the lock from the trigger. She gathered up all the ammunition she could find. Wally always kept the extra ammo in his room or his van, and she had already taken some over the weekend. In total, she collected about 1,000 rounds of Federal Power Flight long shelled .22 calibre ammunition.

She took the new rifle and her old pellet gun and made her way to the front door. On the way, she grabbed her white-handled folding knife and a black-handled hunting knife hidden in her room. She put on her black cotton zip-up hooded sweatshirt and blue trainers. To keep her hair in place, she added her navy fisherman-style watch cap. It was also said to be her lucky charm.

Brenda set everything down on the tile entrance way and picked up a small bottle of Southern Comfort. The front door opened inwards and almost directly into the living room. Either Wally left the screen door wide open, or Brenda opened it outwards to get it out of the way. Police photos showed it was fully open and pressed against Brenda's bedroom window.

The view through the diamond-shaped window panels on the top half of the door was over the driveway and on to Lake Atlin Ave. Brenda probably used the butt of her pellet rifle to break out the lower left and right half diamond-shaped glass windows. She would not want to damage her new Ruger.

The glass fell outside the front door as expected. The upper half of the door was window and the lower half was wooden, so she could easily crouch down behind the door out of sight but still have clear vision of the driveway. A rifle could now easily be rested on the doorframe for maximum stability. By breaking both glass windows, it is assumed that she was considering shooting with both guns. She had the knives just in case.

There might have been a few kindergarten students and parents congregating near the front gates of the western part of the building. The view of the kindergarten was partially obscured from Brenda's vantage point by the pick-up truck in her driveway and parking lot bushes.

Brenda could hear the bell clearly from her house just across the 35ft-wide road but had no view of the kindergarten door. Her bedroom window looked onto the driveway but was blocked from the school by the overgrown tree in the front of the house. For whatever reason, Brenda did not fire at the kindergarteners or their parents.

By 8am, the parking lot across the road at Cleveland Elementary School was filling up with teachers' cars, and students would soon be arriving.

Seven hours later two people were dead, nine injured and Brenda was being led away in handcuffs.

17

MAKING THE CASE

AS EXPECTED, TWO days after the shooting on Jan. 31, 1979, the district attorney's office filed a petition with the juvenile court charging Brenda with two counts of murder, one count of assault with a deadly weapon on a police officer, and nine counts of assault with intent to commit murder.

Chuck Patrick, chief trial deputy in the D.A.'s office, asked that Brenda be tried as an adult, in Superior Court. The petition alleged *special circumstances*, making it clear that Brenda could be given a maximum sentence of life without the possibility of parole, if she were found guilty. If the trial was held in juvenile courts, the maximum sentence would be custody for seven years.

William L. Todd Jr. was selected as Superior Court judge to hear the case. As a legal formality, Judge Todd scheduled a detention hearing that morning to decide if Brenda would be kept in custody or released pending court action. A juvenile court hearing also could make a formal determination whether she would be tried as an adult, but Todd did not schedule one.

A question of whether Brenda should be tried at all centred on her sanity, and many thought she might never see the inside of a Superior Court because of her age. As her arraignment – her first appearance before a judge – was being organised, locals outraged by the horrific crime were rallying in a bid to make sure she was never released. The *San Diego Union* reported that more than 2,000 already had signed a petition sent to the district attorney asking that Brenda be tried as an adult.

Because Brenda had previously been released to her parents after shoplifting and vandalism, it seems she believed she would soon be released and did not understand the severity of her crimes. Judge Todd soon ordered her to be held without bail at juvenile hall, until the outcome of a trial.

Police homicide division chief Winston Yetta said the tests taken after Brenda's arrest showed she was not under the influence of alcohol. It took more than two weeks before police were able to determine she was not under the influence of any drug or alcohol.

Detective Olson and Tribune reporter Steve Wiegand both told me they agreed with the findings. Brenda was coherent and spoke normally during their phone calls with her. Officer Kasinak, who accompanied Brenda on the trip to police headquarters in downtown San Diego after the shooting, told me she did not speak at all on the journey and showed no signs of stumbling.

For her arraignment in juvenile court on Thursday, Feb. 1, Brenda's brother, Scott, had arrived from Texas and was positioned at the defence table next to her. Defence attorney Robert Butler sat next to her parents on the other side of Scott. Dot and Wally were sitting together and holding hands in between wiping their tears with tissues.

Butler was a San Diego native who lived about five miles from the Spencers' home in La Mesa. He spent little time with the Spencers leading up to the hearing and purposely did not allow himself to be photographed next to Brenda.

Normally, cameras would not be permitted in the courtroom, but this was possibly the biggest criminal court case in San Diego history, and Judge Todd allowed them.

"Under the unusual circumstances of this case, I recognise I cannot un-ring the bell," he said. "I cannot change what facts already exist."

Todd said he might allow any defence motion to bar photographers from future hearings, but this hearing would go ahead with cameras present.

The cameras and their operators took up much space, about 10ft from the defence table.

Wally tried his best to hide his face from the cameras, sometimes dropping his head and crying.

Wally and Dot held hands and continued to cry. Occasionally, they looked at their daughter, who never once turned to face them.

Judge Todd asked Brenda if she understood the charges against her. In a low voice, she responded inaudibly.

"Speak up, young lady," he ordered. She swallowed and said loudly, "Yes, I understand the charges."

There was no objection when she was ordered to be remanded in custody without bail. Defence attorney Butler told the judge she should be kept in juvenile hall for her own safety, and the judge agreed. She would remain there until the hearing to determine if she were to be tried as an adult or a juvenile.

Brenda sat motionless except for a brief moment when she turned and whispered to her brother sitting next to her. She gave a small smile as she turned to face the judge again.

The hearing was scheduled for Feb. 16 – two weeks away. That allowed time for Butler and the Spencers to get an adequate psychological profile. The court appointed two psychiatrists: Dr. Haig Koshkarian and Dr. Thomas Rodgers. Immediately after the hearing, Butler told waiting reporters that Brenda showed no emotion towards him and was difficult to read.

Koshkarian came to San Diego in 1970. He had worked on US Navy bases during the Vietnam war and decided to settle in the Pacific coast community of La Jolla. Rodgers, who was from

Colorado, later would become director of San Diego's Psychiatry and Law Center.

The day after the hearing, Scott Spencer was seen wandering the neighbourhood, looking for Brenda's cat. The family also started to receive death threats and hate mail. Someone also damaged Dot's car and Wally's van by pelting them with eggs and rocks over the next few weeks.

Brenda, who seemed not to be faring too well in juvenile hall, was refusing sessions with social workers. She and her family spoke to no one as they prepped for the trial.

On Feb. 8, Brenda's lawyer, Robert Butler, asked to be relieved of his duties, citing earlier commitments. He had been subjected to death threats and his application was granted.

The new court-appointed attorney was to be Michael McGlinn, who was given time to familiarise himself with the case. McGlinn had graduated from Washington D.C.'s Georgetown University and studied law at the University of California during the 1967 summer of love in San Francisco. He started practicing juvenile law in 1970 and had given evidence as an expert witness in child abuse hearings.

Deputy district attorney Charles Patrick was named to represent the prosecution. Patrick, known as "Big Chuck," attended the University of California at Los Angeles in the '50s, then went on to Southwestern Law School and straight into the district attorney's office in the coastal city of Santa Barbara in 1964. He was taller than McGlinn by almost a foot, with a long face and greying hair.

Judge Todd rescheduled Brenda's fitness hearing to allow McGlinn more time to prepare.

McGlinn's first action was to try to remove the media from it. He petitioned Judge Todd, and a determination was set for two days before the hearing. Judge Todd had said sensitive material would be discussed at the fitness hearing, and it might be material that was not allowed at the actual trial.

McGlinn argued that this material, if the news media were allowed to attend, could be published and might prejudice a fair trial.

Brenda sat alone with McGlinn at the hearing. She wore the light blue T-shirt, blue jeans, and dark slip-on shoes provided by juvenile hall. She was completely blank-faced and did not sit up straight for a single part of the hearing.

McGlinn opened by arguing that some San Diego news media was irresponsible and had reported untruths about the case. He said this prompted threats toward the family and Brenda's previous counsel.

"There is no guarantee that that type of [news] coverage will not continue," McGlinn told the judge.

He argued that Brenda might be denied a fair trial if evaluations by the two psychiatrists who interviewed her were to become public.

He also said he would be reluctant to speak about sensitive areas and would "not be able to openly and frankly discuss the case with the court."

Deputy district attorney Patrick rebutted the argument, saying he couldn't believe that McGlinn would withhold sensitive material if it were critical to protecting his client.

"Clearly this is a case that has news value. It's hard to conceive of what will come up at a fitness hearing that hasn't already come up in the press," Patrick told the judge.

He also noted that Brenda spoke to reporters on the telephone while hiding in the house.

"It is impossible to conceal the fact that she acted as a participant in disseminating information."

Attorney Edward J. McIntyre was on hand to represent the Copley Newspapers company, which owned *The Evening Tribune* and *San Diego Union*. He argued the community at large had a legitimate interest in being informed about the proceedings.

But Judge Todd agreed with McGlinn and banned journalists from the fitness hearing taking place that Friday. He also said that had Brenda been an adult, the media would not even have attended the preliminary hearing earlier that month.

At the fitness hearing on Feb. 23, Judge Todd ruled Brenda was "unfit to be treated as a juvenile".

The Tribune reporter Steve Wiegand was called to testify and gave the court a copy of his notes. He was asked to recount what had happened. He told me, "I recall the judge complained he couldn't read my scribbled notes."

McGlinn had called a representative from the California Youth Authority as his only witness. The hearing, held behind closed doors, without media present, took just 90 minutes.

Todd ordered Brenda to be turned over to adult court and scheduled her next court appearance as an arraignment in Municipal Court the following Tuesday, Feb. 27.

McGlinn told reporters he was "disappointed with the ruling" as he shuffled out of court. Wally was in tears as he left and refused to speak to the press.

Brenda was marched in and out of court in handcuffs behind her back. She had been in custody for about 30 days and looked as skinny as a rake. She wore a light mustard turtleneck tucked into white jeans without a belt. Her hair was brushed and parted down the middle, and she wore her signature glasses. Brenda was kept at juvenile hall without bail until the arraignment.

Later, Municipal Judge Lewis Wenzell postponed Brenda's arraignment until March 8. McGlinn had asked for more time to file a writ to the California Court of Appeal contesting Todd's previous ruling.

McGlinn's appeal argued that Judge Todd used a wrong legal standard in deciding which court she should be tried in.

"As it stands, Brenda faces little if any hope for rehabilitation in state prison, and even if rehabilitated, she would not get out of prison. While under the Juvenile Court's direction, Brenda can be treated and helped, with the good chance of becoming a responsible person in the community," he said.

The appeal said McGlinn's single witness – California Youth Authority official Richard J. Holler – had made a key mistake in his testimony by saying Brenda could be incarcerated only until she was 23. McGlinn argued that if she continued to pose a danger to society as a juvenile, she could be kept in custody for successive stints, theoretically forever.

He also said two psychiatric reports on Brenda were not considered. Both had agreed that she was best suited for a juvenile court.

Dr. Haig Koshkarian's psychological profile of Brenda said she was not a sophisticated criminal, and both he and Dr. Thomas Rodgers questioned whether her disorder could be treated successfully by the time she was 23.

Koshkarian's report said Brenda was "a sick and very disturbed girl, who appears much younger than her age but tries to act much older. She shows characteristics of both schizoid and a psychopathic personality, both severe." It would be "in the best interests of Brenda and society that basic changes and rehabilitation be affected on her personality… While the prognosis for this is not good, the best chance for it to occur is in an age-appropriate, therapeutic setting, rather than in an adult penal setting."

Rodgers wrote she was "a sick adolescent… her personality is such that a combination of her youth, her rigid naiveté, and her frail physical stature would make her a target for physical and sexual abuse in the adult prison system. It may be possible to rehabilitate this youngster through the facilitation of the Juvenile Court; however, it would not be easy to accomplish. A plan of intensive psychotherapy would need to be devised."

McGlinn said Brenda was a young, unpopular, misfit who was

out of place at the school and troubled by her parents' divorce seven years earlier. In her father's custody, she rarely saw her mother, even though they only lived blocks away.

He described her home life as "a rather bleak residence, totally lacking in feminine interest, softness, or any organization. It would almost border on a deprived existence… One senses the mother did not initiate a great deal of requests for her to come over."

McGlinn's brief included the counsellor's report by Noreen Harmon that described Brenda as "unwilling to discuss any future plans, or even acknowledge that the future existed" with a "lack of self-esteem and isolation from peers and parents that Miss Spencer was referred to a psychiatrist, whom she saw on Dec. 20, 1978."

Harmon says the report was filed with Youth Services, but Wally maintains he had never seen nor heard of any report before the court hearings began.

Prosecutor Chuck Patrick argued that in a first-degree murder case, the burden is on minors to show in court why they should *not* be tried as an adult. He suggested that expert opinions were based solely on Brenda's own non-responsive interviews over the past weeks.

Patrick said none of the reports quoted Brenda and almost all information was taken from her background as described by McGlinn. There was no information to suggest Brenda's state of mind during the day of the crime, and it was clear the defence had not proved anything, he said.

Therefore, he argued, Brenda Spencer, by default, should be tried in the adult courts.

McGlinn argued in return that even if the burden lay with him and his client, the testimony of the two concurring psychiatrists and California Youth Authority officials should be enough evidence to keep Brenda in the juvenile court.

But Judge Todd, once again, agreed with the prosecution, saying the defence failed to prove that Brenda's trial should stay in Juvenile Court.

He ruled that Brenda would be tried in Superior Court and if convicted would be sentenced to a maximum term of life in prison without parole.

McGlinn argued in rebuttal that he felt the decision was not supported by the evidence and raised the question of his client's right to equal protection under the law. He requested a delay in Brenda's upcoming arraignment, which Todd rejected.

On March 8, 1979, Brenda entered a plea of not guilty. During the short hearing, she said only the word "yes" when asked if she waived her right to a preliminary hearing. Judge Wenzell set the hearing for March 27, and McGlinn reiterated that he intended to appeal to the California Supreme Court for her right to be tried in juvenile court.

Nine-year-old shooting victim Cam Miller attended the hearing with his parents.

"When I saw her, the look she gave me – her whole appearance was very evil and scary... blank, empty stare. She just sat there and glared at me," he told the *San Diego Union*.

Before the hearing, Cam had seen the Spencers only on television a few times. The first was from his hospital bed on the day of the attack. He watched the news from his gurney as it showed police taking Brenda away.

18

LETTER FROM BRENDA

BRENDA'S LAWYER ADVISED her not to contact anyone outside of juvenile hall. She was allowed visits by her family but was told not to write letters or correspond with anyone else. Her parents visited with her often but almost never together. The bond they showed in court had since disappeared. Wally brought her brother Scott on occasions, and Teresa visited at least once.

On the sly, Brenda started writing to the Minors in Potrero. Her father took the letters during his visits and passed them on. She is believed to have written more than a dozen letters over the months she was locked up in juvie.

In the first set of letters, she said she wished Wally could sneak the Minors in as long-lost cousins. Brenda added she felt they were more like family than anyone else in her life and repeatedly asked if all of their animals are getting along. She was particularly worried about their dog named Van.

She offered them her four-and-a-half-ft bull snake named Willis, to be set free in their woodpile. The name came from the TV Show *Diff'rent Strokes*, which first aired earlier that November. The name Willis became a famous catchphrase by star Gary Coleman, "What'chu talkin' 'bout, Willis?"

Brenda told the Minors that juvenile hall was not that bad except for the food. She said she had to negotiate with the nurse to get a decent pair of shoes and bragged about hitting a door frame and breaking her hand. She said she was placed on room confinement and suicide watch, then given her own toilet and sink, considered a luxury by incarcerated juveniles.

Her daily job was cleaning the bathrooms, and she said she thought she was in good enough physical shape to help around the Minors' new house. She made friends with the coaches (guards), other inmates, and seemed to think she was behaving well, despite being confined on suicide watch.

Most interestingly, Brenda said she might be sent to California Youth Authority detention centre in the city of Ventura before being freed. At this early stage, Brenda still seemed to believe that this would all blow over and that she would soon be home.

She ended her letters with the occasional poem. This one is taken from her letter dated March 2.

There was a young cat from Cann.
Who loved to run so he ran.
He slipped on some rice.
The fall wasn't nice.
So now he just draws with a crayon.

Brenda continued her letters to the Minors. In one dated March 11, she wrote to Jan expressing a multitude of worries. Brenda indicated that she was keenly aware that other inmates were nervous and scared of her and did not fight with her anymore.

She described herself as a drug addict for the last five years and said Jan was the only person she could relate to. She said she needed drugs to help her through being locked up and said she'd been in a head spin without drugs and questioned her own sanity.

A week later, she was apologetic and promised to show more resilience in future letters. Brenda said she stayed up all night, so she could sleep during an electroencephalogram (EEG) test scheduled the next day. The test was intended to determine brain activity. Brenda also said she was looking forward to personnel putting water in her ear to see if her eyes would move back and forth, although she had no idea what that might prove.

She said she was trying to keep studying so her father would continue putting her allowance in her bank account. Wally and Brenda had agreed her allowance would continue if she continued with her schooling. She said she thought she might have enough money to buy her own dog when her incarceration ended.

Brenda wrote of a new girl in juvenile hall named Sheila who was sharing a space with her. She told the Minors that Sheila looked enough like her to pass as her sister. She joked that Sheila spoke quickly, like her brother Scott. When Brenda introduced Sheila to her father on one of his visits, the two struck up a strange friendship. Unbeknownst to Brenda, Wally began to correspond directly with his daughter's roommate.

Sheila McCoy was born on August 29, 1962, and was just five months younger than Brenda. She had been arrested for arson of a new apartment her family recently moved into. She had lived with her mother, stepfather, and one-year-old brother in the country town of Ramona. But the family moved to an apartment in suburban Santee to Sheila's displeasure.

Being moved into a smaller residence and away from her grandparents and friends did not sit well with Sheila, investigators said, so she and a boyfriend concocted a plan to set fire to the new apartment and force a move back to Ramona.

She was arrested shortly after the blaze and taken to juvenile hall and into Brenda's room. Sheila had seen Brenda on the news and was well aware of who she was. As it turned out, Sheila's family did move back to Ramona but without their daughter.

"She was just a weirdo, like a groupie," Brenda said years later of

Sheila, who looked up to the older girl in many ways. "She thought what I did was something great, and I just can't go along with that kind of thinking."

Their local notoriety made both Brenda and Sheila very popular in juvenile hall. Other inmates never bothered them. Brenda's father continued to visit regularly and often visited Sheila when his daughter was away at a testing facility.

Brenda underwent a series of neurological tests at a local hospital, Scripps Memorial. McGlinn would say only that results will "remain confidential until such time as they may be released". The tests included X-rays of her skull and the EEG brain wave diagnostic tests for a multitude of potential issues including brain tumors, inflammation, stroke, sleep disorders, and epilepsy.

Brenda told the Minors she was sick from the tests although EEGs are said to be non-invasive and usually just involve placing electrodes on the head. Normal side effects are said to include tiredness or drowsiness but considering many people who take these tests suffer from sleep problems, no side effects are attributed to most patients.

In a further letter to the Minors, Brenda said she went to the hospital for more EEG tests and had to pee into cups and have her blood drawn. She said she had spent some time in a rubber room wearing only a paper gown and had been restrained with leg chains.

She said she was still on suicide watch and had to leave her shoes outside the room because of her "whack-attacks". Jokingly, she said that if she wanted to kill herself, she wouldn't need to do it with shoelaces. Brenda told the Minors she did not understand why she was locked up and believed she was still coming down from drug addiction.

The late 70s were a strange time for psychiatry with doctors giving many varying reasons for the shooting. Brenda had read in the *San Diego Union*, writer Paul Krueger sarcastically suggesting her lawyers could use bad biorhythms as a defence. He published findings from a North Carolina biorhythms expert saying her emotional cycle was "critical," her intellectual cycle was "peaking," and her physical cycle was "very high" on the morning of the shooting.

The expert also determined that Brenda's biorhythm cycle was 36% aligned with negotiator Detective Olson's but had 0% in common with bull horn wielder Detective Thurston. This must obviously explain what Brenda and Olson got along so well during the phone calls. I shared this report with Olson, and he thought it was funny but totally irrelevant.

19

EPILEPSY

ON MARCH 28, McGlinn filed a writ of *habeas corpus* with the California Supreme Court, in essence asking for authorities to prove Brenda's detention was lawful, or to release her. *Habeas corpus* writs often are based on new evidence that might cause a judge to reconsider an earlier ruling.

McGlinn, who sought a ruling that Judge Todd should conduct a new fitness hearing, entered fresh reports from a new doctor who hadn't previously examined Brenda. He offered new conclusions on Brenda's EEG test by psychiatrist Dr. William DeBolt. The DeBolt report said Brenda had a mental illness from her bicycle accident two years before. In his opinion, Brenda had abnormal brain waves and epilepsy.

McGlinn said this new information about her mental condition was not available when she was first remanded to the adult courts. He argued that Brenda had been treated by the stricter procedures of the adult court and that constituted a denial of her rights as a child.

Dr. Rodgers, one of the two psychiatrists who earlier treated Brenda, told the court, "Dr. DeBolt reported to me that the neurological examinations and scan tests were normal. However, the EEG is grossly abnormal and shows a definite seizure disorder.

"Brenda has epilepsy. Further tests, mostly blood and urine tests, have been requested to help delineate the etiology of this seizure disorder. It is my opinion that the trauma, bicycle accident, of one-and-a-half to two years ago likely was the cause of the problem.

"If you will remember, I pointed out that it would be very difficult to treat this youngster. I do think that if a significant part of her illness is this seizure disorder, then she most probably can be treated successfully. This would include both anti-convulsive medication and a trial of psychotherapy. Both can be offered by the California Youth Authority."

His colleague Dr. Koshkarian said, "Further tests are needed, as well as a trial of treatment with medication. This discovery now raises the possibility that with treatment of this medical condition, Brenda may show measurable changes in her personality disposition and behaviour patterns. As such, it improves Brenda's prognosis and raises the possibility that changes in her personality could be made in a more definitive period of time."

Both doctors agreed it that while it would be difficult to rehabilitate Brenda, any treatment would certainly not be concluded by the time she was 23 and within the Youth Authority's care.

This was a key factor why Todd sent the case to the adult court following the first hearing.

The Supreme Court refused McGlinn's earlier appeal without comment and began to consider his new writ of *habeas corpus*.

Experts on epilepsy have concluded no evidence exists of a connection between epilepsy and violence except for a rare form of the disease, then called psychomotor seizure, which affects the temporal lobe of the brain. But some experts say that even though violence has been associated with psychomotor seizures, it is so rare that it is almost never seen. As it turns out, Brenda *was* diagnosed with this rare form.

Publication of the psychiatric conclusions on Brenda swamped the San Diego County Epilepsy Society with calls seeking more information. Prominent neurologists and neuropsychologists carefully distanced themselves from judgments about Brenda's mental state or guilt as they offered opinions on epilepsy.

One of them, Dr. Charlotte McCutchen, co-director of the neuro-seizure clinic at the Veterans Administration and University Hospital in San Diego's La Jolla district, offered, "To equate temporal lobe epilepsy with mental disability to the extent that someone is psychotic is not appropriate for the majority of people who have temporal lobe epilepsy.

"There are no reports of violence in any epileptic who was being intensively monitored, and intensive monitoring has been going on at the National Institutes of Health and many other centres for more than 25 years. The probability that such violence could come during an epileptic seizure is extremely low."

Dr Paul Schultz, co-director of neurology at Children's Hospital said, "The people we are treating for it are no more violent than the patients down the hall who are being treated for diabetes or asthma."

Neuropsychologist Dr. Melvin Schwartz said, "There have been some instances of violence under laboratory conditions (by stimulating violence-sensitive areas of the brain with electricity), but there have been, perhaps, 999 patients who have not had violent episodes for everyone who has, even when electrically stimulated."

He also said that any violent behaviour resulting from epilepsy would be very short episodes, several seconds to a minute at most and would be undirected at any specific recipient. Schwartz said he had worked at 25 laboratories in the USA in which only two patients exhibited any kind of violence when their brains were stimulated with electricity.

Most doctors who gave opinions said temporal lobe epilepsy produced a seizure that was more likely to make a patient fall and convulse. But it was possible a patient might stagger and make unintelligible sounds. All said doctors commonly accepted that neither this type nor other kinds of epilepsy was a form of mental illness.

During her multitude of tests and examinations, Brenda met with Dr. Dorothy Otnow Lewis, who became one of America's best-known crime psychologists. Among others, she interviewed killers Ted Bundy, Arthur Shawcross, Joel Rifkin, and Mark David Chapman, the man who slew John Lennon.

Dr. Otnow Lewis, who insisted on speaking with Brenda's parents at length and even evaluated Wally's mental stability, reached many of the same conclusions about the girl as the other experts.

But in her report on Brenda, she mentioned something that was only rumoured at the time, possible abuse. Taken from her 1979 report:

> *"In contrast to Ms. Spencer, Mr. Spencer presented as a man extremely, if not excessively devoted to his daughter Brenda. He expressed great concern at ever leaving the house and leaving her alone. He was quite open about the fact that for years he and Brenda shared a room, and he saw nothing peculiar of the fact that Brenda, according to him, frequently came into his bed and fondled his hair."*

Brenda turned 17 on Tuesday, April 3, and a juvenile hall coach nicknamed Ma Kettle made special arrangements for her to have a party with girls in her unit. Brenda wrote to her parents and friends saying what a nice event it was, praising her coaches for arranging it and for attending.

At her arraignment on April 10, Brenda formally pleaded not guilty to the two counts of murder and 18 felony counts, including attempted murder and assault with a deadly weapon on a police officer. Judge Howard J. Bechefsky initially scheduled the trial for July 23 in San Diego Superior Court, and McGlinn agreed for

Brenda to undergo more medical and psychiatric examinations before trial.

In early June, McGlinn filed an application seeking a change of venue for the trial, arguing that Brenda could not have a fair trial in San Diego County because of what he called excessive publicity and outlandish stories told by San Carlos residents.

He demanded production to the court of all broadcast tapes, television footage, and newspaper articles of the Cleveland Elementary shooting incident from 16 different news agencies that reported from the scene.

At a hearing on the issue on July 5, presiding Judge William T. Low watched two-and-a-half hours of news footage at the studios of KFMB Channel 8, a local television station. He also heard from a reporter from the UPI news agency and employees from the district attorney's office about the amount of news coverage of the shooting and the days after.

A representative of the county's Epilepsy Society also gave evidence about the effect the news had on its hotline number.

Judge Low recessed the hearing until the following Thursday when McGlinn produced countless reports in which classmates and neighbours called Brenda a menace and animal torturer. He then presented the court a petition signed by more than 2,000 people:

> *"We the undersigned concerned citizens of our community feel that due to the heinous murder of Mr. Burton Wragg and Mr. Michael Suchar of Cleveland Elementary School, and the injuries inflicted both physically and mentally on innocent children, that Ms. Brenda Spencer should be tried as an adult. She should not be allowed to be back in our society where 'another dull Monday' could occur. She was adult enough to plan her crime far enough in advance. In the name of justice for all, she must be tried as an adult."*

McGlinn also was armed with the results of a public opinion poll by Dr. Oskar Kaplin, psychology professor at San Diego State University, and professional opinion-taker. Kaplin gave witness evidence from seven polls taken about pretrial publicity before court cases.

"More than a reasonable likelihood defendant cannot obtain an unprejudiced jury in San Diego," Kaplin said in his report to the court.

> *"Results show 96 percent of San Diegans have heard or read that Brenda Ann Spencer is accused of killing a principal and a custodian and wounding 8 pupils and a policeman at an elementary school in January. Further, 64 percent have an opinion as to guilt or innocence. Another 6 percent are not sure whether she is guilty or innocent. A full 29 percent are of the opinion Brenda is guilty of premeditated murder. 16 percent are not sure. In addition, 34 percent of San Diegans believe that it would not be safe to release Brenda into the community after eight years if she was given psychiatric treatment. Another 50 percent were not sure if it would be safe."*

The prosecution argued the polls were not accurate because of the manner in which the questions were presented. Deputy District Attorney Ronald Prager said the poll relied only on whether the public could identify Brenda. The mixed answers showed how confusing the initial questions were, he said.

In his ruling, Judge Low granted the motion and ordered Brenda's trial to be moved outside of San Diego.

McGlinn pushed for Los Angeles, the big high-crime city 120 miles north. But prosecutors favored the more suburban residential Orange County. They cited its proximity to San Diego and cost implications of transporting witnesses and other travel considerations. The district attorney's office also knew Orange County as one of the most conservative counties in the state, seeing far less crime than its big city neighbour to the north.

Two days after Judge Low upheld the motion to change venue, he ordered the case moved to Orange County. The trial would be held at the Superior Court in the county seat of Santa Ana, about a 90-minute drive from San Diego.

The rationale behind moving the trial there was that potential jurors in the area would be less likely to have heard of the Spencer case and less likely to have already formed an opinion about it.

Brenda did not appear in court for any of the five-day venue change hearings, remaining in juvenile hall to prepare for her adult trial.

San Diego County Supreme Court sources said this was the first successful change-of-venue motion in the county since the 1960s.

20

CIVIL SUIT

POLICE OFFICER ROBERT Robb was still recovering from his bullet injury when he decided to join the Selvig family in taking legal action. Lee Selvig was leading the other parents in how to initiate a lawsuit on behalf of their children. But, as a police officer, Robb was on his own if he wanted to be compensated for his pain and suffering.

There is a long-standing legal convention in California known as the "fireman's rule" that first responders could not sue homeowners for damages and/or injuries suffered on duty. But Robb, who says he'd always believed "getting injured is part of the job," chose to challenge the "fireman's rule" after seeking legal advice.

"After I got released from the hospital, the city had me transferred to the care of the city contract doctors," Robb said of his medical treatment for his injuries. He was struck by a bullet in his neck that nearly hit his carotid artery.

Robb was seeking unspecified general and punitive damages plus medical expenses and loss of earnings. His suit charged Brenda's father with negligence and "wanton disregard" for the public. It says he was aware that his daughter "had a history of antisocial behaviour, a dangerous propensity towards violence, had in fact committed acts of violence and had a history of drug use and emotional problems".

Robb's lawyer was Ron Mix, a former member of the San Diego Chargers American Football team. The two were introduced by Robb's police supervisors. Mix, a popular figure in San Diego and a member of the American Football Hall of Fame, was friendly with dozens of police officers and city authorities.

Westfield Insurance Company held the policy on Wally Spencer's home. The unique insurance policy covered any damage caused from inside the house. So, as the bullets came from the entrance way, the insurance company could be held liable for up to $100,000 for each occurrence. But if he were to be found negligent or to have shown wanton disregard for the public by giving Brenda the weapon, a jury potentially could award millions of dollars to victims.

The legal interpretation of *per occurrence* was what concerned the insurance providers. Eleven people had been damaged by Brenda's shooting spree. Was this incident to be deemed as 11 different occurrences, in which case the Westfield could potentially be liable for $1,100,000? Or as one single occurrence of negligence against Wally for giving Brenda the gun and, thus, being liable only for $100,000?

Westfield Insurance hired John Netterblad as lead attorney to defend Wally on his homeowner policy. Netterblad was nearing 50 with a deep tan and snappy wardrobe. He was well known in political and legal circles and had mingled with the mayor and police chief at functions.

Netterblad, from southern Wisconsin and a standout athlete in his younger days, came to San Diego in 1961 and spent the rest of his life there. He was the district attorney before joining the prestigious Higgs, Fletcher, and Mack law firm, becoming a partner in 1970.

I knew Netterblad when I contributed items for a local newspaper in Ocean Beach and found him to be straightforward and an interesting man. He was also an elder at his church in the harbourside district of Point Loma and volunteered his time at a soup kitchen near the beach.

Wally retained local lawyer Jack Phillips to handle his personal issues. It was assumed he would only have to play pick up after Netterblad and Westfield did their lengthy investigations and claims adjusting.

Private investigators for Westfield Insurance interviewed family and friends to gather further information and affidavits for Wally's defence. Netterblad had to prove that Wally was a great father and not responsible for Brenda's behaviour. He possessed all the psychologist reports that basically said they had no idea why it happened.

Netterblad said the investigators interviewed more than a dozen witnesses with mixed results.

Later, many of the witnesses I contacted either did not remember being interviewed or said flatly that they were not contacted. These alleged interviews were heavily focused on Brenda's influences, musical tastes, and relationship with her father. Almost all witnesses appeared to go out of their way to say Wally was a great guy.

Published notes from Wally's interview said he was baffled why his daughter had so much anger towards him during the negotiation. Wally said he would never have alcohol in the house. He acknowledged his son smoked pot but said he never gave it to Brenda.

The interview gave little detail into the shooting, but Wally made a point of saying Brenda's menstrual cycle could have played a role. Wally also made it clear that he did not like Brenda's friend Brant Flemming and was happy he moved away the August before the shooting.

Insurance investigators interviewed Brenda's brother Scott and sister Teresa at the Spencer house at their father's request in late April. Published notes say Scott admitted he smoked pot with Brenda but did not want his father to find out. He said he knew she made drug references but doubted she was a druggy other than occasional experiment.

Teresa was reluctant to be interviewed and just wanted the incident and consequent embarrassment not to have happened in the first place. Published notes said Brenda wanted the gun for Christmas and had virtually nagged her father for it. Teresa said Brenda bragged about doing heavy drugs and getting in fights but said she did not believe her.

Brenda's mother Dot was the last of the family to be interviewed. She took a similar position as her eldest daughter and felt shame and embarrassment over the shooting. She said Brenda enjoys her own company, unlike her siblings, and was annoyed that Wally never spanked her. Dot said Wally would do whatever Brenda said because he was a weak push over.

Dot visited Brenda in juvenile hall and was appalled by her foul language and violent thoughts. Brenda told her it was easier to get drugs than chewing gum at Patrick Henry High and bragged about being a drug addict since she was 11. Dot refused to believe that.

The Minors gave Brenda's letters from juvie back to Wally because they thought they might help her defence. Wally passed them on to Netterblad, hoping they would help with the civil case and might save his home. The letters illustrated Brenda's current state of mind and showed how unaware she was of what was to come. They were never used in her defence, and it is unknown if Wally ever showed them to McGlinn.

Insurance investigators met with the Minors without any serious revelations. They said Brenda started to talk more about fighting and drugs and was very capable of shooting targets from a long distance. Both Tom and Jan said Brenda smoked pot and appeared to be a loner without many friends.

Published notes say Westfield investigators interviewed underaged friends and neighbours of Brenda by phone and in person. They prowled the neighbourhood knocking on doors and speaking to anyone who said they knew the Spencers. Their report said no one identified Brenda as doing anything to threaten anyone before the shooting.

Most neighbours said they knew Wally enough to wave and say hello but did not know him well. Some said Brenda would play with their children when they were younger and had no issues with her behaviour. One neighbour remembered seeing television interviews about burning cat's tails or wanting to kill cops but did not know what was true.

The O'Connell sisters, who lived behind the Spencers, were named in the Westfield reports. Their alleged quotes in newspapers and on TV about harming cats became legend in the area.

When I interviewed Colleen O'Connell at length in 2020, she denied ever saying that Brenda hurt cats or harmed animals in any way. "No, I don't remember anything like that," she told me.

I reviewed all her interviews from 1979 and she was correct; Colleen's only comments were about the gossip. But in a television interview she did say she had heard it might be true.

Susie Stewart considered herself as Brenda's best girlfriend for years and was with her when she injured her head in the bike crash. She told me, "I was so young when all this happened. It very much affected my life, and I have *not* spoken publicly about it ever."

The Stewart family had a beach house they rented each summer in Mission Beach. They would invite Brenda along like a family member. Brenda told me, "They would rent a house for a week, and they would take me along. I always had fun."

The girls slept over at each other's homes, and Susie would often join them on their day trips to the Potrero property. Susie said they were like sisters, especially when Susie had a broken leg and could not get around easily in 1977.

The two friends apparently drifted apart in the months before the shooting because they did not share any classes in high school. Susie became interested in boys, but Brenda was still a bit shy and did not speak with too many guys at school. She was underdeveloped for her age and didn't have Susie's confidence.

Brenda did have a crush on a surfer kid named Steve that never went anywhere. She said he definitely didn't know she liked him. They sat next to each other in a class at Pershing Junior High. Brenda never mentioned any other boys when I asked her.

Susie's insurance interview is remarkably similar to the interview she gave police after the shooting. I contacted Susie to ask her about its validity. She said, "It's funny that I don't recall any interviews. Back then there was no protocol to protect kids under 18."

In her insurance interview, Susie was adamant that nobody knew Brenda as well as she did. The girls would shoplift together but never committed any serious crimes. She said trouble followed Brant Flemming, and she denied any drug use.

Some reports said Susie visited Brenda in juvenile hall with her mother, father, and brother, but years later, she remembered visiting only with Brenda's father.

"I visited her right after she went in with her dad. We were so young," she told me.

Susie was reported to have told Westfield investigators that Wally was the perfect parent and could not see how anyone could complain about him.

I asked Susie to elaborate on her relationship with Brenda and her father. She respectfully declined, saying, "Still figuring out how I feel. I have not yet asked Brenda how she feels about me talking about what I know" and "sadly really no one really knows what happened. Only Brenda, and to some degree me. But we were so young."

I told Brenda we had corresponded and would give Susie details on how to reach her. She replied, "Gosh, it's been a long time since I've heard from her. Thanks for giving her the information."

Susie now lives in Florida and began to correspond with Brenda again. "It's funny, even after all these years, we just kinda pick up where we left off," Susie said. The two write to each other as often as they can.

None of the insurance interviews ever referred to Brenda being an epileptic or if she ever had seizures. The insurance investigators allegedly interviewed more than a dozen people but never spoke with Brenda herself or to Brant Flemming.

Westfield Insurance conducted its interviews between March and June 1979, with investigators for the plaintiffs also contacting the same people. It is not known who spoke to whom first. One of the neighbours told me she first heard from a lawyer representing the victims long before the insurance company.

Westfield Insurance tried to make sure the negligence case was limited to one occurrence, making the company liable for a mere $100,000. It hired separate law firms to cover Westfield against any punitive damages that might arise after any initial award.

Lawyer Netterblad said he would personally represent Wally but only if Westfield wanted to fight the case and contend that Brenda's father was not negligent. Westfield hired another lawyer to represent Brenda in the event she was found negligent.

The Insurance company also hired an independent law firm to legally define "per occurrence" and its interpretation in the case. With a possible 11 separate occurrences looming, and no statutes or case law in such instances, it needed to gain a clear understanding. Westfield filed what was known as a "declaratory relief case," seeking an early decision on the meaning of "per occurrence."

Westfield, believing it would lose at least the policy limit of $100,000, deposited that amount with the court for safekeeping.

The family of principal Wragg began their suit against Wally. They aggressively instructed a talented up and coming lawyer named Dan Broderick. They had no intention of participating in a joint settlement with the other victims and looked to end it quickly.

Westfield Insurance said it was happy to discuss a possible settlement, and the pair soon reached an agreement. The parties agreed to settle for the maximum amount guaranteed by Wally's insurance policy: $100,000.

Broderick believed this was the absolute maximum he could gain for the Wraggs. Westfield was obligated only up to this amount, and both agreed that fighting the Spencers for more would go nowhere. Wally was, by all appearances, broke.

Netterblad said settling with Broderick and the Wragg family would be instrumental in the conclusion of all the cases against Westfield. They offered the agreement to the courts for a formal sign off.

San Diego Supreme Court Judge Jack Levitt was unhappy with the agreement and issued an injunction against any payment of damages against Wally Spencer. He ruled that all settlements be suspended pending the outcome of the criminal trial of his daughter. Levitt consolidated all the lawsuits by victims into one file and said he would make no determination on the "per occurrence" point until that time.

This meant that Broderick would not secure the $100,000 for the Wragg family until the end of the trial in Orange County. He then argued that his clients should get the first $100,000 from the deal because he settled first. Both decisions would have to wait until the end of Brenda's trial.

21

PLEA DEALS

ON AUG. 17, 1979, in the new Santa Ana Courthouse, Brenda pleaded not guilty by reason of insanity. Many people in San Diego expressed shock that Brenda entered a not guilty plea. How could she be innocent, some thought, when she was caught red-handed and had confessed?

Standing before the judge in a flood of tears, the 17-year-old had the change of plea explained to her in detail.

Legal insanity is a difficult concept and juries often need to debate over the issue for days.

Essentially, the court would have had two general types of insanity to consider in the late 70s.

In the first analysis, courts would have to consider whether a defendant was able to distinguish right from wrong: in layman's terms, whether a person is mentally ill all the time and does not know what he or she is doing.

The second category is more intricate. It involves a defendant being delusional and believing actions were justified because of the delusion. This is the so-called "God made me do it" defence, as used in the case of the New York "Son of Sam" killer David Berkowitz. He told the court his neighbour's dog told him to kill people, although he did plead guilty in the end.

Legal psychology experts say a crime requires criminal intent and a person not in his right mind would not have the intention to commit crime. A person who is insane should not automatically be considered a criminal.

A convicted murderer who is sane would go to prison. But an insane person who kills someone would be confined to a mental hospital indeterminately, getting support, until regaining sanity.

In a San Francisco murder case just two months before the Cleveland Elementary shooting, a disgruntled colleague called Dan White shot the city's Mayor George Moscone and politician Harvey Milk to death. Reports on White's defence centred on claims of diminished capacity based on his eating too much junk food. The idea became known as the "Twinkie Defence" after the name of a popular sugary snack cake. White was convicted and served five years of a seven-year sentence. Less than two years after his release, he killed himself.

Judge Byron McMillan told Brenda the new plea meant that a jury could declare her insane, and she could spend the rest of her life in a state mental hospital. He ordered two new psychiatrists to examine and assess her. The trial was set for Oct. 1, with a pre-trial conference on Sept. 21.

If found sane and guilty of first-degree murder, Brenda stood to be sentenced to life in prison without parole. She was exempted from California's death penalty because she was a minor at the time of the crime.

When prosecutor Chuck Patrick accused Brenda of "lying in wait" to commit murders, her attorney McGlinn argued there was no evidence of that because Burton Wragg and Mike Suchar would have heard shots before they ran into the line of fire.

He asked to have Patrick's allegation stricken from the record, a motion Judge McMillan denied, saying, "unfortunately we'll never know what they were thinking," adding that it was something a jury would have to decide.

By September 1979, five more psychologists had examined Brenda, including two court-appointed doctors and the others hired by her defence attorney, McGlinn. Prosecutor Patrick arranged for big-hitter Beverly Hills psychiatrist Dr. Ronald Markman to offer his opinion on the diminished responsibility defence.

"We just want someone to examine her on our behalf. And if this risky report is beneficial to the defence; then we will be obligated by law to turn it over to McGlinn," he told reporters.

When Markman's report concluded Brenda was legally insane, Patrick and McGlinn began talks on a plea deal.

Rumours began to swirl throughout San Diego that Brenda wanted to change her criminal plea to guilty after Dr. Markman's examination. The *Los Angeles Times* reported there was to be another evaluation on the Wednesday before the trial. Markman's final report had not been submitted to the courts but was lodged with McGlinn.

A change of plea would mean no lengthy hearing, sparing Brenda's family and the victims' upset. It would mean no jury selection and would save Wally scrutiny of his personal life.

On Monday, Oct. 1, Brenda stood next to her attorney in the Santa Ana courthouse and pleaded guilty to two counts of murder in the first degree. She also pleaded guilty to several counts of assault with a deadly weapon. She was unemotional until Judge McMillan asked her what happened that day.

With tears in her eyes, she replied in a low voice, "I shot from my house and killed two people."

To the 11 other charges, she simply whispered "guilty" to the judge when asked for her plea. Brenda's parents joined her at the defence table after she gave her official pleas. Her father placed his right arm around Brenda as her mother cried quietly.

The judge asked the parents if they fully understood the impact of the plea. They nodded.

In a last-minute plea bargain to her sentencing, Chuck Patrick agreed to drop the charges of attempted murder in each of the non-fatal shootings in exchange for her guilty plea. Patrick also dropped the "lay in wait" special circumstance allegation, which, upon conviction, might have seen her incarcerated without parole.

McGlinn said he agreed to the guilty plea because juries were reluctant to acquit anyone using the insanity defence.

He told the press that Brenda lost control of herself that day because of her temporal lobe epilepsy. He said he believed she would have a good chance at early release as long as she continued treatment for her condition. But Patrick countered that California's Community Release Board would keep Brenda locked up for at least 44 years because of the severity of the crime.

Only Brenda knows why she accepted the deal. She faced a sentence of 25 years to life in prison but with the chance of parole one day. If sentenced to the maximum prison term, she could be paroled in just under 17 years. But she still could face a lifetime in prison if the parole board found her unfit for release.

Many teachers, parents, and Cleveland Elementary students who were expected to give evidence in the case found the plea a great relief. Two teachers, Mary Jeffcoat and Paul Woodburn, who were scheduled to testify, said students had nearly succeeded in burying their memories and the trial could have stirred them back up.

"I wasn't really dreading it," Woodburn told reporters. "But I wasn't looking forward to it, either. Three days after it happened, they'd had enough of it; they didn't want to hear any more," he said of the children involved.

Judge McMillan ordered Brenda to undergo a 90-day diagnostic study by the California Youth Authority and set sentencing for after that. The action was a formality required by law, intended to help determine whether she should spend her first eight years in a

CYA detention centre or go straight to Frontera Prison for women in the Central California city of Chino.

"She is too young, too physically frail, to go to a women's prison," defence lawyer McGlinn told reporters.

In Santa Ana, Judge McMillan ordered Brenda to transfer from her holding cell in the local juvenile hall to the California Youth Authority in Ventura, about 100 miles north. The hearing lasted about a minute, and the judge said he would not pronounce a permanent move pending more tests. Brenda was ordered to undertake extensive diagnostic evaluations by the end of November 1979.

McGlinn told reporters he was still hopeful Brenda would be sentenced to stay at the CYA centre until she was 25, rather than go directly to state women's prison at Frontera.

He pledged a legal challenge if Brenda were forced into an adult prison.

He said he feared for her safety "for a combination of reasons – her age, her size, and the offence she committed".

McGlinn said he was pleased with Brenda's progress in juvenile hall but she "doesn't recall the actual incident itself. She's blacked that out of her mind. She's got a lot of very serious psychological problems".

Brenda turned 18 the day before the sentencing on April 4, 1980. She arrived in court and was escorted to the usual position next to her lawyer. She made no eye contact with her parents, who sat behind her in the front row.

Wearing a printed brown dress, tan vest, and her usual glasses, Brenda stood silently waiting for the judge to speak. McMillan asked her if she understood the purpose of the hearing, and Brenda said, "Yes". This was the only thing she would say in the short hearing.

Her parents stood, and each put a hand on her shoulder as the judge read the agreed sentence, 25 years to life for murdering the two men, with concurrent sentences of seven years for shooting a police officer and eight six-year sentences for the wounding of the children.

D.A. Patrick had already worked out the sentence with McGlinn and Judge McMillan. Under law this was the only sentence possible, based on her guilty plea. With time served, Brenda would be eligible for parole in 15-and-a-half years shortened by up to a third for good behaviour.

Brenda showed no emotion outside the courthouse as she was escorted back to the CYA centre.

McGlinn stood to speak with reporters, "Brenda's very depressed about the amount of time of the sentence. She's very scared, but I think she's going to do really well in custody. There's a lot of outrage there. She blames her parents for certain things. She's terribly paranoid. She has been an empty shell all her life."

McGlinn said the evaluations at the CYA concluded she had mental issues stemming from troubles at home. But these determinations had no effect on the sentence.

"She's determined to pursue her diploma. She intends to become a veterinarian and will take college courses while confined at the CYA facility," he said.

"I think justice has been served," parent Norm Buell told the Union. "I still think 16 years seems like a long time to pay for a mistake, even though Brenda killed two people."

Wally, asked by reporters if Brenda was holding up well, replied, "Um, I don't want to talk about it right now, if you don't mind."

Patrick was asked if he would like to see her free one day.

"Well, I don't think that's something I can answer at this time. You know, after 30 to 40 years who know[s] what she will be like then."

Under a new law co-written by Patrick, Brenda would serve the first part of her sentence at the CYA in Ventura, which could be as long as seven years. When Brenda pleaded guilty in October there was nothing in the law that said a girl must be sent to prison when she turned 18. But the newly passed law allowed Brenda the possibly to stay at CYA until she was 25.

Once Brenda's prison term was done and dusted the state appellate court ruled the Spencers were now partly responsible for their daughter's legal fees. In a bizarre turn of events in October 1983, it was decided Brenda's father would pay back just $5,000 of the $46,698 spent to defend his daughter. Her mom was ordered to pay even less, just $1,000.

As homeowners with decent incomes the court felt the Spencer's were obligated to contribute something to the ongoing costs associated with their daughter's crime. The secret land owned by Wally near the Mexican border was never taken into consideration. It appears he was able to keep information private once again.

Justice Edward Butler was pressed on why the Spencers' fees were so low. He wrote in his decision, "We cannot say; determination of the parents' financial liability is not supported by substantial evidence."

22

CIVIL SETTLEMENT

ONCE SENTENCING WAS confirmed, the Wragg family instructed Broderick to formalise their financial agreement. Six weeks later Westfield Insurance and their attorney Netterblad agreed to a tentative settlement with the remaining victims. It was decided that all involved would share a $350,000 payout, including Officer Robb.

The Wragg family had previously agreed to get the first $100,000 which saw $85,000 going to Burton Wragg's widow, Kathe, and $5,000 to each of the fallen principal's three children. Tina, widow of slain janitor Mike Suchar, who had only just filed her suit after Brenda pleaded guilty, was awarded $85,000.

Because both men were on duty at the time, the San Diego school district also awarded each family an additional $55,000 in workers compensation.

Settlements for the injured children appeared to hinge on the amount of time they spent in the hospital. The largest sum – $52,000 – went to Christy Buell who was still in and out of the hospital having physiotherapy on her injured foot at the time.

Monica Selvig received an amount negotiated by her father of $33,000. Eight-year-old Greg Verner, who still had a bullet lodged near his pelvic bone, received $30,000. Brave Mary Clark, who did not tell anyone she was shot in her lower torso until she arrived at Pershing Junior High School, was awarded $16,000.

Cam Miller received just $5,000 for being shot two centimetres from his heart. Julie Robles, who was shot in her side, got $4,000. And Crystal Hardy, who was shot straight through her wrist and released from the hospital in record time, received $3,000, as did the youngest victim, Audrey Stites, for her elbow injury.

Judge William Yale approved the Buell settlement first and then the others one by one as they were presented. By making the individual decisions on each case, he effectively rendered moot the dispute over the "per occurrence" point that had arisen earlier.

Most parents said they placed the money into trust accounts until the children were old enough to make use of it.

Lawyer and father Lee Selvig was not particularly talkative to reporters after the settlement, telling the Union, "We're very happy it's over." And saying of daughter Monica, "She's going to be fine."

"It's finally over," agreed Norm Buell. "She'll need that money," he said of daughter Christy. "By the time she can have it, houses will cost a half-million dollars each. Maybe she'll be able to buy a couple gallons of gas with it." Norm bought high-yield U.S. Treasury bills with Christy's award.

"My daughter's doing well now, but she has another year to go. She occasionally trips or stumbles when she is barefoot because her toes just hang there."

Asked what he thought of Brenda's trial, Norm said, "She's just a girl that was screwed up. I told her father... it wasn't that little girl shooting that gun, it was whatever she took that made her pull the trigger. I told him, he and his family could be a guest in my home any day, including Brenda. We feel no animosity against her."

Officer Robb's claim was also part of this settlement but was not so straightforward. He was awarded $19,000 for a bullet through the neck, which remained lodged near his spine. He also was awarded an additional workers compensation claim from the city for $8,000. Observers believed Robb's injuries also could qualify him for possible disability payments and retirement benefits in later years.

The shooting left Robb entangled in lengthy legal wrangling for years. Robb needed years of medical treatment and was often in pain while police lawyers argued over who was responsible for paying the bills. Neither Wally Spencer nor Robb were present for a series of very confusing hearings.

A year after being shot, Robb had a second operation to remove the bullet from his back. It had moved toward his spine and was causing more pain. He was having problems with wearing a bulletproof vest and driving. On a routine traffic stop, the vest pushed the slug into his spine, and he was paralysed from the waist down. He was unable to perform his assigned duties, and a supervisor had to help him at the roadside.

"In a week, I was walking and within a few months I was back on active duty," Robb said.

He says San Diego authorities took away his medical benefits, accrued holiday time, and sick leave, leaving him broke. He said the city billed him for his hospital costs and also said he was told it wanted any money he was awarded from his legal claim against the Spencer family. Robb was angry that the police chief who set him up with his original lawyer, Ron Mix. He asked his police union for free legal representation to get the matter sorted once and for all.

After a few years, Robb says, the city decided to retire him "rather than try and keep fixing" him all the time. He became a stay-at-home father for a year or so before looking for a new career.

The State of California later disbarred Robb's first lawyer, the former star football player Ron Mix, after he pleaded guilty to federal tax charges. Mix's former practice often dealt with worker compensation claims for former athletes but only dabbled in police business.

Not long after the settlements, the San Diego Supreme Court honoured Netterblad for easing case backlog. He had helped draft rules for arbitration proceedings that reduced court congestion by 25 percent and cut the time it took to get a civil suit to trial from 29 months to 14 or 15 months.

He was involved in more than a dozen cases surrounding the Cleveland School shooting. All were settled within a year. It was rumoured that he opened and closed multiple civil cases to make the overall numbers look good.

To celebrate, Netterblad and colleagues from multiple law firms across town and executives from Westfield insurance arranged a party at the posh Westgate Hotel in downtown San Diego. When the hotel opened in 1970, it was the most expensive hotel in the country. Lawyers for the victims were invited to attend, but only Dan Broderick showed up.

Broderick was a well-known and well-liked 35-year-old. The Wragg family was extremely thankful to him for taking care of all the financial affairs during such a hard time. Dan attended the celebration alone. He and his wife, Betty had just lost a child two days after birth, and it was also a sad time for his growing family of four.

A year after the shooting, Broderick wrote to the editor of The *San Diego Union*:

> *"Tribute to spirit – I read with interest Carl Cannon's article (Jan 27, 1980) on the tragic aftermath of Brenda Spencer's mindless attack on the Cleveland Elementary School one year ago this week. The article is a fine tribute to the spirit of those who survived the attack and to the memories of the two courageous men who did not. Most of us in the community never knew Burton Wragg or Michael Suchar, but thanks to your article they will not be forgotten. It is reassuring that in these self-indulgent, narcissistic times, there are at least some among us who are prepared to risk their lives without hesitation to protect the lives of others."*

Almost 10 years after the settlements, Dan Broderick was murdered in what became the most famous divorce scandal/love triangle in San Diego history, the focus of numerous reports and television movies.

In 1983, Dan began a relationship with his 21-year-old legal assistant named Linda Kolkena. He left his wife Betty and filed for what became a very acrimonious divorce a year later.

Four years later it was finalised and Dan married Linda, but six and a half months after the marriage, at 5:30am on Nov. 5, 1989, Betty let herself into her ex-husband's house, crept upstairs in the dark and shot Dan and Linda to death in their bed.

Betty pleaded not guilty and claimed justification as a battered wife. She said her husband's actions drove her over the edge. The jury found her guilty of two counts of murder, and she was ordered to serve two consecutive terms of 15 years to life in prison.

Because of her celebrity, she was interviewed many times on every major American television network, including a session with Oprah Winfrey. She has been rejected on each parole application she filed and remains incarcerated.

23

WALLY AND SHEILA

DURING BRENDA'S PLEA bargaining, sentencing and countless psychological tests her juvenile hall roommate continued her visits with Wally Spencer. Sheila McCoy was still telling other inmates that she was Brenda's best friend as a form of security while in the hall.

Wally and Sheila had formed a very tight connection from his frequent visits to see his daughter. After Brenda transferred to Orange County and then to the Ventura facility, Wally continued to see Sheila on his own. In August 1979, Sheila was transferred from juvenile hall to a youth facility across the road and was preparing for release.

Sometime in early November, Sheila simply walked through the front door of the building and got into Wally's cluttered van and escaped. He took her to his home on Lake Atlin Ave. to hide out until the coast was clear. Having previously cleared out his garage to protect his cars against vandalism, he drove Sheila straight into the garage so she would not be seen.

Brenda believes she moved in after telling Wally and his son Scott that she had nowhere else to go. But Sheila's family believes she was manipulated into making the move.

What is for sure is that Wally appears to have known what he was doing was illegal. Sheila had just turned 17 and should only have been on day release from juvenile hall. Wally also appears to have told her he was just 40, when he was, in fact, 50. It wasn't until his next birthday party at his brother Vern's house that his actual age was revealed. It shocked Sheila.

She began to clean the house and continually tidy up after the bachelors. Scott moved from the house as Sheila was moving in, but he would come and go over the years.

Even though her father was enjoying alone time with her old cell mate, Brenda told me, "I never had a good relationship with Sheila. I thought she was creepy."

Exactly when Sheila and Wally started a romantic relationship is unknown, but at the end of 1979 Sheila became pregnant with Wally's baby.

During the pregnancy, Wally tried his best to shield his new partner from prying eyes. He hid her on his Potrero land near the border and eventually rented an apartment across town. Sheila had once attended the hospital after taking a bottle of his prescription pills, but Wally was able to smooth over the incident with the doctors, and they returned home.

Shortly after moving in, a neighbour reported seeing her leaving the Spencer family house. The neighbour called police saying they had seen Brenda go in the front door. Detectives followed up the call by contacting her lawyer, McGlinn.

"I can recall, about a year after Brenda was committed, getting a call from one of the detectives wondering what Brenda was doing out," McGlinn said in a television interview. "This girl looked very similar to, very much like Brenda."

Sheila did vaguely resemble Brenda because of her long hair at the time. While in juvenile hall, Brenda thought the pair could pass for sisters.

The week before Brenda's sentencing hearing, Wally took the day off from work and drove Sheila over the state line to Arizona for a shotgun wedding. They were met in Yuma by her mother and stepfather, Sandy and Robert Elmore. The parents were to act as witnesses at the quickly arranged ceremony.

California law requires anyone under 18 to have the consent of both parents and court permission to marry. But the state of Arizona requires the permission of only one parent and no court order.

Wally and Sheila were married by Justice of the Peace William Steen. Their residences were both listed as Lake Atlin Ave. Brenda's new stepmother was about four months pregnant and younger than she.

"Sheila tried shit when we were in juvenile hall," Brenda wrote to me in a letter. "She wanted to have a relationship with me, and I didn't want that. She married my dad, so she could come in to visit me. Even the cops didn't like her. She's just a generally evil person who will do anything to get what she wants."

The question of Wally and Sheila's marriage was never raised during the hearing, though McGlinn knew about it.

But on May 30, Wally's attorney, Jack Phillips, wrote to the probation department on Sheila's behalf to explain the marriage and living situation. The probation department immediately referred the letter to the district attorney's office and asked detectives to determine if Wally had committed a crime.

Contributing to the delinquency of a minor, harboring a fugitive, and statutory rape could be possible charges against Wally. A further charge of helping Sheila abscond from custody was also a possibility.

Elsa Norbeck, Sheila's appointed probation officer, published this statement:

"Mr. Spencer met our court ward, Sheila McCoy, in the San Diego County juvenile hall when his daughter and Sheila were

both confined therein. Sheila was placed in a treatment facility in August of 1979, but she left that facility in November of 1979. Sheila's whereabouts were unknown until May 28, 1980, when an attorney, Jack Phillips, informed us that Sheila and Mr. Spencer were married in Yuma, Arizona, on March 26, 1980.

Mr. Spencer was previously informed and was aware that Sheila was and still is a ward of the Juvenile Court. He was also advised that she was a runaway from a court-ordered placement. He was additionally aware that she was a juvenile. We are therefore specifically requesting that the case of Wallace Spencer be reviewed for possible criminal charges against him."

Assistant district attorney Kennedy replied:

"The probation department referred it to us for screening for possible charges and prosecution. Because of the lack of evidence available, I have requested the SDPD to make a more complete investigation to determine if any criminal acts occurred in San Diego County involving Spencer and the 17-year-old girl."

After a police investigation, the district attorney decided not to prosecute. Local and national newspapers reporting the story would identify Wally as being only 41 when he was, in fact, about to turn 51.

Sheila Spencer (nee McCoy) gave birth to Bree Ann Spencer on Sept. 17, 1980 and took her home to be raised at the house on Lake Atlin Ave. Wally and Sheila moved into Brenda's old room with a view of Cleveland Elementary across the road.

The name Bree was taken from a new local television news reporter, Bree Walker. Wally was known to be a fan of hers beginning with her days at radio station KPRI. At the time, she was the afternoon drive-time DJ Bree Bushaw and known for her big red sultry lips in TV advertisements for the station.

When her daughter Bree was five years old, Sheila left the family home, also leaving the girl behind. Sheila's family said Wally was physically abusive and forced her out. They also believe Sheila tried to take Bree, but Wally prevented it.

The family said Sheila intended on getting a better job so she could find her own place and have a car. The plan was to return later and take Wally to court, seeking custody of Bree. But this never happened. She visited the child as often as she could, but eventually Wally refused access and they lost touch.

Sheila did not have the skills nor support to fight an experienced single father like Wally. But Wally's sister-in-law continued to send Sheila pictures of Bree until she was six. Sheila keeps them in a photo album, but mother and daughter have never reunited.

Brenda said about Sheila, "She didn't want anything to do with Bree. To my knowledge I don't think they have any connection." But members of Sheila's family say they are desperate to reunite with Bree and welcome her into the family.

24

CLEVELAND ELEMENTARY SCHOOL

A FEW MONTHS after the event, students voted unanimously for some kind of marker of the shooting, and education authorities erected a two-foot-high granite memorial to the victims. The memorial is situated on a grass plot directly in front of the flagpole and not far from where both Wragg and Suchar were killed. Everyone entering the school passes by it.

Its marble plaque reads:

> *"Presented by the student body in memory of Burton Wragg & Mike Suchar, who died in the service of helping others Jan. 29, 1979."*

Framed photos of both men were hung on the office wall just next to those of the then-current President Jimmy Carter and the school's namesake, 19th century President Grover Cleveland. Below the photos are the words from a San Diego City Council resolution commending the staff on that day "for the calm bravery and quick and effective actions".

Paint-covered bullet holes could still be seen on the woodwork near the office door. Tyre prints from where Officer Ted Kasinak parked the garbage truck were still slightly visible long after the event.

Exactly two years after the shooting, the San Diego Unified School District commissioned a 50-stone solid aluminium sculpture as a memorial. It was to reside on the lawn at the school district's Education Center building.

Serra High School art teacher Joe Nyiri spent almost a year constructing the large blocks and more than 100 hours shaping them with a bandsaw. He collected the materials from scrap yards throughout Southern California.

The widows of both fallen men attended the unveiling.

"I don't think of the sad, negative things. I think of the good people are trying to do. It is a wonderful commemoration of my husband," Kathe Wragg told the Union.

At some point over the weekend of Feb. 7, 1981, vandals cut out large sections of the sculpture. It had been in place only for two weeks.

Sculptor Nyiri said, "It took hours and hours of time. I haven't seen it yet... but I understand it's pretty bad," when reporters called him to ask about the vandalism. He said he had no idea how much it would cost to replace the piece.

Only the plinth remained after the vandalism. Police and school security officers contacted recycling centres in search of anyone trying to trade in large pieces of aluminium for cash. No one was ever arrested for the vandalism, and the memorial later was replaced with something similar but less recyclable.

Cleveland Elementary School, where enrolment had begun to dwindle, shut its doors in 1983 after newly built Gage Elementary opened around the corner. Cleveland was just one of many San Diego County public schools that closed in the 1980s.

The building sat on an 8.67-acre parcel and was later leased to the private San Diego Hebrew Day School. Years later, it was leased to a charter school, Magnolia Science Academy. Wally still lived across the road with Bree.

In 2015, after a 4-1 school board vote, the campus was sold to developers. It was part of a major reform to balance the school district's budget. The property sold for $6.1 million and in its place about 40 affordable houses were built .

Before the old school was demolished, two students at the then science academy noticed a man lighting candles and praying near the Cleveland Elementary tragedy memorial. Two youngsters, Madeline Garrett and Julianna Mullen researched the tragedy online and began landscaping the surrounding area as a project for their Girl Scout troop. Other local children pitched in to help.

The former school walkway was demolished and turned into a street and a bold public campaign saved the old memorial plaque and flagpole. Developers of the property moved them to a nearby intersection where they still can be visited today.

Eerily close to the 10-year anniversary of the San Carlos tragedy, another Cleveland Elementary School in California also came under fire, this time with a higher death toll.

On Tuesday, Jan. 17, 1989, 24-year-old Patrick Purdy drove his Chevrolet station wagon to the back of Cleveland Elementary in Stockton, California, and set the vehicle on fire. He waited for it to explode and then fired his Chinese-made Norinco Type 56S semi-automatic rifle and Taurus PT92 pistol into a group of students and teachers who had gathered nearby.

Purdy fired more than 100 shots in less than three minutes, killing five children and wounding 32 other people. As people ran for safety and sirens signaled approaching police and fire vehicles, he shot himself.

Even before he turned 20, Purdy had been arrested for multiple crimes. At 13, he assaulted his mother and moved to the streets, eventually finding himself in foster care. His crimes: BB gun offences, court violations, drinking underage, and possession of marijuana. These led to prostitution, stealing weapons, and armed robbery.

Purdy joined the Army to avoid jail but was unceremoniously discharged. By 1989, he had long since left the forces and was a full-time drifter, drug addict, and racist. Speculation on why he attacked the school centred on the fact that it was known to have a large population of immigrant children.

Purdy had scratched the words "Hezbollah," "freedom," and "victory" on the rifle and "death to the great satin" (presumably a misspelling of Satan) on the flak jacket he wore.

Purdy bought his assault rifle in Oregon about five months before the incident. That state did not require a waiting period for buyers of such weapons.

The Purdy shooting became the lead story in San Diego media as the anniversary of Brenda Spencer's crime approached. Reporters contacted as many of the original victims as possible for comment.

Christy Buell said while shaking, "I was scared for those people. I felt really sorry for them because I know exactly what they're feeling. I went through the same terrible thing."

Christy, by then 19, worked at a day-care centre near the site of the old Cleveland Elementary, where Bree Spencer, Wally's new daughter and Brenda's half-sister, was an attendee,

"There is no other way to say it. I'll just never get over it," she said.

Christy still lived in the same house with her father and brother. She would often see Wally as he came to collect his new young daughter. Christy was unsure if Wally knew who she was when he politely said hello.

She said Bree, who looked a lot like Brenda, once told her, "My sister's in jail." Christy answered simply, "Oh really?"

Monica Selvig, who was now 18, would not comment, and her father spoke for her.

"A child has the right to grow up feeling that they're out of harm's way," he said. "They have a right to a childlike aura of invincibility. Brenda Spencer took that away from Monica forever."

Monica left high school early and was fighting her own personal battle with drug abuse.

"The Stockton thing was terribly upsetting and disturbing," said Julie Robles. "I was very upset by the date being so close to the 10th anniversary of our shooting and the name of the school being the same."

Julie, 20, said that when she told people she was a Cleveland Elementary victim.,"They just look at me stunned. Their reaction is one of total disbelief. They say, 'No way, Julie.'

They just can't believe it."

25

"SIR" BOB AND THE SONG

ON THE MORNING of Brenda's rampage, Bob Geldof and Johnnie Fingers from the Irish new wave band, The Boomtown Rats, were driving in Los Angeles. They were on their way to meet Paul Rappaport of Columbia Records at a downtown FM radio station. The band was in the States promoting their upcoming shows and previous release.

The news of the shooting was reported on the local radio as they were travelling. Once they arrived at the station, they asked for the teletype machine printouts. Geldof was desperate to crack the US market, and Columbia Records had strongly suggested they write songs that would relate to Americans. The Boomtown Rats need a song that Americans would understand.

"You need to write something that's going to resonate in this country," Rappaport told them. Using direct quotes from Wiegand's phone conversations, Geldof and Fingers would hastily pen the song "I Don't like Mondays." By pure coincidence, The Boomtown Rats' first two shows in the USA just happened to be in San Diego the month following the shooting.

Over the years, Geldof has given many variations of these events, but this is his most recent account, told in 2020.

His story has Geldof and Fingers in the middle of an on-air interview at WRAS, the Georgia State University student radio station, as the story came through the telex machine. Former students have doubted this story as the tiny college station never had such a fancy machine. WRAS focused on music and would not have jumped on breaking stories from the west coast, more than 2,000 miles away.

While he and The Boomtown Rats were trying to crack the American market, they stumbled upon one of the most horrific news events of the decade. Geldof, appalled and entranced by the Brenda Spencer incident and what he thought it said about American society, raced to get a tune published.

Geldof played the song on guitar and sang it for Rappaport over the phone.

Rappaport told him, "This is exactly what you need, and you should go out and play this for people… and start doing this now".

Armed with their new song, and poised to break into the American market, the Boomtown Rats wasted no time. Rappaport had pushed them to have a new song to identify with Americans, and there was no point in waiting to play it.

Less than a month after the event, Geldof and the band were about to debut the song around the corner from the scene of the crime. He called the song 'I Don't Like Mondays,' taken from the words Brenda told Evening Tribune reporter Steve Wiegand over the telephone as she was shooting.

On Feb. 27, 1979, The Boomtown Rats took the stage at the Roxy Theatre in San Diego, a shabbily converted cinema on Cass Street in the hip community of Pacific Beach that was becoming known as a venue for an up-and-coming international act.

This was the Boomtown Rats' first date on their first tour of the States after just having a No. 1 hit in the UK and their Irish homeland. Like many travelling artists in America, they started at one end of the country and planned to make their way to the other. Their final date was scheduled at The Palladium in New York City that May.

The first two dates were back-to-back gigs in San Diego, the second being at what was then the Fox Theatre downtown, now known as Copley Symphony Hall. "Mondays" was the penultimate song on the playlist.

Over the next 10 days, the Boomtown Rats would play seven shows in six cities on the West Coast.

During one of their Los Angeles shows, Geldof was recorded giving this intro before starting the song (taken from the authorised documentary *Citizens of Boomtown* 2020):

> *"I don't know if you remember about a month ago, down in San Diego. This girl called Brenda Spencer used to get a gun every Christmas from her father. And one day last month she decided that she'd go down to her school with her toy, and she'd shoot her friends and the janitor and the headmaster of the school." The small crowd began to cheer, and Geldof singled out one person close to the stage, looked straight at him and said, "What are you clapping for, man? She was an idiot!"*

Earlier in the show, while introducing another song, Geldof said he read two newspapers in town and hated them both. In 1979 at the height of the punk rock movement, it was important for aspiring musicians to be rebels and to lash out against the media and authority. The Sex Pistols had enormous success with their "Cash from Chaos" approach.

Geldof was also aware that a large group of radio programmers had journeyed over from a nearby convention and were watching intently. He singled them out and said they were to blame for all the horrible music heard on the radio. The programmers left early, and Geldof later said he believed his statement was why they all pulled his music from playlists in top markets.

As Cleveland Elementary School was getting back to normal, The Boomtown Rats finished their small-venue tour of the States, flew to Holland, and recorded an album, *The Fine Art of Surfacing,* at Phonogram Studios.

They also quickly released a single of "I Don't Like Mondays" in Europe. It topped the UK charts on July 22, staying at No.1 for four weeks. The song also would win Britain's prestigious Ivor Novello Award for Best Pop Song and Outstanding British Lyric of the year.

In the United States, Columbia Records weighed its options for releasing the song as Brenda's lawyer McGlinn urged the company not to do so. He also wrote to local radio stations urging them to not play it for fear of jeopardising a fair trial.

"It is extremely insensitive to the victims. It makes fun of a very tragic situation and a very sick girl," McGlinn said.

The prosecution agreed.

"I think it's pretty sick. It's obviously an attempt to commercialise a very tragic situation," said Chuck Patrick. "The judge should take the proper measure to make sure prospective jurors are not affected by it."

San Diego rock radio station KGB-FM played "Mondays" on Aug. 14, 1979, to determine what locals thought of it.

"We got about 400 calls from listeners and the poll ran about 3-1 against," station manager Jim Price told the Union. "Based on that response, our station does not plan to play it again and would urge other stations in the area to follow suit."

Other San Diego stations agreed.

"San Diego is just not digging it,'" said Glen McCartney, music programmer at B100-FM.

A spokesman for KFMB-AM radio station said, "The contents of the song are sick for our adult audience. I don't think it merits play."

KMJC, a local family-oriented station, said, "It's a very negative song. The subject matter and what it will remind people here of is very morbid. We will not play it even if there was an overwhelming response to it."

Despite the negative feedback from San Diego, Columbia Records pushed ahead with plans to release the album that October. The company also made plans to release "Mondays" as a single and hoped that things would have died down by then. Brenda's trial was scheduled to start the same month, and The Boomtown Rats would have known they would be cashing in on the publicity.

McGlinn told reporters he did not know "what legal ramifications we have. It would be terribly difficult unless people don't want to hear it. How can we prevent Columbia Records from disseminating it? I'm not sure. Some smart civil attorney may have a good idea of how to pursue that. I would welcome any help".

After hearing the lyrics, he said, "Something tragic could result from making fun of a serious and tragic situation. It's terrible, degenerate, sick, and insensitive."

In regard to releasing it during Brenda's trial, McGlinn said, "A lot of people will lose sight of what the issues are. This community has a vested interest in finding out why a 16-year-old girl would do this. It's insane to think it was because she doesn't like Mondays. For us to think this couldn't happen again is very naïve."

The San Diego district attorney's office agreed once again.

"It's a tragic situation, and they are being commercially exploitive," said assistant D.A. William Kennedy. "Their timing also creates an unnecessary legal issue. The judge will have to poll the jurors to find out if they have heard the song and if it has influenced them. Then he will have to admonish them not to listen to it."

Michael Jensen, an associate publicity director at Columbia Records, told local newspapers that Columbia would release the album containing the song. But he said the company was now undecided whether to release the song as a single, even after it sold more than 650,000 copies in the U.K.

He insisted the date of release, and the trial dates were purely coincidental, saying, "the song is not really about Brenda Spencer. It's about the incident."

In a 2007 interview for the BBC Radio 6 program "Classic Singles," Geldof says the opening line of the song about a silicon chip was inspired by Steve Jobs. In 1978, the Apple Computers founder contacted The Boomtown Rats about playing a gig for him in Northern California.

"We'd been contacted by a guy called Steve Jobs. And the reason I remembered it was because I thought I had got a text or letter from The Beatles. Cause Apple was at the top of it and Apple wanted us to come and play. And I thought, wow, that's cool and then it turned out it was like four guys in a garage in California or something, ya know. And I said nah, I don't want to do that, ya know."

Considering the Boomtown Rats were already scheduled to play in Northern California, I find this version of events to be questionable. Apple Records was founded by The Beatles in 1968 and their label had not released anything new since 1976. Apple Computers did not go public until 1980, more than a year after the shooting.

A week before the trial was to begin, Columbia Records announced it would still release the album in 10 days' time, as expected. The company said the timing of the release so close to the media exposure of the trial was "coincidental." The Boomtown Rats were really hoping for their first hit record in the States and must have thought it was a sure thing.

"There is nothing I know of we can legally do about it," McGlinn told the Union. "Under the First Amendment, they can do what they want. It's deplorable." In a letter to Columbia, he reiterated his concerns for the trial and pointed out the emotional stress he thought it inevitably would cause victims for years to come.

As expected, "I Don't Like Mondays" was nationally released as a single, followed by the full album in October 1979. KROQ in Los Angeles was the only radio station with Southern California to sporadically play the song in the weeks surrounding the trial.

The band had also been trying to promote the album on a number of national television shows including American Bandstand (in December 1979) and the short-lived sketch comedy show "Fridays" (the weekend before the San Diego show) but without success.

Despite enormous sales in almost all other English-speaking countries including Canada, *The Fine Art of Surfacing* failed to break the top 100 in the USA's Billboard album charts. The song peaked at 73 on the Hot100 singles chart. It fell from the charts completely by Thanksgiving. So much for the Boomtown Rats dream of hitting it big in America.

More than a year later the Boomtown Rats were back again. In April 1980, they were finishing their next US tour and found themselves back at the Fox Theater in downtown. The shooting was still raw to locals and a large parent-led protest began forming months before they had even started the tour. Just days before the show, the band felt it had no choice but to cancel the gig.

The Los Angeles-based promoters spoke with the *Union*: "Obviously, the band didn't want to incite the situation any further. They didn't want to look like they were cashing in on it."

Lead singer Geldof was quoted as saying he wrote the single because the whole crime appeared to be peculiarly Californian to him. It lacked any reason or logic and was pointless, much like most of America to him, he said. Geldof was openly mocking San Diegans.

He told the *Union* that the protests were spurious and said, "We will not be party to cheap morality. Our presence there would only fan the slowly cooling embers."

A day before the show the Boomtown Rats had sold only about 600 tickets for the 2,400-seat venue. It was cancelled.

Around the same time, Geldof became annoyed about a negative article in *Rolling Stone* magazine and told his fans he wanted people to buy his records so he could become rich enough to buy the publication.

In his autobiography, *Is That It?*, he said he had told the San Diego crowd a year earlier, "For some reason, we don't get played on American radio, which says more about American radio than it does about us."

As a band, the Boomtown Rats never played in the United States again. But Geldof grew to solo international celebrity status in 1984 when he spearheaded humanitarian efforts in Africa. He rallied a star-studded cast of British pop acts to record for a charity he formed called Band Aid and co-wrote a song that became one of the biggest selling singles in history, 'Do They Know It's Christmas?'

Geldof organised Live Aid charity concerts featuring pop stars in London and Philadelphia in 1985 that were watched by millions around the globe. In the middle of the 16-hour fund-raising show, he took to the stage and shouted, "Give us your fucking money!"

The Boomtown Rats performed 'I Don't Like Mondays' as their only song during the event. Geldof paused for 20 seconds after singing the line "the lesson today is how to die," creating drama to signify the starvation in Africa. It would be one of the last times the group would play together. Live Aid raised more than £150 million for famine relief in Africa.

A year later, Queen Elizabeth II awarded Geldof an honorary knighthood for his fundraising achievements – honorary because as an Irish citizen, he was not, technically, entitled to be knighted. Geldof is allowed to use the letters KBE after his name (for Knight of the British Empire).

In 1986, The Boomtown Rats technically broke up, and Geldof embarked on a mediocre solo career. He returned to play San

Diego only once more. On May 3, 1993, Bob Geldof and his new backup band played the Belly-Up Tavern in Solana Beach.

Local alternative rock station 91X handed out free tickets as a promotion, making sure it was a full house. This was the first time he had been back to San Diego since the poor reception he received in 1980. The show finished without protest, and the small venue was packed.

At the time of this solo tour, Geldof was on the outs with his TV star wife Paula Yates. She and Geldof met in 1976 and had been together ever since. They married in 1986 and had three children – Fifi Trixibelle, Peaches Honey Blossom, and Little Pixie.

"Sir Bob" was trying to resurrect his shambles of a musical career by touring around the States. Back in England, his wife Paula began a torrid affair with Michael Hutchence of the Australian pop band INXS. She and Geldof soon split up, and Paula took off to Australia with the kids to stay with Hutchence. Yates and Geldof officially divorced in May 1996.

Hutchence later killed himself and Yates also passed away following a heroin overdose.

In an online retrospective interview about his most famous song, Geldof claims Brenda once wrote to him.

"She wrote to me saying she was glad she'd done it because I made her famous, which is not a good thing to live with," he said.

In one of my interviews with Brenda, I asked her directly: Is it true you wrote to Bob Geldof and thanked him for making you famous? She replied simply saying, "No, I didn't."

Jonnie Fingers, The Boomtown Rats' piano player, had a long-running dispute with Geldof over who actually wrote 'I Don't Like Mondays.' Fingers says he was never credited with writing all the music and some of the lyrics. In a UK High Court case in 2016, he sought two-thirds of the royalties.

During these negotiations, Geldof now claimed he first played the song at a Dallas radio station without Fingers present. Fingers said he helped with the lyrics and wrote the piece's famous piano riff once they were back in the UK.

He believes they were not in the USA at the time of the shooting.

In the high court action, Fingers says Geldof told him not to claim royalties and promised him he would get his "fair share" in time. The case was finally settled with Fingers being credited as a co-writer and receiving an undisclosed financial settlement.

26

INCARCERATION

BRENDA WAS HELD at the CYA in Ventura from late 1979 to early 1981. Wally and her new stepmother, Sheila, brought Bree to meet her half-sister. They visited often, but Brenda always found it awkward with her younger stepmother and former cellmate.

While incarcerated, Brenda graduated from high school, completing the 12th and final high school grade as a remote student at Mary B. Perry High school.

Brenda's life in Ventura seems to have been turbulent. Her letters to the Minors indicated she was often taken to a rubber room and placed in solitary confinement. No information about these incidents was included in official files on her.

But it is documented that she did make an unsuccessful suicide attempt at the CYA. Alone in her room, she broke a coffee cup and slit her wrist with a shard. Quick emergency attention meant that she was released from the CYA infirmary after sustaining only small wounds.

After the incident, Brenda was watched closely for weeks and eventually deemed a low risk. Then in 1981, she received a major disciplinary citation for setting her room on fire. She claims to have been angry at herself and said she was simply burning something as she sat on the bed.

Authorities did not consider this a suicide attempt because none of her personal items were damaged. Her room had many possessions including the TV she won from the photo competition in 1978. They allowed her to have the TV in her room, and she had it with her for years as she travelled to various facilities.

California penal institutions are laws unto themselves and can transfer a prisoner at their own discretion. Though Brenda was just about to turn 19, CYA authorities deemed her an adult and transferred her to the California Institution for Women Prison at Frontera. The official date is listed as April 14, 1980, in all prison records, but it is also documented, curiously, that she was at the CYA in 1981.

I asked Brenda about her incarceration journey. She told me, "Getting locked up was a wakeup call. I went from San Diego juvie to Orange County juvie then Ventura then here. I was in Orange County juvie while I was going through court."

The Frontera prison for women was built in the middle of nowhere outside Chino in Riverside County in Southern California. It is now known as the CIW after the state dropped the formal name. Farms and agriculture surround the prison on all sides. The smell of manure from the nearby San Bernardino County Dairy Preserve hangs heavy in the prison air.

From the outside the building looks more like a large 1960s elementary school than a prison. Officials proudly say on their website that the campus-like design was "in keeping with the 1950s progressive notion of rehabilitation".

The various buildings (or units) are shaped like bear claws, separated by trees and grass patches. The painted stucco and concrete walkways are not unlike that of Cleveland Elementary.

The heat in the summer can be almost unbearable, and inmates are allowed to wear muumuus, the flowing Hawaiian-style dresses, but Brenda chooses not to. Smoke from the frequent forest fires is a familiar sight and smell. Snow can be seen on the mountains surrounding the valley, but it never gets very cold.

The wind is the biggest daily challenge for inmates. As most of the pathways and spaces are outdoors it can be a real chore for prisoners to get themselves to chow or to work details.

Brenda was the most famous arrival at the CIW since women from the murderous Charles Manson gang were placed there 10 years earlier. She was internationally known, and other inmates would whisper behind her back as she walked by. As a small, underdeveloped girl in a general population prison, she kept to herself for almost a year.

She withdrew even further and failed to eat properly. Most days, she stayed in her room reading. Eventually, her confidence grew, and Brenda started to participate in prison activities. It would be more than 12 years before her first parole hearing, so she decided to get to work on her rehabilitation.

From day one, she attended both Alcoholics Anonymous and Narcotics Anonymous activities but failed to fully complete the 12 step programs until 1991. She did complete countless anger management courses and Co-dependents Anonymous programs.

Over the next decade, Brenda went on a progression of self-help courses and learning programs. She studied animal grooming, took vocational electronics and hobby/ craft classes, attained a qualification as an electrical test technician, and worked as a repair tech for more than 12 years.

She earned top marks in upholstery and maintenance warehouse courses. Brenda worked for years as the prison's Fire Department clerk and made long lasting friendships with the staff. She is also an accredited forklift driver from her time in the warehouse.

She got her driver's license so she could start working in the prison's auto shop, where she currently works at time of writing.

Brenda became a tutor for the Project Read program, helping other inmates learn to read. She played for the prison softball team, performed in a musical group called "One Heart Band," helped to rebuild the recreation auditorium, and participated in World AIDS Day and HIV education programs.

For many years she was able to create a garden at work in the prison.

"I used to have a garden when I worked at the warehouse. I grew everything I could get seeds for. I grew corn one year out of corn I got from a microwave popcorn bag before it was popped. My boss was truly amazed. I had cantaloupe one year from seeds I got out of the kitchen, stuff like that. Sometimes when they serve the melons, they leave some of the seeds in them. I love gardening. That's another thing I am looking forward to when I parole," she told me enthusiastically.

In the evenings, she spent countless hours digging up legal arguments and self-studying law. Brenda filed several appeals with the state but though her arguments were articulate, they went nowhere.

For every appeal letter written by Brenda, another lengthy psychiatric evaluation was ordered. There was a revolving door of doctors coming and going at the prison. She finally gave up this tactic and started to prepare for her first parole hearing.

Brenda became a fairly good prisoner, and her Central File or C-file shows she had no serious disciplinary issues and just seven minor incidents in her file. In her time at the prison, Brenda missed only a few days at work duty or educational assignments classes.

Her file includes a favorable mention relating to an incident in the hobby/craft room. A prison staff member cut her hand, and Brenda took control and "gathered up all the tools and organised the situation."

Brenda was relocated to the Emmons A Unit and was given the cell across the hallway from Manson family member Leslie van Houten, who was convicted of murder and initially sentenced to death. The two became good friends and worked together helping other prisoners to read.

She is also friendly with Manson family member Patricia Krenwinkel, who also was convicted of murder for her part in the crime spree that terrorised California in the mid-1960s. Krenwinkel has become the longest-serving female member in the California penal system.

"Both of the ladies are very sweet and will always do what they can to help you out if you have a problem," Brenda said when I asked about Van Houten and Krenwinkel.

"One of them trains helper dogs for the handicapped, and the other one is in the executive inmate advisory council, which is a liaison between inmates and administration."

The year before her own crime, Brenda had read the book "Helter Skelter" by Manson case prosecutor Vincent Bugliosi and Curt Gentry about the horrific crime spree by drifter Charles Manson and his so-called family of followers who killed actress Sharon Tate, among others. The book is the biggest-selling true crime story in history. Thus, she had known of the pair long before arriving at the prison.

"There's an unwritten rule here that you don't ask. You usually pick up from the gossip going around what people are in here for. Unless you're like me or Leslie or Pat and it's blared all across the news and true crime shows. Then they whisper behind your back when you walk by. I just don't care what people say anymore," Brenda told me.

After Betty Broderick was sentenced for killing her ex-husband and his new wife, she, too, was incarcerated at the same prison. Brenda got to know Broderick, but they did not become friends. Both were unaware of the connection with Dan Broderick until I told Brenda about it.

"That Betty Broderick thing is funny. Small world. Her husband did right by my victims, got them some money I'm sure they could use. I just wish the Wraggs the best. It saddens me to know that I affected them so badly. They didn't deserve that," Brenda said.

The Manson girls, Betty Broderick and Brenda are all eligible for the "Golden Girls" program at the prison, earning special treatment because of their age.

"We get a few things general population don't get. We get to be first in line for shopping canteen. We get two mattresses, two pillows, and three blankets. We used to go out first for meals," Brenda said.

Brenda's siblings have rarely visited her while she has been incarcerated. She signs up for a phone call once a week and tries to keep up with family events.

Her brother Scott married in 1982 and started his own family. He occasionally visited with their father Wally, but it was rare. Her sister Teresa went to see the incarcerated Brenda just once.

Brenda said Teresa really liked the cowboy boots Brenda was wearing when she visited her at the CYA. She tried to bargain for them, but Brenda refused to trade.

"No, I didn't give my sister my boots. I was wearing them. She could buy her own boots… I guess maybe she thought staff wouldn't notice me going back to the unit wearing just socks," she told me.

Teresa married in 1983 and moved to the San Francisco Bay Area, where she lives today.

"Me and my sister aren't close," Brenda said. "We don't hate each other, but we just don't have much contact with each other. I try not to bother her about things. It must be hard to wake up one day and find out your baby sister is a murderer. I don't take it to heart."

"My mom showed me a picture of my sister, and I didn't recognise her. Mom told me she swears that is my older sister. So, I just have to take her word for it."

Brenda's mother visits occasionally, sometimes bringing a relative or a family friend.

Father Wally would come often and bring her half-sister Bree on occasion. In the early stages, Wally would visit every weekend but that soon dwindled as they both grew older. Brenda and Wally began to argue during visits, but they worked through it.

27

PAROLE

BRENDA'S FIRST PAROLE suitability hearing was scheduled for Jan. 21, 1993, at the CIW in Riverside County, almost 14 years after the day of her arrest.

She had recently completed a course called the Breaking Barriers Program, intended for inmates hoping to be paroled. If she were to be released, Brenda would move in with her Uncle Vern in Ventura County and hoped to continue with electronics. Vern was Wally's older brother and owned a successful precision machine business. Brenda was fond of both him and her Aunty Barbara, who was deeply religious.

A three-person parole suitability panel would consider Brenda's life of crime and post-conviction factors along with a representative of the San Diego County district attorney and her court-appointed lawyer, Richard Jallins. The panel would consider all written evidence from both sides.

Two key board members were very familiar with Brenda. Carol Bentley was a member of the California State Assembly from the San Diego County community of El Cajon, and Manny Guaderrama was a former San Diego assistant police chief who knew many of the investigating officers in the Cleveland Elementary shooting case.

The two major newspapers in San Diego, the *Evening Tribune* and the morning *San Diego Union*, had recently merged into one newspaper called *The Union-Tribune*. Two reporters from the new paper got an early start and made the 90-minute journey to the CIW for a 9am start.

As the hearing was about to begin, Brenda announced she would not attend. In her absence, she submitted a document similar to a press release and asked her lawyer, Jallins, to read it to the panel.

None of the victims or their families made the journey. It was later rumoured they were not told of the hearing. Wally, Dot, and the Spencer siblings did not show either.

Brenda's statement was the first time the public would have heard directly from her. The statement is written in the third person, with spelling and grammatical mistakes, and with a newspaper headline:

"CONVICTED GIRL KILLER BREAKS 13-YEAR-OLD SILENCE AND WILL NOT SEEK PAROLE"

"Brenda the shy, diminutive, 16-year-old, pixy-face San Diego red-head, who on January 29th 1979 barricaded herself in her family home and began firing at students and teachers in the elementary school yard across the street.

Leaving the school principal and janitor dead, and six children wounded. After an hour's long stand off with the San Diego SWAT team, announced Wednesday from California Institution for Women in Frontera, California that she is waiving the January 21 scheduled appearance before the Board of Prison Terms for parole consideration, and will instead file before the end of the month a petition for Writ of *Habeas Corpus* to challenge her conviction.

Now, thirty years old, but little changed in physical appearance from 13 years ago, Brenda Spencer is serving twenty-five years to life sentences for first degree murder, plus eight five-year terms for assault with a deadly weapon. In explaining her reasons for waiving her parole board hearing Brenda stated, "I am not trying to dodge responsibility for anything I did. I live with the unbearable pain everyday of knowing that I was responsible for the death of two people and caused many others physical and emotional pain and suffering. No one can know just how hard that is to live with, but I'm not a murderer.

"I was and had been for many days before that incident heavily under the influence of a lot of drugs I had been taking. I had been doing uppers and downers combined with PCP and straight alcohol for several days before the incident. Then that morning I stayed home from school and started doing more.

"I started taking some pills, which I thought were secondals, that I had got from someone on the streets, and I was taking these while smoking PCP and drinking straight whiskey. I started to hallucinate. I saw these commando types. All these people in para-military gear advancing on me from out of the school yard. It was so real. I barricaded myself in, got my rifle and started firing.

The SWAT came I guess, but by then I was so stoned I just gave them the weapons. I remember talking to someone over the telephone from inside the house, but I sure couldn't tell you what I said.

Over the years the press has written some pretty wild tales about what I said, but whatever I said it was the liquor and the drugs talking. Anyone who knew me knew that I wouldn't hurt anyone or anything, but when it was all over in January of 1979, two people were dead and some little children were wounded.

"I must tell you that there's not a day that I don't see those people and those children in my mind and not a day I don't wish, with all my heart, I could bring them back. But, I'm not guilty of murder.

"I don't know what I was doing. You can't for malice a required element for a first-degree murder conviction when you are under the influence of that many drugs and that much alcohol. And more important after all these years some serious inconsistencies have come to light about just who fired all those bullets that killed people.

"For sure the SWAT team lied in court about how many shots they fired, and in what direction they were fired. A big question now emerges as to who, if anyone, was hit from fire from my rifle and who was hit by police fire.

"Clearly when the SWAT team first arrived and before anyone had been shot, they acknowledged that they did not know what direction the shots were coming from. They lied about not firing at me in the house, and they also apparently lied about not firing toward the school yard.

"Also, although the police stated during my court hearings that the lab results showed no drugs or alcohol in my system at the time of my arrest; we, some people who are helping with my writ, have gotten hold of independent lab results which the prosecutor had done from the same blood sample and which show that I had potentially lethal levels of drugs in my system at the time.

"The prosecutor and my own defence attorney covered up this fact and withheld this evidence from the court and withheld it from all the doctors and psychiatrists who did reports and evaluations on me trying to figure out what made me do it. So, I was convicted as a cold-blooded killer, which I'm not.

"On top of that once they arrested me and got me to juvenile hall, they gave me massive doses of powerful, mind altering, psychotropic drugs which kept me completely stoned for the next two years. And until I was finally transported to prison and was finally able to get off the drugs. I wasn't aware of anything at all while I was going through the various court hearings.

"People who saw me say I was a zombie. They said what they told me to say, I did what they told me to do. I didn't even know until a few months ago that I had signed a plea bargain agreement for first degree murder. I can tell you for sure that getting my court papers out of my prison file after all these years and learning that I was plea bargained was the biggest shock of my life. I sure didn't know anything about the law then and being stoned on top of it well they could have told me to sign anything, and I would have.

"Funny thing was none of the doctors, psychiatrists, and other specialists who did expert reports on me and who gave me no kind of neurological and psychological tests bothered to really talk to me, and none of them ever asked what happened. I thought that was really strange. I still think it's strange. They just wrote the reports based on what the police told them, and the police were hiding a lot of information and evidence from them. So, all their special reports are just so much garbage. That's also an issue that I'm raising on my *Habeas Corpus* and Civil Rights lawsuit.

"At the California Institution for Women, Brenda is active in a group called Women Prisoners Convicted by Drugging. A group of approximately fifty women who all can document that they were given psychotropic drugs while being detained in the county jails and going through their trial.

And who are all seeking to overturn their convictions or get new trials or sentence modifications because of their being drugged.

Brenda points out that the drugging of a pretrial detainee without their informed consent is a felony in violation of California Penal Code Section 2670. She says that none of the women gave their informed consent and those who resisted the drugging were coerced, threatened, thrown into the rubber room, or had worse happen to them until they complied and took the drugs. And some were beaten and left in rubber rooms for days, naked and with no food, water, and provisions for hygiene.

Forty-two of the women in the group, including Bernadette has sought and received help from various State Legislators and

Congressmen, and an investigation is currently under way by the FBI and the US Justice Department.

State Senator Robert Presley, of Riverside, has been most active in demanding and getting the investigation by the FBI, Brenda reports. Two of the group also have *Habeas Corpus* in the State Courts and one has filled a large Federal Civil Rights suit.

Brenda states that in addition to her Writ of *Habeas Corpus* which will be filed on the end of the month in State Court, she will also be filing in the southern District Federal Court a Civil Rights suit for damages due to violations of her federally protected Constitutional rights. In addition to charging that she did not get a fair hearing due to being given the psychotropic drugs, Brenda's *Habeas Corpus* charges prosecutor Charles Patrick and the San Diego Police Department with falsifying, fabricating, and withholding evidence and her own defence attorney Michael McGlinn of San Diego with willful misrepresentation.

In her Writ she also challenges the vigil and political opportunities that marked her prosecution, obviously referring to the political aspirations of Governor Pete Wilson, the former Mayor of San Diego and arguing that the desire of many to benefit politically from the notoriety of her case caused perverse police and prosecution evidence, fabrication, and suppression and prevented her from being granted fair representation of receiving a fair hearing.

Now enrolled in a vocational training electronic program and taking college courses at California Institution for Women. Brenda states further that she is working to formulate an outreach program which she hopes to launch soon in cooperation with persons on the outside of the community, which has its objective to attempt to reach other troubled youth like herself and in an effort to intervene before their lives come to tragic consequences like hers.

Although she has in the past thirteen years categorically refused all contact with the media, Brenda states that she will now do interviews with selected newspapers, magazines, and television programs. Deciding on these an individual basis, and after careful consideration of each prospective interview.

Brenda's statement was annexed with her contact details for media requests. Panel members and members of the press observed Brenda through a glass window but did not speak with her.

The panel deliberated for 35 minutes and refused parole. The board commissioner, Jim Nielson, said Brenda Spencer's crime was "carried out in an especially heinous, atrocious, cruel, and callous manner." The findings determined she still was a risk to society and had much to resolve before she could be released.

"Until progress is made, the prisoner continues to be completely unpredictable and a threat to others," it said.

She was denied parole for another three years. But Brenda appealed the decision and was back in front of the group in less than two years.

Her former lawyer, McGlinn, although not in attendance and technically no longer representing Brenda, vehemently denied that any evidence was hidden, lost, or tampered with during her arrest and trial.

"It's just absolute nonsense. There was never any indication that any test results were in any way falsified," he told reporters. McGlinn said he gave her the best defence he could.

Former Cleveland Elementary teacher Daryl Barnes said, "Everybody makes mistakes and should be forgiven but to me it's a capital crime. If the sentence is 25 years, she shouldn't be paroled until the 25 years are up."

But Christy Buell's father Norm said he believed Brenda was abused and deserved a break.

"Those things put together are not a good chemical mix, and I could see where it would happen. I personally would say that she's served her sentence," he said.

Wally Spencer, contacted by reporters at the Spencer home on Lake Atlin Ave., chose not to comment.

Almost every news operation in California approached Brenda, all hoping to be first to interview the "I don't like Mondays killer." She chose a few local TV broadcasters who came to the prison to conduct sit-down interviews with the prisoner.

In a large prison office with steel-framed chairs, Brenda sat facing interviewers. She wore her prison blue jeans, sweatshirt, and her signature aviator-style glasses. With a hint of modern trend, her orange hair was in a mullet style – long in the back, cropped short on top.

At 30, Brenda still looked young, with a freckled-face and tiny frame. She swallowed frequently with nerves and simply repeated what was in her parole statement. A few times she appeared to hold back tears when asked about the victims.

Brenda does not speak with a typical California accent, and at times a slightly southern accent as her family was from Arkansas, came through. (Later, she told me about this, "I still have a trace of the accent; when I get tired, it really comes out." Her cellmate "would look at me funny and say, 'do you realise you have an accent?'")

She made no apologies during her interviews. But said she is the one who has to live with the knowledge of taking two men's lives. She also denies saying the famous phrase "I hate Mondays." Brenda says she would like to hear recordings of the conversation, knowing it was not recorded.

In one hand, she held up the SDPD toxicology report from Poisonlab/Enbionics. It said she was drug and alcohol free. In the other she held a report from The Center for Human Toxicology saying she had imbibed a cocktail of drugs and alcohol.

Brenda said both were taken from the same blood sample at

different times. She repeatedly says there were lethal drug amounts in her system and the second report was hidden on purpose.

McGlinn responded, "It's an outrageous statement. We were not aware of any PCP use around the time of the offence. Brenda did have an abnormal brain wave. She was diagnosed as being epileptic. And we believed that the reason for what occurred was more of a result of her being in a dissociated state than any kind of intoxication defence or illegal drug usage."

"I think it's nonsense, to put it politely," said prosecutor Patrick. "Here you have a 16-year-old kid who, granted, was maybe not the best adjusted kid in the world, to all of a sudden, for no good reason of any kind, to start blasting away at totally innocent school children. It just leaves you flabbergasted. That's all I can say. It's just the utter senselessness of it."

"If I had no drugs or alcohol in my system then I am just a cold-blooded killer," Brenda told Mitch Duncan of San Diego's KFMB television news in one of the interviews.

28

PRISON LIFE

BRENDA, LIKE MANY of the incarcerated, began intimate relationships with other inmates.

Prisoners jokingly say there are two kinds of homosexuals: genetic queers and generic queers. Generics are people with opposite-sex partners on the outside who have flings with other inmates for convenience. Genetics are people who identify as homosexuals in and out of prison. Brenda is self-described as a genetic queer.

She moved in with a new cellmate named BranDee in 1993. Brenda always had the lower bunk because of her continued seizures. For the next 15 years, they would share a very small space. The two bunkies did have a short sexual relationship but settled on a friendship. They became close for life and shared everything, even when BranDee was released.

BranDee Sisemore was convicted of murder the same year as Brenda. Her stepfather convinced her to kidnap and kill a 10-year-old girl to cover up his molestation of the child. BranDee, her husband Hilton Tripp, and his best friend Randy Cook, abducted and the men strangled little Tami Carpenter in Avila Beach, near San Luis Obispo, California.

Brenda knew the area from her trips with her dad to Morro Bay. They would drive the coast roads very near the crime scene and take photographs.

BranDee's stepfather, William Record, had been accused of molesting Tami. Days before she was to testify against him, he hatched a plan to kill her. BranDee was a family friend and she arranged to take Tami on a swimming trip. Instead, they went to a secluded campsite she shared with her husband and Cook. BranDee watched as the two men tortured and strangled the girl.

Her young and scared husband soon confessed. The police found the body buried near their tent, just as Hilton said it would be. In 1981, BranDee pleaded guilty in a plea deal to second-degree murder and was sentenced to 15 years to life.

Record died in prison four years after his conviction and the other two defendants are serving life sentences with little hope of getting out. BranDee divorced Tripp in 1982 and resumed her maiden name.

When BranDee was just three, her younger brother died at 10 months old. Her mother, Mary Jenkins, never fully recovered. When BranDee gave birth to a daughter, Kaitlyn, in 1978, Mary wanted to adopt her grandchild. She later adopted a girl named Venna and would raise both children as sisters after BranDee's arrest.

BranDee says her stepfather molested her from when she was seven, and she was afraid of him. She says this was the reason she complied with his demand to help kill Tami Carpenter.

She and Brenda shared horror stories about their home lives.

Brenda had made no official statement about abuse in her family despite multiple rumours after her father's marriage to Sheila.

BranDee told her parole panel that it took years for her to be able to deal with her molestation.

"He had a lot of control over me," she told the panel. "He manipulated me into doing things that a normal child would never, ever do. And it took a lot of counselling to get past that."

The first 10 years of BranDee's incarceration were turbulent. She made homemade liquor in her cell and often fought with other inmates. Her behaviour began to improve after she attended group therapy for incest survivors.

Brenda's legal team never submitted the writ of *habeas corpus* she spoke about in her parole panel statement. But the lawyers did persuade the parole board to schedule another hearing in 1994. No victims, family members, or journalists would be allowed; Brenda would have the right to object to the panel's composition.

1994 PAROLE HEARING

This time, Carol Bentley was to be joined as a panel member by former SDPD police lieutenant Tom Giaquinto who had presided during the parole hearings for members of the Manson Family and was highly experienced.

In September 1994, three months before the hearing was scheduled, Brenda was taken to hospital, suffering from an overdose of her seizure medicine after being found unconscious in her cell. She denies this was a suicide attempt.

She says it happened because doctors were trying new prescriptions and dosages to control her attacks. Brenda was also being treated at the time for a continued viral infection and believes the mix of prescriptions might have been a factor.

The hearing started as planned at 12 noon on Dec. 12. Brenda gave no objection to the panel members, and it got under way. Immediately, she was asked about the crime and her behaviour leading up to it.

Asked about suicide, she told a new story of consuming glue and aspirins while at Patrick Henry High School. She said she was released to her parents and went back to therapy just weeks before the shooting.

"Well, I had tried and completely failed," she said, when asked why she tried to kill herself.

The panel asked Brenda if she was attending anger management courses and she replied, "Yeah, I'm getting a lot out of it."

Asked about the focuses of Alcoholics Anonymous and Nicotine Anonymous courses she was supposed to be taking, Brenda was unable to be specific about any part of the programs. The panel was unconvinced of her attendance.

The ninth of the 12 steps of the AA program is called: *"Make direct amends to such people whenever possible, except when to do so would injure them or others."*

Ten years after starting AA, Brenda says she wrote letters to her victims. They were addressed to her lawyer with the intention that they should reach surviving victims. Brenda says she has no idea if the victims ever received her letters, but she is certain she received no response.

Brenda said the AA meetings became repetitious with inmates telling the same stories over and over again. "Basically, I learned to tell their stories as good as they could." When a psychiatric report was read out saying she was anti-social with a false sense of reality, Brenda began to cry. That stunned the panel.

Asked why she had not shown similar emotion in a meeting with the doctor who wrote the report, she said, "well, he left me waiting in the hallway for three hours." The panel said this may have been part of the test. Brenda responded, "Maybe."

The panel heard that Brenda's continued seizures had an impact on how much work she could do with study groups. She had been prescribed the drugs Geodon, Telazol, and Zoloft to help with the condition, but the seizures continued.

Brenda told the panel that despite her medications and seizures, she was proud of her work with the prison's Native American religious services and had just become sergeant-at-arms of the Long Termers' Organisation.

Only a single letter from her Uncle Vern supported her parole application. No one else from her family was heard from.

The panel's presiding commissioner told her it was important for the group to know she had support outside and that it reflected badly if she didn't.

PRESIDING COMMISSIONER: DO YOU THINK YOU'RE READY FOR PAROLE?

INMATE SPENCER: RIGHT NOW?

PRESIDING COMMISSIONER: UH-HUM

INMATE SPENCER: OBVIOUSLY, NO.

PRESIDING COMMISSIONER: NO, YOU DON'T THINK – YOU DON'T THINK YOU ARE?

INMATE SPENCER: NO.

In final arguments, Richard Jallins, Brenda's court-appointed lawyer, chose to read newspaper quotes from Norm Buell.

"That's from a father of one of the children," Jallins said. "I mean, there's some attempt – some point in time we have to say enough is enough and try to put this... tragedy behind us."

In less than an hour, Brenda was denied parole for at least another five years.

1998 PAROLE HEARING

A parole hearing scheduled for Brenda in January 1998 was not what anyone expected. Minutes before it was to begin, Brenda withdrew. She gave no precise details for why she refused to attend, but Keith Stanton, her new court-appointed lawyer, said Brenda was remorseful for the killings and would not be there for tactical reasons.

Brenda had just been told that victim Cam Miller, by then 27, and a San Diego probation officer and thus part of the police fraternity, might be present at the hearing. In fact, the San Diego district attorney's office had asked Miller to write a victim's statement, and he opted to deliver it by hand.

Cam and his wife arrived early at the prison and hung around for hours waiting for a chance to confront Brenda.

In the end, he was able to see her only through a window as she was leaving the holding room.

"I was psyching myself up," Miller said in an article in *Good Housekeeping* magazine later that year. "My wife saw her through the window and said, 'There she is.'"

Miller still had scar tissue on his back and chest from the bullets. It continued to cause pain when he stretched the wrong way. Through his high school years, he would deny being a victim and always wore a T-shirt to hide his wounds when he went swimming.

San Diego deputy district attorney Andrea Crisanti spoke with reporters after the parole hearing.

"She knew she would be denied. There's nothing she could say at this time to sway the board," Crisanti said. "We think she should still do life. She killed two people. How can she repay that? How could we take that risk again, if she were released?"

Brenda's specific reason for withdrawing from the parole hearing was never made clear. Her Uncle Vern was unwell at the time, and her father was struggling at home with Bree, by then a 17-year-old misfit. Emotionally, Brenda may not have wanted to be confronted by Miller.

Vern died four days later.

Her half-sister Bree would continue to be a source of frustration for her father and for Brenda. It would be a further three years before Brenda would gain another opportunity for parole.

In February 2000, she tattooed herself by scratching her chest with a hot paper clip. She branded the words "Unforgiven" and "Alone," using Viking runes.

Authorities first interpreted this self-mutilation as "Courage" and "Pride." Brenda originally agreed this is what it said, but later changed her mind.

She cited many reasons for her self-mutilation, including depression and stress. She was worried about a job change at the prison and concerns about her half-sister. She also was stressed because a prison-reform activist named Jennifer Furio had published some private letters of hers.

"Letters from Prison – Voices of Women Murderers" was a subjective collection of letters from women condemned for murder who had replied to letters from Furio. Her book was written with the assumption that the female murderers were victims of some form of abuse.

"Jennifer Furio was just an author who started writing me a while back. I haven't heard from her in years. I guess she got what she wanted and then just quit writing," Brenda told me later.

It is not unusual for killers' letters or cards to be published or sold without the writer's consent. Letters from Brenda are for sale on the internet and in crime-memorabilia circles. Any time Brenda is in the news she receives a batch of letters from short-term pen pals.

But I believe the strongest cause of Brenda's breakdown was a separation from her prison girlfriend. For some years she had been in a relationship with a woman named Chris. Not much is known about Chris other than that she was in and out of different prisons and eventually was paroled.

Because of her various prison stints, Chris was doing a life sentence on instalments, as they say in prison jargon. Toward the end of their relationship, Brenda and she could communicate only by telephone. Eventually, when Chris was released, she vowed to stay out of prison and severed the relationship. Brenda was devastated because she had relied heavily on Chris to make major decisions for her life inside.

All issues with her half-sister Bree resolved themselves. After running away from home, Bree returned safely to the old house she shared with Wally. After meeting a boy while working at Sea World, she would soon leave again to get married in Las Vegas. The neighbouring state of Nevada was an easier proposition than California for a quick marriage.

Brenda's relationship with Bree as an adult was strained and would never develop. Wally and Scott kept her up to date on all family activities by letter and during visits.

29

ANOTHER SHOOTING

LIKE CLOCKWORK, THREE years and three months after the last hearing, Brenda was up for parole again. Now 39, she was far better prepared this time round. Prison security officers escorted her to the hearing room in chains, flanked by her team of lawyers.

The tone of Brenda's latest hearing was greatly affected by a horrific incident in San Diego County just five weeks before, which bore remarkable similarities to the Spencer case.

A troubled teenager unleashed a volley of gunfire on a school, killing two adults and wounding 13 students. Charles "Andy" Williams, 16, was arrested on his knees trying to commit suicide inside Santana High School in the San Diego suburb of Santee.

Like Brenda, Williams also chose a Monday for his rampage. He used a small .22 calibre handgun. Again, like Brenda, he came from a troubled home. His father gained custody after a messy divorce, and the boy had little contact with his mother.

Brenda was familiar with Santana High School. Brant Flemming studied there for two years in the 1980s, and Sheila McCoy attended before her arrest. The son of former Cleveland Elementary teacher Daryl Barnes taught at Santana High at the time of the shooting and helped usher students to safety.

2001 PAROLE HEARING

Brett Granlund, a former Republican member of the California State Assembly, was presiding commissioner of the three-person panel for Brenda's hearing. Joining them in the wood-paneled room were a half-dozen reporters, Cam Miller with a representative from a victim services organisation, and Richard Sachs, a San Diego deputy district attorney.

Miller sat at the back of the room, staring intently as he waited for Brenda to arrive. She was seated and told she would have to keep her restraints on throughout the hearing. Normally, a prisoner is allowed to have the chains removed if two guards are present. Granlund denied Brenda's request to remove the restraints.

All questions during the parole hearing were given more weight because of the current climate. Brenda also had adjusted her answers to suit the line of inquiry. The panel followed the usual format asking her about her memory of the event, toxicology reports, and rehabilitation, etc.

Asked why she thought her father would buy her a gun, she responded, "I felt like he wanted me to kill myself."

The panel did not probe deeper. Growing sceptical of Brenda, Granlund kept to the agenda and pressed on.

The following is taken directly from the parole hearing transcripts:

COMMISSIONER GRANLUND: WELL, IS THERE ANYTHING MORE YOU WANT TO SHARE WITH US ABOUT THE DAY OF THE SHOOTING, THE EVENTS THAT LED UP TO THE SHOOTING, SOME OF THE FOLKS THAT YOU RAN AROUND WITH, OR WHY YOU THINK YOU DID IT?

INMATE SPENCER: WELL, (INAUDIBLE) AND ABUSIVE HOUSE.

COMMISSIONER GRANLUND: AND WHAT WAS ABUSIVE ABOUT THE HOUSEHOLD?

INMATE SPENCER: I WAS SEXUALLY ABUSED BY MY FATHER.

COMMISSIONER GRANLUND: IS THAT - HAS THAT EVER BEEN INDICATED IN THE RECORD IN THE PAST?

INMATE SPENCER: JUST (INAUDIBLE) BUT I NEVER TALKED ABOUT IT.

COMMISSIONER GRANLUND: BECAUSE I DIDN'T SEE IT. I READ YOUR FILE AND YOUR TRANSCRIPTS AND PRIOR HEARING TRANSCRIPTS. I DIDN'T SEE ANY MENTION WHATSOEVER OF (INAUDIBLE).

INMATE SPENCER: (INAUDIBLE) TILL I WAS 14.

COMMISSIONER GRANLUND: AND YOU NEVER TOLD YOUR PROBATION OFFICER OR YOUR COUNSELLOR?

INMATE SPENCER: NO. (INAUDIBLE) MY PROBATION OFFICER.

COMMISSIONER GRANLUND: WELL, IS THERE ANY MORE YOU WOULD LIKE TO (INAUDIBLE) WITH US?

INMATE SPENCER: I JUST WANT TO TAKE FULL RESPONSIBILITY FOR IT. THERE IS NOT A DAY THAT GOES BY THAT I DON'T THINK ABOUT IT AND ALL THE PAIN IT CAUSED.

What should have been a revelation was quickly glossed over by the panel. They noted it and moved on. Granlund re-joined the topic much later in the hearing:

COMMISSIONER GRANLUND: NOW, YOU'RE TELLING US THAT YOUR FATHER BEAT YOU AND MOLESTED YOU?

INMATE SPENCER: YES, HE DID.

COMMISSIONER GRANLUND: DO YOU THINK HE BEAT AND MOLESTED YOUR SIBLINGS?

INMATE SPENCER: I DON'T KNOW. I DON'T THINK SO. I'M MORE LIKE MY MOTHER THAN ANYBODY ELSE. AND HE HAS A PROBLEM WITH MY MOTHER. (INAUDABLE) EVEN AFTER ALL THESE YEARS.

COMMISSIONER GRANLUND: WHY DO YOU THINK THE COURTS AWARDED CUSTODY IN A CUSTODY BATTLE?

INMATE SPENCER: BECAUSE MY MOM DIDN'T HAVE ANY EMPLOYMENT (INAUDIBLE). IF I STAYED WITH MY MOM, I PROBABLY WOULDN'T BE HERE.

COMMISSIONER GRANLUND: SO, YOU THINK IT'S YOUR FATHER'S FAULT?

INMATE SPENCER: NO.

COMMISSIONER GRANLUND: WHY WOULD IT HAVE BEEN DIFFERENT IF YOU HAD STAYED WITH YOUR MOTHER?

INMATE SPENCER: THE ABUSE WOULDN'T HAVE BEEN THERE.

COMMISSIONER GRANLUND: AND YOU NEVER REPORTED ABUSE?

INMATE SPENCER: NO. I WAS SCARED TO.

COMMISSIONER GRANLUND: OKAY. YOUR MOTHER, SHE MAINTAINED A RESIDENCE WITH ANOTHER WOMAN, A FAMILY FRIEND?

INMATE SPENCER: UM-HMM.

COMMISSIONER GRANLUND: AND THE TWO HOUSEHOLDS, THE HOUSE WHERE YOUR MOTHER LIVED WAS WITHIN WALKING DISTANCE.

INMATE SPENCER: YES, IT WAS.

COMMISSIONER GRANLUND: DID YOU EVER TELL YOUR MOM THAT YOU WERE BEING ABUSED?

INMATE SPENCER: NO.

The panel reviewed a handwritten letter from Brenda to Wally saying he had visited her twice a month since she was incarcerated. Granlund was surprised to hear there was still a relationship between father and daughter. He asked if she welcomed her father's visits:

INMATE SPENCER: YES. WE'VE LEARNED TO DEAL WITH THE ABUSE AND THE ISSUES, AND WE HAVE GOTTEN TO BE FRIENDS.

The panel moved on to a large file full of psychological reports and multiple letters for objection and support. Confidential notices had been sent out to all concerned parties and answers had been arriving at the prison for five months.

The hearing watched an emotional video statement from Kathe

Wragg and heard a similar audio tape from Crystal Hardy. Mike Suchar's son submitted a letter. It was read aloud, but the panel reviewed it privately.

Members also received generic letters from the parents of Santana High victims. The parents of Trevor Edwards, who was injured in the shooting, said all school shooters should never be freed.

Grunlund read out a short letter asking for forgiveness for Brenda from the mother of the injured Officer Robert Robb. He also read an excerpt of a birthday card sent to Brenda by a former Cleveland Elementary pupil called Lorra Craig. She was still coming to grips with the events 22 years later.

At the time of the shooting, she had been a 12-year-old member of the class of Darryl Barnes and began corresponding with Brenda after the Santana High shooting. Her hope was to communicate with Brenda and try to understand why it all happened. She began what she called a "journey of understanding" by setting up a post office box and writing to Brenda.

Lorra visited Brenda twice a month for the next two years. On occasions, she'd bring a police officer friend or her daughter to meet Brenda. A few visits were photographed.

About Lorra's outreach, Brenda told the panel, "Well, I was kind of surprised at first, and then I was a little scared because I didn't know how she was going to act. But I knew I had answers that she needed."

Communications between the two later ceased when Lorra moved out of California.

The most damning evidence before the panel was the psychological report authored by Dr. Robert McDaniel. It says her schizoaffective disorder was under control at present but would need a lifetime of prescription. Dr. McDaniel said he considered Brenda to be a threat to society and he could not recommend parole.

In closing statements, the presiding commissioner asked to speak with Brenda again:

COMMISSIONER GRANLUND: I AM VERY TROUBLED WITH THIS ALLEGATION OR RECENT DISCOVERY THAT YOUR POSITION IS YOU WERE MOLESTED. YOU WERE ACTUALLY SEXUALLY MOLESTED BY YOUR FATHER?

INMATE SPENCER: YES.

COMMISSIONER GRANLUND: OKAY. AND YOU BELIEVE THAT THAT (INAUDIBLE) MOLESTATION CONTRIBUTED TO YOUR PERSONALITY THAT CONTRIBUTED TO THE CRIMES – TO THE CRIME THAT YOU COMMITTED?

INMATE SPENCER: YES.

COMMISSIONER GRANLUND: WHAT WOULD HAPPEN IF THE DISTRICT ATTORNEY WOULD ELECT TO FILE (INAUDIBLE) MOLESTATION CHARGES AGAINST YOUR FATHER?

INMATE SPENCER: I DON'T ANYTHING (INAUDIBLE)

COMMISSIONER GRANLUND: BUT YOU WOULD SUPPORT OPENING AN INVESTIGATION AND PROCEEDING CRIMINALLY AGAINST YOUR FATHER?

INMATE SPENCER: THERE HAS ALREADY BEEN AN INVESTIGATION DONE.

COMMISSIONER GRANLUND: BY WHOM?

INMATE SPENCER: RIGHT AFTER I GOT ARRESTED.

COMMISSIONER GRANLUND: WHO INVESTIGATED?

INMATE SPENCER: THE CITY OF SAN DIEGO.

COMMISSIONER GRANLUND: THE CITY?

INMATE SPENCER: YEAH. (INAUDIBLE) INVESTIGATION.

COMMISSIONER GRANLUND: POLICE DEPARTMENT? BUT YOU TOLD ME YOU HADN'T TOLD ANYONE ABOUT IT.

INMATE SPENCER: I HAD TOLD MY COUNSELLORS (INAUDIBLE)

COMMISSIONER GRANLUND: WELL, THERE AGAIN, I'M JUST GOING TO TELL YOU THAT EITHER YOU'RE INVOLVED IN A SITUATION (INAUDIBLE) BUT NONETHELESS, I THINK IF I TOOK THAT POSITION, I WOULD WANT TO HAVE IT INVESTIGATED AND I WOULD PURSUE IT TO EVERY REMEDY AVAILABLE TO ME IN THE LAW. AND THAT WOULD MAKE YOUR STORY MORE CONVINCING.

Brenda was given the opportunity to say why she was suitable for parole:

> INMATE SPENCER: I'M REALLY DEEPLY SORRY FOR WHAT I HAVE DONE TO MY VICTIMS AND THEIR FAMILIES AND FRIENDS. I KNOW THAT 'I'M SORRY' DOESN'T MAKE IT ALL RIGHT. NOT A DAY GOES BY THAT I DON'T THINK ABOUT WHAT I DID, AND I REALISE THAT NOT ONLY THE PEOPLE I PHYSICALLY HURT ARE VICTIMS, BUT EVERYONE WHO WENT TO THAT SCHOOL, THEIR FAMILY AND FRIENDS ARE VICTIMS AS WELL... WITH EVERY SCHOOL SHOOTING, I FEEL THAT I AM PARTIALLY RESPONSIBLE."

Immediately following Brenda's plea, Cam Miller recounted his memories of the event and subsequent nightmares. The hearing was closed with his final statement, "No one forced her to commit this brutal and senseless crime. She clearly has no regard for human lives. She was shooting to kill any human target that walked into her path. She is a cold-hearted ruthless murderer who needs to be in prison for the rest of her life for the safety of the community. I urge this parole board to deny Brenda Spencer's parole for as many years as possible. Thank you."

The panel unanimously agreed to deny parole. Brenda would face a parole board all over again in four years' time.

30

BRITISH DOCUMENTARY

2005 PAROLE HEARING

In September 2005, Brenda sat in front of newly appointed commissioner Stephen Lee. In an unusual move by prison authorities, a British documentary producer had also been given access. The director set up his single camera on the opposite side of the room, to Brenda's left.

The panel was presented with the normal stack of letters for and against her release. Cam Miller was once again in attendance, and the same audio and video evidence was resubmitted from earlier hearings.

Wally's support letter said there was plenty of room at her mother's house if Brenda were released. Brenda had not heard from her mother in more than five years, and Dot did not confirm this offer with a letter of support.

Despite her father's letter, Brenda had new plans to live at Crossroads Halfway House in the nearby town of Claremont if released. Crossroads is a well-known refuge for released female inmates that was founded by religious dairy farmers who worked near the prison and wanted to help with rehabilitation.

Brenda described the extent of her abuse to Commissioner Lee:

INMATE SPENCER: I REMEMBER JUST, DIFFERENT NIGHTS WHEN HE WOULD JUST ALMOST RAPE ME.

COMMISSIONER LEE: YOU SAY ALMOST…

INMATE SPENCER: IT WAS LIKE THAT, LIKE HE DID.

COMMISSIONER LEE: I DON'T UNDERSTAND.

INMATE SPENCER: LIKE HE WOULD TOUCH ME INAPPROPRIATELY. I DON'T KNOW HOW TO SAY IT.

COMMISSIONER LEE: THE STATEMENT THAT YOU GAVE IN THE PAST THAT APPARENTLY YOU GAVE TO THE DOCTOR INDICATED THAT THERE WAS SOME FONDLING?

INMATE SPENCER: YES.

COMMISSIONER LEE: OKAY. AND DID THAT LEAD TO DIGITAL PENETRATION?

INMATE SPENCER: YES.

COMMISSIONER LEE: AND LATER TO INTERCOURSE?

INMATE SPENCER: YES.

COMMISSIONER LEE: SO, ARE YOU NOW INDICATING THAT THERE WAS ACTUAL INTERCOURSE SERVICED?

INMATE SPENCER: THERE WAS, I GUESS YOU'D CALL IT SODOMY.

COMMISSIONER LEE: OKAY. I HAVE NO REPORTS WHATSOEVER IN REGARDS TO ANY INDIVIDUAL WHO HAS INTERVIEWED YOU TO INDICATE THAT. SO NOW YOU'RE INDICATING THAT IT WAS ONLY SODOMY, OR IT WAS INTERCOURSE AND SODOMY. SO, THERE WAS NO INTERCOURSE?

INMATE SPENCER: NO.

To support her claims of abuse, Brenda's lawyer pointed out a recent Bureau of Public Health investigation that interviewed family members and recalled police statements. Her lawyers concluded the abuse claim was credible based on new witness statements.

In the report, Brenda's mother, Dot Spencer, said she now believed abuse occurred, and Brenda's half-sister Bree also reported an amount of abuse and control by Wally. The discrepancy of where Brenda slept was inconclusive, with friends saying they saw one bed in Wally's room, but her older sister said there was a separate bed.

The BPH report also said if believed Wally's character and judgment also must be considered.

It said his marriage to Brenda's teenage former cellmate Sheila was testament to his poor parenting.

"There may be family secrets that others will never acknowledge or discuss, and this is not an uncommon situation in such families where abuse occurs," the report said.

Wally still regularly visits Brenda, but both say they do not want to discuss the issue of incest. She said she confronted him once but got nowhere and he just doesn't want to talk about it.

Her closing statement:

> INMATE SPENCER: I REALISE THAT NOTHING I DO AND NO AMOUNT OF TIME WILL BRING MR. WRAGG AND MR. SUCHAR BACK. IT DOESN'T ERASE THE... STUFF THAT I'VE GIVEN TO THOSE KIDS AND MRS. WRAGG. I JUST WANT THEM TO KNOW THAT I AM VERY SORRY, AND I DON'T KNOW HOW TO MAKE IT UP TO THEM, BUT I TRY EVERY DAY TO MAKE MYSELF A BETTER PERSON SO THAT THAT DOESN'T HAPPEN AGAIN, AND I DO EVERYTHING I CAN TO MAKE SURE THAT NOTHING LIKE THAT WOULD EVER HAPPEN. I DON'T WASTE MY TIME IN HERE JUST SITTING AROUND. I GO THROUGH THERAPIES, AND I WORK HARD AND EVERYTHING. BECAUSE I DON'T WANT ANYTHING THIS HORRIBLE TO EVER HAPPEN AGAIN. THAT'S ALL.

Just as four years before, the panel heard from victim Cam Miller and adjourned to make its decision. Twenty minutes later, the panel denied parole for another four years.

"She expressed remorse, but she came across as fragile, someone who's not all-together. She says she doesn't remember the crime, and she provided no insight into what happened," Richard Sachs, San Diego deputy district attorney, told reporters waiting outside.

In regard to Brenda's self-mutilation by tattooing, he said, "That demonstrates she can't handle the bad things that happen to her. It's a very good result, and we're very happy." Sachs made no public comment regarding abuse or claims of sodomy.

The TV documentary for Britain's Channel 4 was released throughout Europe in January 2006. The program interviewed both parents separately and would be the only videoed conversations with Wally and Dot to date. Both answered questions about her upbringing, the rifle, and claims of abuse.

When Dot was asked if she knew of father and daughter sharing a bed she said, "Yes, unfortunately, I am. Actually, he didn't have much furniture. I think they slept on a mattress on the floor." She does not say when this information was provided, or by whom.

Asked specifically about abuse, she said she wasn't aware but had suspicions.

"Just the way she would be acting and very evasive. If you asked anything... and it wasn't just her, so I knew something was wrong."

Dot never felt strongly enough about either situation to seek custody of Brenda. She said she could not afford the legal costs and assumed that Wally would "take care" of things.

Dot does show remorse for what happened, but evidently only enough to blame Wally.

"I thought if I could have held the family together, if he hadn't been out, you know, fooling around and maybe if I had been more tolerant and let him have his little fling for a while. And that we would have stayed together, then maybe it wouldn't have happened. So, I do feel a little bit responsible. "

Dot said Wally should be in prison instead of Brenda.

In his interview on the programme, Wally was in total disbelief when confronted by the abuse allegations:

"Brenda said that? Well, it's not true! No! Well that never happened, you know. I would take a lie detector on that. I never did anything like that."

He admitted the two shared a bedroom at one point but said they did not share a bed. He refused to discuss the marriage to Brenda's cellmate and her subsequent disappearance, saying only, "She did not want her daughter, OK? And that is the only statement that I'll make."

Wally seemed baffled when asked if he shared guilt for buying Brenda the rifle.

"Uh well, all I'll say is, you know, it's none of their damn business if I bought a rifle for her Christmas."

Wally said he was not responsible for Brenda's actions and knew nothing about her being suicidal. He said his focus was to make sure his daughter could take care of herself if and when she was released from prison. Like everyone else, he said, he had no idea why she did what she did.

The documentary interviewed many of the police and victims at the scene of the crime. They gave their lasting thoughts about the event and Brenda's possible release.

Crystal Hardy, by then 36, was interviewed standing on the spot where she was shot. "Certainly, it affected my life. Something that is that traumatic... would of course affect your life," she said.

Monica Selvig, 35, says through giggles, "She's evil looking…to me. She had these glasses and that long red hair. She's creepy, yeah. Uh, someone from like a horror flick. I mean, I've never heard her voice and never heard her talk. But just…she is eerie... looking."

Officer Robert Robb said that if Brenda were paroled, "I'd get my guns out and put 'em back together and I would load them, and I would start carrying a weapon again. Because I think if she got out, she would try and finish the job."

Robb, whose mother once wrote to the parole board asking forgiveness for Brenda, later regretted speaking to the documentary makers and said it made him look like a bitter ex-cop.

"I'm not really bitter," he told me. "or I try not to be."

Robb, who never fully recovered from his injuries, moved to Bakersfield, California, where he became a school security officer and started a family. He died from cancer in 2018.

Detective Chester Thurston was filmed at the house re-enacting how he used a bullhorn to distract Brenda.

"The human side, the compassionate side, says let's let her out. Twenty-seven years, it's time to go. The police officer side and of course the retired police officer side says hey uh-uh, let her die in prison," Thurston said.

The television exposure in the UK filled Brenda's mailbox, and she made lasting relationships with two of the writers. Luciana Buccini and Irene Lemos became friends with her, and both wrote letters of support. Lemos flew to California to visit Brenda in prison and thank her for helping with personal issues.

In 2007, Brenda's health began to suffer, and she was hospitalised for depression. She entered into correctional clinical case management prison and was assigned to meet regularly with a psychotherapist. She was diagnosed with a schizoaffective disorder, a condition marked by a combination of schizophrenia symptoms, such as hallucinations or delusions and mood disorders. She was prescribed more medication.

Along with her epilepsy, Brenda also was diagnosed with hypertension, high cholesterol, and hyperthyroidism. She takes many separate medications for all these ailments and probably will have to continue for the rest of her life.

She stopped having seizures.

"They finally found the right drug combination for me," she told me.

Rain or shine, Brenda attends the prison Medline outdoor bank of windows daily to receive her medications.

"All the nurses say, 'Hi, Spencer' when I show up for meds," she told me. "Some of them try to wave me off to another window or pretend to run away. I take so many different meds that it takes them a while to fill my order."

A man named Hanger was assigned as her prison counsellor and to keep a closer eye on her. If her symptoms become more severe, he could order her moved into the Enhanced Outpatient Program, which would require therapy four to five days a week. Part of her current therapy was to take care of prison cats. She tended to about six at any given time.

Brenda had a countless number of pets while in prison. Most recently she cared for a crow named Jacob. He was popular with inmates and staff.

"I paroled him to staff who took him home. He was so cool," she said.

Two of her favourite cats were Crook and Sammy. As a kitten, Crook trapped his tail in a door and ended up with a permanent bend. His name had no connection to his incarceration, but he was paroled in the same way as Jacob the crow. Sammy was a calico who would sleep on her lap with his tongue out. He died of feline leukaemia. He was the last cat Brenda cared for.

In 2007, Brenda began to study the religion known as Wicca, or as she describes it, Pagan Witchcraft. Wiccans celebrate the cycles of the moon, much like Native American faiths.

Brenda says she self-practiced before being arrested with the help of a book she read about Wicca.

"Unfortunately, in here we can't celebrate it. I can't wait until I parole so I can finally keep the holidays again. It's been a long time; it will really feel like coming home once again. And I'll be able to get out into nature, that will be wonderful," she said when I asked her about Wicca holidays.

31

PHYSICAL AND MENTAL ABUSE

2009 PAROLE HEARING

Like a broken record, Brenda's 2009 parole hearing went much like the others, and she was again denied release. Cam Miller attended again, and there was a large collection of letters from victims and friends. But this time her parents sent no support letters.

The presiding commissioner was Timothy O'Hara, a lawyer and an expert on mentally disordered offenders for the state of California. He and the panel read out Brenda's prepared statement before grilling her for more than two hours.

Brenda elaborated on her abuse claims. Not only was her father still guilty, she said but she also accused her brother and sister of participating in abusing her.

In her statement, Brenda said:

"There are many factors that could have led up to my crime, such as sexual abuse, physical abuse, depression, verbal abuse, neglect, problems in school, drugs, and alcohol. Sexual abuse. When I was nine years old, my father started touching me and fondling me.

I had to sleep in the same bed with him, and almost every night he would do something. He would tell me it was all right, and that this would confuse me because at school they told us this was wrong. It created quite a turmoil inside me. How and why would my father, who was supposed to take care of me and watch over me, do things that were so very wrong to me? It really messed up my head.

While I have been locked up, I have taken groups such as Adult Survivors of Abuse, a lifers' group on abuse, and therapy with the psychiatrist and psychologist, and try to understand what happened. Also, as one of the steps in a group, I confronted my father about the abuse. He finally admitted to me what he had done and why. He apologised to me for what he had done, which is probably the best I can hope for. Me and my father have come to terms with the past.

I know now that I am an adult, and I don't have to accept abuse from him or anyone else anymore. I can speak my mind and say the abuse was wrong. If it were to try to continue, I could just leave. I am no longer dependent on my father for everything. I can stand on my own.

Physical abuse. When I was young, every time my father got angry, I would get beat. He would smack me in the face, kick me, and shove me around. My older brother would also smack me around and grab me by the throat and toss me around. It was my brother's way of playing. Their anger in play scared me, so I would do everything I could to stay out of their way. I used to hide from them both in a little fort-like place I had made out in the garage.

Sometimes I stayed out there for days on end. It was the only place I felt safe. Neither one of them could get inside it. Now, through the self-esteem groups and the CODA groups, I know I don't have to be anyone's punching bag. As a person, I matter. I am more secure in myself as a person, and after living with the anger of my father and brother, I am extremely anti-violence because of my committing offence and all the damage it has done to everyone. I am extremely anti-violence.

Depression. From a young age, about 10 years old, I have suffered from depression. Some of it was caused by all the turmoil going on in my home, some of it probably genetic. My father has been treated for depression also. I was never placed on medication for it until I was incarcerated. A month prior to my crime I was taken to a psychiatrist, and his recommendation was that I be hospitalised because I was a danger to myself and possibly others. I was suicidally depressed and had numerous suicide attempts prior to my crimes, all failures.

The weekend prior to my crime I had overdosed from drugs, but I woke up from them. I had failed once again. I tried to commit suicide because my life was more than I could bear, and I never saw it getting any better. With all the failures, I felt like I was such a loser. I couldn't even kill myself right. It only made the depression worse, and I had no one I could turn to for help. Now after groups and coping with depression, therapy, reading, self-help books, and medication, my outlook on life is drastically different.

I know now where my depression comes from, and that it is not something I can't heal from. I know there are people willing to help me with this problem, and I know how to contact them. I know not to give up looking for help if I need it, and I know the medication works, and I'm prepared to take it for the rest of my life. If it works, why would I stop it?

Verbal abuse. My father, brother, and sister all verbally abused me, constantly telling me I was a piece of shit who would never amount to anything. They would go on and on about what a loser I was and always would be. Not all at once, but whenever one would get mad about me being there in the room when they wanted to do something, they would constantly tell me I was never going to amount to anything. This was an almost constant, every day, all day thing. The only way to get away from it was to hide from them or leave.

Their words were devastating to me. They wore my spirit down, and I started believing what they were saying. My self-esteem and self-worth were in the dirt. Now through groups and therapy, my self-esteem and self-worth don't rely on other peoples' opinions. I have dealt with the put downs and name-calling and verbal harassment over my crime for 30 years now and have learned to deal with it in an adult manner. My self-esteem and self-worth come from my inner strength, not on what other people say.

Neglect. I was neglected by my mother and father. My mother by being emotionally distant, and my father in my day-to-day care. I was pretty much left to fend for myself. I had to cook my own meals every day from the age of eight. I was what they used to call a latchkey kid. I made my breakfast every morning and got myself off to school. I came home from school to an empty house every day. I didn't mind the empty house because everyone was abusive when they were there. It was quiet, but it was still neglected.

I did my own laundry. I did everything for myself. Even when I was sick, I took care of myself. I know now that most households aren't like this. Most households the children are taken care of by the parents. They don't have to take care of themselves. One thing I learned from growing up that way was how to take care of myself. I know how to provide for myself. I have no worries that even though it will be hard, if I'm ever allowed to parole, I will be able to provide and take care of myself.

Problems at school. I wasn't the cleanest, most well-taken care of kid for my age. I got picked on constantly about my looks, my clothes. I wore torn up and dirty clothes to school. I was very small for my age also and very quiet. I guess I was just an easy target when I was young. Having red hair didn't help. Redheads are horribly teased by all the kids. Now I don't let other people control how I see myself. There will always be bullies in the world, but I don't have to let them control my life. I am secure in myself. If the bully won't listen to reason, I just leave the area. Fighting doesn't get either one of you anywhere.

Drugs and alcohol. I started using drugs and alcohol at 12 years old. It was easy to get the drugs at school, and I would get the money for them by shoplifting and then selling what I shoplifted. It's amazing what a kid could walk out of a store with 30 years ago. I used drugs and alcohol as an escape from all the craziness at home. They made it so I didn't have to think or feel. When I was drunk or high, I didn't feel any pain emotionally or physically.

My father used to buy me beer every week, and it was just really easy to get everything as often as I could. I used the drugs and alcohol. I didn't want to think or feel anything. Now through AA/NA and group therapy, I know that all I was doing was self-medicating the depression and trying to escape all my problems. I don't need the drugs and alcohol anymore. I have been clean and sober for 30 years now, not just because I'm locked up but because I chose to be. All that stuff is available in here in prison. I just chose not to deal with my problems that way.

If I have a problem, I talk about it and get help from therapists or people who have been through what I might be having a problem with. When or if I get a second chance, I hope to get a sponsor through AA. I know drugs and alcohol aren't the answer to anything. They only bring a whole new set of problems. I don't want to live my life under the influence. I want to be able to think and feel clearly at all times. Drugs and alcohol just aren't an option for me. I have no desire to use them, even when I'm under stress. I know any one of these things could have brought me to prison, but the combination of all of them together made it more definite.

I had already been arrested for shoplifting and breaking and entering, so I knew prison was in my future. I just didn't think it was going to be for a crime as horrible as this one. I have grown up a lot through the years. I'm no longer the crazy, mixed-up kid on drugs. I have become a responsible adult, one that is trusted and relied on by staff and inmates alike."

Brenda's exit strategy still was to move into Crossroads Halfway House in Claremont until she was ready for her own place. At the time of her parole hearing, BranDee Sisemore, her roommate for 15 years, was an administrator at Crossroads and had a guest room at her home in nearby Pomona.

BranDee had been released after her 21st parole hearing in 2008 and kept in touch. But she moved to the state of Arizona when she found California becoming increasingly unaffordable. She still speaks to Brenda once a week.

"We got along like sisters. We would bicker sometimes, and then in the next 10 minutes we would make up. You know? Just like sisters. When she paroled, I was kind of out of it for a while. I would open the door and expect her to be there. It took me a while to get used to her being gone," Brenda said.

O'Hara and the panel deliberated for 30 minutes and denied Brenda parole for an unprecedented 10 years. Brenda legally challenged this decision and was granted a parole hearing seven years later.

Reporter Steve Wiegand was working at the Sacramento Bee when he was asked to testify by Brenda's court appointed lawyers. He was never called and has not been contacted since.

Wiegand told me one of Spencer's lawyers "asked if I would be willing to testify at a parole hearing. I told him I would do so reluctantly, mostly because I was busy and didn't have much to add other than what was already known. He asked me a bit about my recollection of how she sounded and state-of-mind stuff, and that was it. I never heard anything more".

32

DEATH IN THE FAMILY

BRENDA'S HALF-SISTER, NOW known as Bree Ervin, divorced her husband, Patrick, moved back into the old house and was attending the University of California-San Diego for sociology and studied Japanese but did not graduate. She dropped out of college to become a massage therapist and had unsuccessfully tried her luck at owning a massage studio in San Diego.

She and a new boyfriend, Justin Connor, moved to the state of Colorado and had a daughter. They bought a house together but broke up a couple of years later. Justin moved back to San Diego by himself, and she sued him for child support. In late 2015, Wells Fargo Bank foreclosed on Bree's home in Colorado City. She was virtually homeless with a small child when Wally became very ill.

Around the same time, Brenda wrote to the parole board asking it to bump forward her next hearing. She also wrote to her old lawyer, Michael McGlinn.

The full content of the letter has not been released, but McGlinn shared excerpts with reporters.

In very neat handwriting, she said, "What I did was horrible, so I don't really complain about the amount of time I've done." McGlinn says he wrote back, but he never made his response public.

The California Board of Parole Hearings agreed to move Brenda's hearing forward to Feb. 2016, on compassionate grounds because

Brenda's father was so frail. The board notified all parties of the change, but it was too late. Wally Spencer died on Feb. 11, 2016.

Wally was 87 and still lived in the messy old house on Lake Atlin Ave. He never remarried after Sheila took off and was living with his son. Scott had moved back in after being arrested for driving under the influence and given probation at the end of 2013.

Over the years, Scott was known to move in and out of the house when he got in trouble. Even in the early 80s when Sheila was about, Scott would arrive in trouble and leave again after a bust up with his father. The cycle repeated for decades.

Scott married Elyce Harris in 1982 and fathered two children before the couple divorced in 1998. He remained in the area, as did his children and ex-wife. Scott often deposited cars at both his mother and father's houses over the years.

Wally's death sparked a bitter financial dispute between his four children. In 2008, eight years before his death, he transferred ownership of the house, and Potrero land to the Wallace Spencer Family Trust. All four children would then act as trustees in the event of his death.

Immediately after Wally died, Bree contested the trust and tried to take control of the family home. Scott had planned on staying at the property as he was before Wally's death and because he was the oldest. Bree, living in Colorado, consulted a California lawyer without delay and began eviction proceedings against Scott in San Diego Superior Court.

The two older siblings, with Brenda in tow, hired a tax attorney to fight their case. Scott was formally evicted in May 2016 and left the house through the same door his sister shot through.

By July, it was all done and dusted, and a new retroactive will was deposited with the probate court. The Lake Atlin house now belongs to Bree and still looks the same. She rents out the property through an agent and uses the money to raise her daughter in Colorado.

The other siblings still own the Coyote Holler property in Potrero, but it is empty land full of brush. The Minor family still lives next door in a lovely homestead. The land was allocated to the siblings as a life estate. Brenda believes her stake is worth about $200,000, and she has entrusted her mother with power of attorney while she is imprisoned.

Teresa watched the legal doings with interest from her home in Northern California and was given scattered details by Scott. She was not close to the family and never returned home after graduating from college. She married her sweetheart James Ruth in the summer of 1983 and moved north, near San Francisco.

James and Teresa had a son but divorced in 2001. She married a former police officer in 2020 and is now known as Teresa Halleran.

Brenda still refuses to speak about Bree and does not consider her family. She holds the same resentment for Bree's absent mother, her old cell-mate Sheila.

For years, Wally told his children that Sheila had vanished without caring about her daughter. His children never questioned his version of events even though his story has glaring inconsistencies. Bree has little or no memory of her mother and has refused to correspond with her or that side of the family.

Bree works as an office manager in a small law firm in the Colorado town of Pueblo, where her daughter attends elementary school. She has ignored all attempts to communicate with her.

I found the family of her mother, Sheila, to be kind and authentic. Her brother and sister-in-law say they hope she will answer their messages and join the family once again. Sheila moved to Phoenix in Arizona more than 20 years ago, and she has remarried a few times. Her name is now Sheila Lewis, a single woman making a living as a care worker.

At the time of writing, Bree and her mother Sheila had not been reunited.

2016 PAROLE HEARING

The parole hearing was moved back following Wally's death. But in September 2016, Brenda was back in the same old room, but this time with former San Quentin Prison warden Kevin Chappell as presiding commissioner.

By 2016 there were few self-help courses Brenda had not completed. The panel was impressed by her activity in prisoner organisations and her continuing care for cats. She also said she had started to learn Latin. Brenda told the panel she has heard voices in her head since she was 12. They started about the same time her father started sexually abusing her, she said. Her mother was made aware of the issue, "but she felt that it was not her place to say anything."

Brenda also said her father beat her mother. Dot was interviewed by multiple media outlets over the last 37 years and never said Wally was anything other than weak. The panel saw no evidence to support Brenda's claim.

Asked why she gave herself up after her shooting spree, Brenda said, "When the police shot the front door, it scared me because it's like, wow, this is real, and it's going to happen. And I got scared so I just continued to talk to the negotiator until he convinced me to come out."

In 2009, Bree had written a letter urging Brenda's release. But after Wally died, and the estate dispute, she had a change of heart and wrote a damning letter to the parole board.

She and Brenda had been communicating by mail until things became heated. Bree added a heavily redacted correspondence from Brenda into evidence and it prompted the commissioner to quiz the prisoner:

> PRESIDING COMMISSIONER CHAPPELL: OKAY, AND THEN THERE WAS A LETTER "DEAR BREE," IT'S REDACTED. DID YOU REDACT THAT?

INMATE SPENCER: NO, I DIDN'T.

PRESIDING COMMISSIONER CHAPPELL: WHO DID THAT?

INMATE SPENCER: MY SISTER DID.

PRESIDING COMMISSIONER CHAPPELL: OH, OKAY. DO YOU HAVE - AND YOU OF COURSE WROTE IT, SO YOU DON'T HAVE A COPY. "WHEN I PAROLE, I WILL NEED A PLACE TO LIVE SO FUCK SAN DIEGO! I WILL GO LIVE THERE! AS LONG AS I HAVE MY LIFE ESTATE I WILL ALWAYS HAVE SOMEWHERE TO LIVE. I LIKE THAT." CAN YOU EXPLAIN WHAT YOU MEANT BECAUSE IT DOES SOUND LIKE...

INMATE SPENCER: WELL, PRIOR TO THAT I TALK ABOUT NOT GOING TO SAN DIEGO BECAUSE SAN DIEGO DOESN'T WANT ME. AND IT WAS A POOR CHOICE OF WORDS. BUT I SAID, "FUCK SAN DIEGO" BECAUSE I DON'T INTEND TO EVER GO THERE AGAIN. AND THEN THE SECOND PART WAS TALKING ABOUT MOVING TO OREGON AFTER I AM OFF PAROLE OR MOVING TO BIG SUR OR SOMEWHERE, YOU KNOW, FURTHER NORTH. BUT AS LONG AS I HAVE A LIFE ESTATE, IF SOMETHING HAPPENS, I ALWAYS HAVE SOMEWHERE I CAN GO.

PRESIDING COMMISSIONER CHAPPELL: EXCLAMATION POINT. IT'S A LITTLE... IT SOUNDS A LOT MORE FORCEFUL IN THE CONTEXT AND THE TONE THAT IT WAS WRITTEN THAN YOU'RE ARTICULATING HERE TODAY.

INMATE SPENCER: BUT IT REALLY WASN'T. IT WASN'T. I DO THAT WITH EXCLAMATION MARKS ALL OVER THE PLACE WHEN I WRITE LETTERS.

PRESIDING COMMISSIONER CHAPPELL: SO WHY WOULD YOU USE THAT CHOICE OF WORDS ABOUT SAN DIEGO, KNOWING ALL THE VICTIMS AND THE IMPACT THAT YOU PUT ON THAT CITY?

INMATE SPENCER: IT'S A COMMON PHRASE IN HERE. IT'S COMMON. WHEN YOU DON'T WANT TO DO SOMETHING, YOU JUST SAY "WELL, FUCK IT" AND GO ON ABOUT YOUR BUSINESS. IT'S JUST COMMON SLANG IN HERE.

PRESIDING COMMISSIONER CHAPPELL: DID IT DAWN ON YOU THAT THAT MIGHT BE DISRESPECTFUL?

INMATE SPENCER: I NEVER REALLY THOUGHT ABOUT IT.

PRESIDING COMMISSIONER CHAPPELL: OKAY.

INMATE SPENCER: BECAUSE IT'S JUST COMMON SLANG. YOU HEAR IT 5,000 TIMES A DAY IN HERE.

PRESIDING COMMISSIONER CHAPPELL: YEAH, BUT THIS IS IN A SPECIFIC REFERENCE TO WHERE YOU LEFT ALL THESE VICTIMS. AS I READ IT...

INMATE SPENCER: IT WAS...

PRESIDING COMMISSIONER CHAPPELL: LET ME FINISH. AS I READ IT, AND I LOOK AT IT FROM THE OUTSIDE LOOKING IN, I LOOK AT IT LIKE SAN DIEGO, YOU KNOW, REPRESENTS THOSE VICTIMS. AND BY YOU USING THAT TERMINOLOGY TOWARDS SAN DIEGO, IT JUST DOESN'T MAKE SENSE TO ME WHY YOU WOULD SAY SOMETHING...

The panel rolled through various statements from victims for and against Brenda's release. Her lawyer gave a closing statement, and the San Diego district attorney's office gave its usual reasons for denial. Cam Miller was once again in attendance and would speak once Brenda finished her closing statement.

INMATE SPENCER: OKAY, I JUST LIKE MY VICTIMS TO KNOW HOW DEEPLY SORRY I AM FOR WHAT I HAVE DONE TO THEM. I KNOW THERE IS NOTHING I CAN DO THAT WILL MAKE UP FOR IT OR TAKE IT AWAY. BUT I REALISE NOW HOW WIDESPREAD THE DAMAGE I'VE DONE IS. THAT'S ALL.

Brenda was commended for her good behaviour but was refused parole for another five years. Authorities said she must have another hearing "no later than" September 7, 2021.

Reporters quoted at least one victim questioning whether it wasn't time to let Brenda out of prison.

Mary Clark, who was nine when she was shot, said she "can understand why she (Brenda) went down the road she did… she never got the help she needed." Clark works as a dietary technician caring for psychiatric patients.

Brenda's former lawyer Michael McGlinn still blames Wally for the event, telling the Union-Tribune, "total neglect and unbelievably bad parenting by her father in giving her the gun." He also said, "I never got the impression from her that she was interested in trying to hurt kids."

McGlinn also insisted that Brenda's release date would not be far away and said school shootings were no longer unique or committed solely by crazed teens.

"People are recognising that today's young are capable of doing anything, including shooting each other in school," he said.

Richard Sachs the deputy district attorney, responded, "She claimed she wasn't trying to kill anybody, she was just shooting? What she did was so awful, shooting at children. We feel a life sentence is only fair for someone guilty of all those things."

Cam Miller, who has attended as many parole hearings as possible, simply said, "I have a duty. I want to make sure she stays in there for life. If the victims don't show up, she'll get out."

The press contacted Brenda's mother after the parole hearing, but she refused to comment. Dot was in her mid-80s at the time and appeared active, despite being obese. She had stopped golfing but was a league coordinator at a local bowling alley. Dot was still living at the old marital home on Boulder Lake Ave.

Brenda's life in prison is day to day and little inside has changed in her 42 years of incarceration. Outside the prison fences, Brenda can see the world slowly change.

"It has built up around here," she said. "Everything that was farmland is now housing tracts. You can see some of it from my workplace. Nice-looking houses too. When I go out to the hospital for doctors' appointments, I really get to see it all.

"I am working on the transportation and camp vehicles. Oil changes, changing brakes, replacing radiators and water pumps. I'm not a vehicle whiz yet, but I'm working on it. I want to be able to do repairs on my own vehicle when I get paroled," Brenda told me.

In September 2019, Brenda received more terrible news. Her

brother Scott Spencer fell in the kitchen of his apartment and hit his head, never regaining consciousness. He was put on life support and died in a hospital a few days later.

Scott was only 62, and his sudden loss devastated Brenda. Her brother's two children, Jesse and Wendy, are close to their grandmother but have never had any sort of relationship with their aunt.

The fast-spreading COVID-19 virus hit prisons hard in March 2020, with infections skyrocketing among inmates. Brenda took it all in her stride and joked with me that lockdown was what she's been doing for more than 40 years.

"We are pretty well off here in the prison," she told me. "We have plenty of food and toilet paper. We have to stay six feet apart, no cell visiting, no dayroom, no movies, nothing that puts a lot of people clumped together.

"I've been one of the lucky ones... I still get to go to work. There are only two staff and three inmates in the auto shop where I work. We get to work because they still need the vehicles to transport people. The basic maintenance still needs to be done."

Some prison units went on full quarantine as the virus spread; just before Christmas 2020, Brenda tested positive for COVID-19. Less than two weeks later, she tested negative and was returned to her normal room to start 2021. Brenda received two doses of the Moderna vaccine in Feb and March 2021.

In late 2021, she delayed her next parole hearing by voluntarily waiving her right to the scheduled Parole Suitability Hearing. On advice from her new lawyer, Michael Brennan she delayed the hearing for a year. Brennan, director of the University of Southern California's Post-Conviction Justice Project, was working with Brenda on a brand-new strategy.

Brenda told me, "We put the parole hearing off because we didn't have all of our paperwork done. I'd rather go in fully prepared than just try to wing it with half of what we need… they started something called a Palmer Petition already. It has something to do with repeated denials."

In 1988, the 17-year-old William M. Palmer II pleaded guilty to kidnapping for robbery and was sentenced to life with the possibility of parole. He was denied parole at 10 suitability hearings after becoming eligible in 1996.

He was finally released in 2018 after the California Supreme Court found his imprisonment was grossly disproportionate to the crime. They felt the parole board had failed to give weight to youth offender factors as statutorily required.

Brenda and her new heavyweight lawyer hoped to use this tactic to finally gain her freedom.

Her next hearing was scheduled to take place on August 18th 2022.

33

STIP

THE FIRST EDITION of this book was released in the United States in August 2022. It was believed to be, what is essentially, the first biography of a school shooter. Without much fanfare, it quietly went for sale on the internet. I sent Brenda a copy to her prison address and in less than two weeks she jokingly responded with some feedback. Saying, "Yeah that is really close to what happened, and I also learned some things about my family I did not know. Oh, you got me and my brother's rooms mixed up. Mine was at the end of the hall."

During the editing of the final chapters, a couple events took place that really should have been part of the final manuscript.

Firstly, I was saddened to learn of the death of Brenda's attorney, Michael McGlinn. Mike passed away at his San Diego home on March 22, 2022, of Non-Hodgkins Lymphoma.

I had either not understood or not realised what an amazing man he was and deeply regret not including more of his achievements in the first edition. Mike began private practice in 1973 and specialised in juvenile delinquency and defendants with dependency issues. He retired in January 2020 after practising law for over 50 years in San Diego.

I've interviewed dozens of lawyers and media professionals who said that Mike was a brilliant person, father and friend. It is sad that

I did not get to meet him, but it is now obvious why he was unable to accept my request for an interview. Sadly, at the time I contacted him, he was fighting a courageous battle with an incurable cancer. Sorry for persisting, Mike. RIP.

While agreeing the tweaks to the book's cover art, the second event occurred. I clicked on the TV news to see Robb Elementary School in Uvalde, Texas on lockdown from an active shooter. On the screen I could see police officers hiding behind the school's exterior walls while parents screamed for them to act. A physical altercation broke out between them, injuring three distressed civilians.

Initial TV reports said 18-year-old Salvador Ramos steamrolled students with his DDM4 assault rifle for over an hour after he wandered past officers in the school parking lot. Later, I found out that's not exactly how it happened.

Ramos had legally purchased two assault rifles and 375 rounds of ammo as a present to himself for his birthday. On Tuesday May 24th 2022, Ramos shot and wounded his grandmother and fled from her home in his pickup truck. She contacted the police, who went on alert. Minutes later, he crashed his truck into a flood control channel near Robb Elementary School.

Clad in a tactical vest and a backpack holding extra ammo, he emerged from the vehicle and started shooting at two men who witnessed the crash, missing both. He began shooting at the school as police were arriving at the scene. It was reported that police drove right past the shooter on route to the crash scene.

At 11:33am, Ramos sneaked through an open back door to the school and took control of a classroom. He killed 19 children, two teachers and wounded 17 others. He was eventually shot and killed by a border patrol officer responding to the 911 call.

Two first responding officers were indicted for allegedly mis-handling the response to the shooting. Although this was a very different scene than the one encountered by San Diego Police in 1979, it does highlight how things have changed for the worse. While finishing a book about the heroic actions of first responders saving lives 43 years ago, I watched first responders literally walk away from an active shooter; in the present day.

The two events and many others shatter the long-held belief that all American mass shooters are young white men. Certainly, Brenda Spencer destroyed this myth on her own, but the actual facts show that shooters, (who are overwhelmingly men) and predominately white, are reasonably consistent with the racial demographic. Many do not have many similarities other than access to weapons.

Although there is an argument to suggest abuse may have played a role in many cases involving the younger shooters, this becomes more unclear as the age of the shooter advances. There is also an issue with the ever-changing definition of 'mass shooter' over the years and all data should be scrutinised, especially coming from varied sources like Wikipedia, podcasts and social media platforms.

Brenda's next parole hearing was scheduled for August 2022 and her legal team mobilised to make sure she was ready for the board. I wrote to California Department of Corrections and Rehabilitation's (CDCR) Joe Orlando in hope of attending. As the proceedings were still under California's rigid COVID restrictions, the hearing was scheduled remotely. A single press representative would attend virtually and share their notes.

2022 PAROLE HEARING

At 8:30am on Aug 18th, the hearing was over almost as soon as it began. Parole Board Commissioner David Ndudim was contacted by Brenda's legal team moments before the start of the hearing. It was agreed they would waive this hearing in lieu of a "three-year stipulation" or 'stip' as Brenda called it.

Officially a three-year stip means an incarcerated person agrees they are unsuitable for parole, but for a period of three years only. Effectively postponing the parole attempt without a hearing. Meaning? USC, the post conviction project helping her, felt that Brenda was not ready for this hearing and waived her right to hold it, without it counting against her for future considerations. Commissioner Ndudim agreed with the legal team but also wanted to agree terms with Brenda herself. He called the hearing to order.

Brenda's mobility was now suffering from her diabetes and obesity. Dressed in her usual prison blues, she arrived in a wheelchair and was dressed in her usual prison blues. Her face was obscured by a white surgical mask, as per the COVID guidelines. Cam Miller appeared on screen and looked to be the only victim who would make a statement.

Commissioner Ndudim brought the hearing to order and asked for everyone attending to give their full names and occupations, for Brenda to understand who has attended.

He began proceedings by addressing Brenda directly:

COMMISSIONER NDUDIM: MISS SPENCER, I SEE THAT YOU ARE WEARING YOUR GLASSES TODAY. ARE THOSE PRESCRIPTION GLASSES?

INMATE SPENCER: YES, THEY ARE.

NDUDIM: CAN YOU SEE WELL WITH THEM?

SPENCER: YEAH

NDUDIM: MISS SPENCER, HAVE YOU BEEN A PART OF THE MENTAL HEALTH SYSTEM? WHEN WAS THE LAST TIME THAT YOU ACCESSED THAT PROGRAM?

SPENCER: AHH, 2000.

NDUDIM: DO YOU TAKE ANY PSYCHOTROPIC MEDICATION?

SPENCER: YES, I DO

NDUDIM: WHEN WAS THE LAST TIME YOU TOOK ANY OF THOSE MEDICATIONS?

SPENCER: THIS MORNING

NDUDIM: ARE THOSE GOING TO AFFECT YOUR ABILITY TO COMMUNICATE WITH US THIS MORNING?

SPENCER: NO, THEY ARE NOT

NDUDIM: HAS THE COUNSELLOR PROVIDED REASONABLE ACCOMMODATIONS FOR THE HEARING TODAY?

SPENCER: YES

INMATE'S COUNSELLOR: SHE IS ADEQUATELY ACCOMMODATED

NDUDIM: COUNSELLOR, YOU INDICATED THAT YOUR CLIENT WOULD LIKE TO MAKE A REQUEST TO THE PANEL THIS MORNING, PROCEED

COUNSELLOR: YES, WE ARE REQUESTING A THREE YEAR STIPULATION SO THAT MY CLIENT MAY CONTINUE TO DEVELOP AND FIRM UP PAROLE PLANS AND BE PREPARED FOR THE HEARING.

NDUDIM: MS. SPENCER, YOUR ATTORNEY HAS MADE THE REQUEST AND COMMUNICATED THAT YOU WANT TO HAVE A THREE-YEAR STIPULATION… IS THAT CORRECT?

SPENCER: YES, IT IS, SIR.

NDUDIM: DO YOU, MISS SPENCER, UNDERSTAND THAT YOU DO HAVE A RIGHT TO A HEARING TODAY?

SPENCER: YES.

NDUDIM: YOU UNDERSTAND THAT YOU ARE GIVING UP THAT RIGHT?

SPENCER: YES

The commissioner called the hearing to a quick recess and Brenda patiently stayed on the call with her attorney and a few others. In the background of her attorney's home office, Brenda saw what looked like a pet bird.

Her lawyer said the bird is usually free to fly around her home during the day and, "it would've said hello to you". Brenda giggled through her COVID mask before the commissioners brought the hearing back to order:

NDUDIM: THE PANEL DOES ACCEPT THE STIPULATION FOR ALL SENSIBILITY… FOR THREE YEARS. YOU DO UNDER-

STAND THAT YOU DO HAVE A RIGHT TO A HEARING TODAY, CORRECT?

SPENCER: CORRECT

NDUDIM: YOU ARE MAKING THIS REQUEST FREELY?

SPENCER: YES

NDUDIM: (NOW ADDRESSING THE VICTIM, CAM MILLER) MR. MILLER DO YOU WANT TO MAKE A VICTIM IMPACT STATEMENT OR WAIT UNTIL THE NEXT PANEL?

MILLER: I WILL WAIT, SIR.

And just like that it was over. Brenda would get another chance at freedom in three years.

34

GOLDEN GIRL

MAJOR CHANGES WERE taking place to California's penal legislation with the governor, Gavin Newsom, leading the charge. He outlined an aggressive plan for more fiscal responsibility and ordered the closure of multiple facilities in 2023, including the famous San Quentin. It is the oldest prison in California and will be rebranded as a "rehabilitation centre".

San Quentin had the dubious reputation for holding California's executions on its East Block. It was once known for its famous gas chamber, as seen on TV and films. In 1995 the activity was ruled 'cruel and unusual punishment' and the chamber was refitted into the more clinical lethal injection room. But the room has not seen any action since the execution of the triple murderer, Clarence Allen, in January 2006.

In 2024, the death row inmates began being relegated to 'lifers' and shipped off to other facilities throughout the state. For example, Eric Houston, the infamous 1992 Lindhurst High School shooter from Olivehurst, CA was moved a couple of times, finally landing in the Pelican Bay Supermax in Northern California. He was incredibly pleased with the move and sees his new facility as a chance at redemption. As he is no longer on death row, Houston believes his sentence could also be reduced and he could get out on parole. He has not stopped filing appeals since relocating.

The infamous Scott Peterson who murdered his eight month pregnant wife Laci in 2002, the Menendez Brothers, Joseph and Erik, whose killing of their parents in their Beverley Hills Home in 1989, and countless other murderers and many we have never heard of, are all petitioning to have their sentences changed in one way or another. The new California legislation appears to offer great hope to the incarcerated population in the state, not just the murderers.

But it was the release of Brenda's good friend that would dramatically change her outlook on getting back into society.

Leslie Van Houten, the former Manson sister, had previously been recommended for parole by the commission but blocked continually by Governor Newsom. On May 30th, 2023, a California Court of Appeal set aside the Governor's denial, and she was released. It was her 24th attempt at freedom. She was transferred to a transitional facility, possibly the same one Brenda is prepping for, and quietly disappeared into the parole supervision system.

The other Manson sister, Pat Krenwinkel, was granted parole in 2022 and has twice had the decision reversed by the Governor, most recently in October 2025. They cited the continued threat she would pose to society if she were released

Brenda says she has been trying hard to complete the programs and parole board recommendations or "board packs" as she calls them. The prison counsellors help all inmates put the findings together and into one easy folder. Albeit a large one in Brenda's case.

She adjusted her medications for diabetes to Ozempic in an attempt to lower her glycated haemoglobin A1C levels. She also made drastic changes to her diet to shed pounds and try to gain more energy. Brenda managed to drop almost 70 pounds by eating predominantly ramen noodles.

"I have to take my jacket in and exchange it for one that fits. I've lost a lot of weight. I'm down to 168 (lbs.) now. That's down from 234. I just changed how I eat. Like, if I have noodles to eat, I have to eat it for lunch, so I still have time left in the day to burn it off.

"They've come up with a new way to get people to go to Medline. If you don't go, they shut your tablet off. No messaging, telephone or apps. They leave the games on but shut off the important stuff. They don't waste any time either, if you miss morning Medline, your tablet is off by 8:30. If you get a write up, they shut off your tablet too as punishment," Brenda said.

She spends most of her days going to work in the Hazmat Department (hazardous materials) at the prison fire house. After work she still retires to her lower bunk and watches TV or reads books on her tablet.

"The job is good, we actually mainly go around and confiscate improperly stored chemicals on all the housing units … Our boss is by the book on rules and regulations but that is cool, you always know where you stand. Today they woke us up to do a shakedown of our unit. We were supposed to go sit in the auditorium, but I had taken my bag with me, and they said, 'If you have work, go to work! So, I booked it out of there and went to work. They ran the dogs by us and everything. Try waking up with a drug dog sticking its nose in your ass! Talk about rude awakenings," Brenda said.

Her day-to-day life in prison has not really changed for years. She is still on the Golden Girls programme. Because she is now over 60 and was a teenager at the time of her conviction, she is now eligible for 'Older Parole' and 'Youth Offender' considerations at the same time. "So, I am an elderly youth offender," she joked. Something she clearly was unable to imagine when committing her crime.

"I am a Golden Girl, so I get to go to the head of the line. That's a program they have for the elderly in here. From the Golden Girl program, I also get two mattresses, two pillows and three blankets.

Oh, and I get to go to meals before they call the unit. You have to walk as quick as you can though because they release the rest of the unit five minutes after they call Golden Girls. The youngsters will run right over you to get to meals."

Her lack of mobility means she is now required to wear a high visibility vest when she ventures away from her prison unit. "I am officially an old woman now. I have a bright yellow vest, I have to wear whenever I leave the unit. It says, 'Mobility Impaired'. With that vest, when the yard goes down, I don't have to sit on the ground. My friend Kathy says that now I am a member of the " Hi-lighter Club"... It even shows up at night it's so bright. So now I am officially old," she continued to joke.

Brenda recently broke a toe by hitting it against a leg of her metal chair. She refused to see the medics, electing to stay glued to her old TV shows like Perry Mason and Starsky & Hutch, setting herself reading targets as the latest goal. She says she has a few books 'on the go' at any given time. Some at work and some in her unit. She claims to have already read 55 of the 111 horror books on her tablet in the two years she's had it.

I continue to communicate with Brenda and remain fascinated even though I am no closer to understanding why she did what she did. We exchange messages with one another monthly and there has never seemed to be any pressure to communicate, well, certainly not from my end. And it certainly seems that she only writes when she wants to, often glossing over my inquisitive questions. She told me years ago to ask anything I wanted but she would only answer what she wanted to.

Brenda told me about the gopher problem around her unit's yard and asked if we had them in England. I told her we don't really, but we have moles and hedgehogs. She was not sure what hedgehogs were, so I sent her a few images.

"When we catch the gopher, we will relocate it to the far side of the maintenance area. There is plenty of open space where he can dig his little heart out. And he won't bother anything. Now in our rooms we have all these little spiders hatching out. Those we just smash. People start getting spider bites that get infected. They are horrible to look at.

"Hedgehogs, are those the ones with spines that roll up into a ball when they feel threatened? Don't people keep those as pets? I think I saw a show on PBS about strange animals as pets. Nothing beats the naked mole rats though. They are so ugly!"

Her mother has begun to call more often. Since her brother's death, they appear to have much more to talk about these days. Dot calls about once a week and even rang while she was visiting Brenda's sister for Christmas. Brenda and her sister, Teresa, still do not speak.

Brenda was hit with a great loss in January 2024. Her best friend and former cell mate, BranDee Sisemore passed away from what Brenda called 'acute renal failure, diabetes with nephropathy pneumonia, and pancreatic mass diabetic ketoacidosis'. BranDee left prison in 2008 and kept in close contact from her small place in Mesa, Arizona. They were like sisters, she said.

"She was my best friend. I knew her longer than anyone. I know she would like to talk of how important it is to always take very good care of yourself and monitor your diabetes closely with doctors. She used to get all over my ass because I am diabetic and wasn't taking it too seriously. She was very good to me and always hoped I would get out. Over a year ago and it still makes me cry..."

Her father, Wally, left a decent sized trust fund for his kids after he passed away in 2016. Brenda has joked a few times about how her support mechanism is dying off and how her mother is very elderly. The prison is helping Brenda prepare her will, as she is set to inherit a tidy sum when her mother passes away and her father's trust was split between her, her sister Teresa and her half-sister

Bree. Countless internet bios on Brenda's home life says her family was poor and this was never the case. Her trust fund and restart money is one of the key aspects that may help her gain freedom.

The loneliness of losing loved ones is clearly caving in on Brenda. Might she actually be beginning to understand what her victim's families have felt for over 45 years? Or maybe I misread this as a financial worry?

In 2024, I was invited to speak about Brenda and the case at Crime Con UK in London and Glasgow. When I notified Brenda about the presentations and its content, she was absolutely amazed that anyone would care about what happened so many years ago. I stopped short of explaining the world's fascination with true crime.

I reminded her that her actions might have changed the world forever. She still can't understand. She had not known that the first use of the expression 'school shooter', was about her. Is Brenda still minimising her actions or is she simply living in a very controlled environment and is detached from the real world? My gut tells me it's a little of both.

35

WE DO NOT FORGET

LEADING UP TO Brenda's 2025 parole hearing, the local media aired an interview with Cam Miller. Cam was nine when he was shot and recalls the event like it was yesterday. Like so many at the scene, he never heard the gunshots because it happened so fast.

"You know, it's just a regular day, kids playing and walking up to school. I didn't know what was happening. All of a sudden, I went numb on the left side and I blacked out and one of my neighbours took me around to the school staff and that's where they discovered I had been shot.

"I was shot an inch away from my heart and it went clear through my back. From the back to the front. Fortunately, it missed all my organs and any internal parts.

"We had to go see her in court, testify against her… it robs you of your youth and your innocence at that age. It is a little eerie to see somebody that almost killed me."

Cam has attended all of the previous parole hearings. He has almost acted as a surrogate for the other victims who could either not attend or trusted in his ability to illustrate the families' points of view.

"She's a loose cannon… I think the whole community would be in danger and you never know whether she'll go after somebody who's testified against her, and you just never know what her mindset is going to be. She doesn't deserve a second chance. The two people who were killed did not receive a second chance, so I think that she deserves to stay behind bars," Cam says when asked about her possible rehabilitation.

I asked Brenda about Cam Miller. She said, "I feel sorry for him. But I can always hope he can get better and heal from what I did 46 years ago. I wish him the best."

Burton Wragg's son and granddaughter wrote to the Parole Board after seeing Cam Miller's interview on the local news. Burt was the Principal at Cleveland Elementary and slain while trying to save children. Their mother had recently passed away and they had not received notice of the hearing.

Sadly, the son and granddaughter's formal request to attend the hearing was denied. But the board allowed them to submit a 'victims impact statement', although not to be added to the official record.

Brenda's parole hearing took place on Feb 21st, 2025, at the California Institution for Women. It was scheduled for a video conference using the Microsoft Teams platform, acquired during the COVID outbreak and began as planned.

Brenda was represented by her attorney, Brianna Estevez of the USC Post Conviction Project. As Brenda says, "they are bulldogs and don't mess around". The CDCR presiding commissioner was 46-year-old Teal Kozel, a former Senior Psychologist Supervisor in the Forensic Assessment Division at the Board of Parole Hearings. She has a strong Psychology background and was once the Suicide Prevention Coordinator at San Quentin.

Her Deputy Commissioner was a local defence attorney and Administrative Law Judge, Cristina Guerrero. Representing the San Diego County District Attorney's Office was Deputy DA, Dino Paraskevopoulos.

Unlike the past parole hearings which were held in person,

multiple survivors were able to attend the virtual hearing without having to travel. Usually, Cam Miller would attend alone but, on this occasion, he was joined by Mary Clark, Crystal Hardy and Greg Verner. All were shot by Spencer that infamous Monday morning.

2025 PAROLE HEARING

The hearing began with Brenda appearing noticeably thinner, even on screen. Her attorney started by saying her client has difficulty processing information in the 'abstract and hypothetical'. Prison doctors had previously discussed the issue and believe Brenda is on the autism spectrum.

Commissioner Kozel accepts this prognosis but states she is only here to determine whether Brenda would pose an unreasonable risk to society and not her current ability to process information. The crime, prison record, comprehensive risk assessment (CRA), and parole plans are the only importance to the board. The commissioner agrees that special consideration will be given for her age now (62), her age at the time (16) and the 44 years of incarceration.

Questioning began quickly with Brenda saying she was denied in the past due to lack of insight and remorse but asked the board to review her recent psych report. She says her CRA was favorable with a low-moderate score.

"It was a lot of physical and sexual abuse from my father. I dealt with it by self-medicating with drugs and alcohol," Brenda told the board. She then said she began taking heroin at about 12 years old and it became her drug of choice. She claimed she was using as often as "every three days".

Brenda was unable to remember her first interaction with police and claimed she stole from shops to get drug money. The Commissioner asked if she stole bullets from a drug store, when she was 13, to buy drugs? Brenda replied, saying she stole them so she could sell them to a neighbour.

The Commissioner said Brenda was referred to counselling when she was arrested at 15 for breaking into the elementary school. "We talked about a little of everything," Brenda said, also saying she spoke about her father's abuse, but nothing was done.

Leading up to the crime she said, once again, "I had tried to kill myself the week before (the shooting)" but added, "I overdosed on heroin."

When asked why she used the rifle she replied, "so the police would come and kill me. I knew shooting at kids would get the police there quicker" as she reiterated the suicide by cop concept.

Brenda responded "I don't know" to almost every other question when pressed about what happened that day.

While sifting through psychology reports, Commissioner Kozel asks, "Did she not tell the psychologist that she did not want to hit people during her previous interview? Do you remember saying people attending to children were heroes and that is something she didn't have?"

Brenda replied through tears, "Yes, I said it because it is true. It was sad. They had what I wanted. They had parents that cared about them."

The commissioner quoted a line from Brenda's victim apology letter, "I never considered you would die or anyone would be hurt."

Brenda replied, "I didn't consider the consequences, and I wanted the cops to come and kill me."

When asked about the last time she was angry, she said it was two weeks ago when people kept cutting in line. She said she used her breathing exercises to calm herself down.

As the hearing progressed, Brenda again said she was drinking because "drugs and alcohol made me feel numb". The commissioner reminded the hearing of the blood test confirming there were no drugs or alcohol in her blood immediately after the shooting.

Brenda said the last time she used drugs or alcohol was about 1989 while in prison. "I've used Alcoholics Anonymous, one day at a time. There's a possibility I can relapse. Stress over a family member dying or the smell of heroin or holidays may make me want to use again."

COMMISSIONER KOZEL: DO YOU KNOW WHAT YOUR DIAGNOSIS IS?

INMATE SPENCER: I EXPERIENCE HALLUCINATIONS AND DEPRESSION. IN 2019 WAS THE LAST TIME WHEN MY BROTHER DIED. AS LONG AS I TAKE MY MEDS, I AM OK.

COMMISSIONER KOZEL: WHAT DO YOU PLAN TO DO TO HANDLE MENTAL HEALTH ISSUES?

INMATE SPENCER: FIND A DOCTOR AND A PSYCHOLOGIST FOR THERAPY.

Unlike her other parole hearings, Brenda's medication came into the discussion. She is now taking brand new meds like Geodon (Ziprasidone) for her bipolar disorder and Zoloft for her depression. The board made a note of this in detail.

The commissioner directly asked Brenda why she continued to tell psychologists that she was trying to shoot over people's heads and did not want to kill anyone? Through tears, her simple reply was, "I don't know."

COMMISSIONER KOZEL: WERE YOU HALLUCINATING AT THE TIME OF THE CRIME?

INMATE SPENCER: YES, I WAS, OF COMMANDOS CREEPING UP AT THE HOUSE. I DIDN'T SAY ANYTHING BECAUSE I THOUGHT THEY WERE IN ON IT.

COMMISSIONER KOZEL: DO YOU REMEMBER SAYING YOU DIDN'T LIKE MONDAYS?

INMATE SPENCER: NO, I DON'T.

DEPUTY COMMISSIONER GUERRERO: CAN YOU TELL ME MORE ABOUT WHAT YOU WERE FEELING INSIDE?

INMATE SPENCER: I WAS FEELING ANGER. ANGER TOWARDS MY FATHER.

DEPUTY COMMISSIONER GUERRERO: WERE YOU ANGRY AT SOMEONE ELSE?

INMATE SPENCER: MY MOTHER BECAUSE SHE ABANDONED ME.

COMMISSIONER KOZEL: DID YOU CARRY A WEAPON AROUND AT THE TIME OF THE CRIME?

INMATE SPENCER: I CARRIED A KNIFE BECAUSE I WAS PARANOID THAT SOMEONE WOULD COME AND GET ME, THAT SOMEONE WOULD HARM ME.

This parole hearing was going the exact same way as the others and probably with the same result. Brenda sticks to her story of impairment from drugs and drink and the board looking for remorse and rehabilitation. She was still suggesting that she never intended to shoot anyone, and her only hatred was for her father and mother.

The new information about her addiction to heroin did surprise me. Having researched her case in depth and read every page of her previous hearings and reports, this has never been mentioned. In fact, the abandonment by her mother was only glossed over previously. Is Brenda making headway or looking for new angles to gain release?

The commission was quick to pull Brenda up on her previous conversation with the psychologists. The doctor wrote about a possible substance abuse relapse, "stress is a highly relevant risk factor for violence… she denied she had any external triggers even being around her". When Brenda was asked about this, she responded, "I don't remember saying that."

She soon reversed this and said, "how I feel about my father. I can't think of others other than when I am late for work or when someone tries to bully me" or "could be the smell of heroin, going to a party where people are using, I can't think of anything else.

Internal triggers are depression. That's all I can think of right now."

And later said, "I think when people don't act like adults. All the women on our unit. They scream down the halls and start fights. I go to my room to stay out. I know that I can't control anyone but myself."

The commissioners asked about her plans for the outside, including housing and support. Brenda was vague saying she had not had a response from transition housing but intended on living with her friend, Doris. She conceded, "I may have difficulty finding a job and learning to operate a phone and a computer."

Most remarkably when discussing where she will live on the outside she flippantly said, "Fuck San Diego. I don't want to go back there because my victims are there".

The opposing parties would all have their time to speak but not until the San Diego District Attorney's Office was allowed a small cross examination. Deputy DA Dino Paraskevopoulos went straight at Brenda asking if she was obsessed with killing or murdering cops. Brenda denied this.

Paraskevopoulos brought up her previous statements to Brant Flemming and news reporter Steve Wiegand, about her plan to shoot cops and watching the kids squirm as easy pickings like ducks in a pond. Brenda said, "I don't remember. I did not enjoy watching that". In fact, Brenda said she did not remember any of the event or said anything like what was described.

Throughout the hearing, she maintained she was high on drugs and was aiming over the heads of all of the victims. Under final questions from her own attorney, she tearfully said the voices in her head would "not let her stop shooting" and "it makes me sad because I did it."

Closing arguments began with the DA going first. "She is unsuitable for parole… Her statement in November to the psychologist that she was aiming above the children is patently false... The children were struck in their lower extremities. She was shooting to harm and to kill… It shows deception and an attempt to mislead and minimise. She was shooting to kill... She has been listed as a potential risk to the community. No consistent treatment or self-help. This case involves callous planning and complete disregard for human life. Based on all of that, the inmate should be denied parole."

Her defence Attorney Estevez responded, "During her 46 years of incarceration, she has worked to better understand her life crime. Spencer committed the life crime at 16 during severe abuse by her father. Given her young age and the abuse she suffered, she had diminished culpability. Miss Spencer exhibited signs of someone who is on the autism spectrum. This is not a refusal to take responsibility but an inability to express herself due to neuro-typical responses. If released on parole, Miss Spencer will stay in transitional housing. She has significant savings from her inheritance. The board must grant Miss Spencer parole as she does not pose any risk to society."

Brenda was given the final word before victim statements. "I just want them to know how remorseful I am for what I did."

Crystal Hardy, who was ten years old at the time, was the first of the victims to speak. "I just want to say that our justice system is to treat people fairly and get what they deserve. She deserves to be in prison. She shot children, a police officer, and adults trying to help. I have images of those bodies in the bushes, and they never leave me. Nothing can fix that. There is solace in knowing she is in prison."

Cam Miller was next. "I was nine years old when I was shot and wearing a blue jacket. After lying on the floor of the auditorium and bleeding, I was taken to the hospital. I was fortunate. I did not need surgery. When I returned to school, I did so with fear. I could not go to school without being afraid. I would have my mother walk me around the house… to ensure Brenda Spencer was not in my home. The memory of being shot one inch from my heart is always on my mind. When I hear Spencer is up for parole, I wonder why she thinks she should be released. Spencer decided to hunt for humans because she was bored. The lasting tragedy plays in my mind every day."

Greg Verner and Mary Clarke, both eight at the time, quietly agreed to give no further comments. They trusted Cam and Crystal's words resonated with the panel. The board adjourned to deliberate and came back with a denial of parole with the next suitability hearing set for three years, in 2028.

> COMMISSIONER KOZEL: MS. SPENCER, THIS IS IN DENIAL OF YOUR PAROLE. WE FIND YOU POSE AN UNREASONABLE RISK TO SOCIETY.

Brenda nodded her head and looked down.

The commissioners pointed to the various accounts of the shooting and gave great weight to the youthful offender, her age, mental and physical health, but there wasn't enough to outweigh the current risk to society. The major issues surrounding her failure to continue substance abuse treatment, anger management treatment and underdeveloped release plans played a large role in the decision.

The commissioners said her lack of understanding of the crime and its motivations were evident, even in the letters she wrote to the victims, telling them "she did not mean to hurt them". The panel recommended anger management programming, substance abuse courses, and seeing therapists more frequently than she is currently.

> COMMISSIONER KOZEL: THIS DENIAL GIVES THE BOARD NO PLEASURE, ESPECIALLY AFTER ALL THESE YEARS, AND IT IS CLEAR THERE ARE LIMITATIONS WHEN IT COMES TO YOUR MENTAL AND PHYSICAL HEALTH.

During the 20-minute deliberation the panel reviewed the two letters sent in from the victims' families. There were letters from the Robb family, which was listed as Robert Robb Jr, and Burt Wragg's son and granddaughter.

The Wragg family victim impact statement was dated the same day as hearing. It is an honestly written legal document which reads in part:

IN OBJECTION TO THE PAROLE OF BRENDA SPENCER, SCHOOL SHOOTER AND MURDERER

Regarded as the solo actor behind (one of if not) the earliest recorded elementary school shootings in the United States at Cleveland Elementary School on January 29, 1979. The first of many school shooters, literally triggering a school shooting epidemic our country has been unable to escape for decades since.

My name is Haley Wragg. I am the granddaughter of Burton Wragg, one of the two educators murdered by Brenda Spencer in the Cleveland Elementary School Shooting, the first modern elementary school shooting the US ever experienced. Let me repeat that – the person regarded as the first modern elementary school shooter in the United States is Brenda Spencer.

I write with the support of my entire family, on behalf of my father Tom (only 16 at the time of the shooting), and in the spirit of all victims as we express our vehement objections to any parole being considered or granted to Spencer on any terms.

We do not forgive school shooters.

We do not forget those we lost.

There is no world and no parallel universe in which what Spencer did was pardonable.

Officially the CDCR will have to schedule Brenda's next parole hearing prior to Feb 2028.

Brenda and I corresponded the day after the denial. I asked if she will be taking the parole board's guidance? She said, "I will be working hard on it. They recommended a program called "P.R.E.P." and I sent them a letter already. They had a long list of things to work on, but I will have to wait for the transcript to see all their recommendations. And I will get right on them".

P.R.E.P is the Partnership for Reentry Program by the Archdiocese of Los Angeles. Their goal is to prepare parolees for a 'purposeful, productive future' using the Restorative Justice ethos. Within a few weeks Brenda joined the program and said, "I have fun with it, it's not that hard but it makes you dive down in those deep, dark feelings of emotions. I'm almost done with my first lesson on victim awareness".

More sad news was to follow. Less than a month after the parole hearing I received word that Detective Paul Olson passed away at his home in Lakeside, CA on March 12th 2025. He was 78. Detective Olson, Olé' as he was nicknamed by the SDPD, was the negotiator who managed to peacefully talk Brenda out of the house. It was partly his communication skill that allowed the SDPD to control the scene without any further bloodshed. The SDPD never fired a single shot that day.

Paul was originally from Cokato, Minnesota and served in Vietnam and Laos as a Marine prior to becoming a patrol officer then eventually a detective. Paul served in Desert Storm while still on active duty as an SDPD detective.

He proudly had three daughters who became police officers in San Diego and South Carolina. Paul had a brilliant John Deere tractor addiction and somehow managed to retire on the same Minnesota farm he grew up in. Rest in Peace, Olé'.

In April 2025, Brenda turned 63. I sent her an e-card with a puppy wearing a gold birthday hat and the words 'Happy Birthday Dawg!' across the top. She wrote back the next day, "Thanks for the birthday card, Nick. It's adorable. B"

36

MOTIVE

THERE IS A great deal America could learn from Brenda's actions in 1979. School shootings are now so commonplace in the country that many psychologists no longer consider the perpetrators to be abnormal. Brenda was considered to be so abnormal in her time that the events leading up to the shooting were never seriously considered.

Police had a slam-dunk case. She had already confessed to *The Evening Tribune*, so evidence was not collected in the usual fashion. The case never went to trial, so motive was never formally considered.

Brenda became the most famous criminal in the United States, and her picture was published by news agencies worldwide. The Boomtown Rats' song propelled her to the status of an international poster child for evil.

Almost half a century later, she is still recognisable as the sweet 16-year-old who took the gun her father gave her for Christmas and shot schoolchildren. As in the cases of so many school shooters since, the reason why may never be fully revealed.

PSYCHOLOGY AND PROFESSIONAL OPINIONS

Dozens of psychologists and doctors examined Brenda the year after the shooting. Various experts submitted multiple diagnoses at the time of her trial. Despite massive attempts to understand Brenda, she remains a paradox.

In 1979, the school shooter phenomenon was incredibly rare and for the perpetrator to be a young woman, even more rare. The fact that Brenda is alive to tell the tale is even more incredible. It is rare for a rampage or school shooter to be apprehended after finishing a shooting spree.

Not one psychologist or expert ever has been close enough with Brenda to understand her. Any time another school shooting occurs, her crime is referenced, but we are no closer to understanding why she did it.

Dr. Peter Langman is one of America's greatest minds on the psychology of school shooters. He has written countless articles for Psychology Today and has authored a number of books on the subject.

Langman rose to prominence with his 2009 book *Why Kids Kill – Inside the Minds of the School Shooters.* Brenda's case is mentioned by the author but is not part of the study. Langman considered the event technically not a school shooting because Brenda did not attend the targeted school.

It may be that Brenda is not technically a school shooter because she did not attend the school targeted. But she most certainly was the start of the growing trend of teenage murderers. In the four years that followed the Cleveland Elementary shooting, there were more than a dozen violent deaths at the hands of teenagers in San Diego County alone.

In early 1983, 17-year-old Charles Tyberg drove up next to a police officer and shot him in an eerie recreation of what Brenda and Brant Flemming said they had planned. Tyberg, the son of a police officer, borrowed his father's uniform, patrol car, and .357 Magnum pistol and went for a joyride.

About midnight he pulled up alongside Patrolman Kirk Johnson and from the darkness emptied the weapon. He hit the officer five times, killing him. Tyberg returned home and bragged that he had done something that would make him famous. He was tried as an adult and remains incarcerated.

Less than a month later, paralysed Vietnam veteran Harry Sherwood's naked and partially burned body was found in a mountain ravine near San Diego. He had been robbed, tortured, and dumped from his own van to die of exposure.

Four teenage girls were found guilty of the crime. A 13-year-old and a 14-year-old were convicted as juveniles with two others, Joyce Largo, 16, and Marguerite Benjamin, 17, convicted as adults. By 2014, all had been released from prison.

The perpetrators were listed as not under the influence of drugs, but all had a history of use. Like Brenda's, these crimes were committed against random victims for maximum shock value and without any regard for consequences.

Brenda is named in almost all scientific journals as the mother of school shooters. Most list her as a side note or anomaly among the scores of male shooters. A scientific study of her never has been conducted.

All through the 70s and 80s the Federal Bureau of Investigation studied other murderers and serial killers but dedicated no time toward school shootings. The mass shooting at Colorado's Columbine High School in 1999 that killed 12 students and a teacher would change that, but it may be that the damage has been done. Brenda's fame and its accompanying soundtrack seem to have normalised the phenomenon forever in the United States.

Psychologists have been exceptional at categorising school shooters and branding different types and styles. But they have done little to stop the avalanche of rampage shooters at schools.

DRUGS AND ALCOHOL

Brenda says she was high on drugs at the time she shot up the school and has maintained that position since being arrested. She did TV interviews showing her toxicology evidence and stubbornly refuses to accept another explanation for her behaviour.

It is true that alcohol and drug paraphernalia were found in the house after Brenda's arrest. Alcohol was just three feet from where Brenda knelt to take aim. During the negotiation for her surrender, she also made two comments to Det. Olson about having drunk alcohol.

A half-empty bottle of Southern Comfort was sitting in the entranceway with a missing top. This bottle was the half-size type, and Brenda could easily have lifted it from any liquor store. No extensive search of the house ever was undertaken, so it is possible there was more alcohol on the property.

Wally was not known to be a drinker and would not have left an open container on the floor when he went to work. Brother Scott possibly could have been the owner of the bottle, but he was away at the time and would not have left it there.

Marijuana was Scott Spencer's drug of choice, and he had been arrested for growing it the summer before the shooting. It is possible he shared harder drugs with his sister. Brenda did introduce Brant Flemming and other neighbourhood kids to various drugs in her garage hideaway.

Yet, according to the police, no alcohol or drugs were found in her system.

Brenda certainly had access to marijuana that morning and quite possibly harder drugs. Her father's prescription pills were also mentioned during parole hearings. She also was known to have shown these to local kids.

Phenyl cyclohexyl piperidine (PCP) is also known as Angel

Dust and was very popular in the 70s. It has been the core of many "diminished capacity" claims by perpetrators, much to the dismay of district attorneys nationwide.

It was never determined if PCP was in the hash pipes found in the Spencer garage and in Scott's room. Science in 1979 was not advanced enough to test Brenda's system for PCP.

In October 1979, nine months after the shooting, experts from all over America attended the National Homicide Symposium at the Bahia Hotel on San Diego's Mission Bay.

PCP was the main topic of the first sessions.

Dr. Ronald Mark, professor of forensic psychiatry at the University of Southern California, said, "A hundred people here had a beer with their lunch, and nothing happened. If a hundred people each had one hit of PCP, we'd have brawls all over the place."

Most importantly, Mark said some users become homicidal, and the drug remains in the users' bodies for weeks or even months after they stop using it.

At the same event, Dr. Steven Lerner, California's leading expert on PCP, said the problem was an "epidemic" among young white, suburban, affluent youths. The drug causes "agitation, excitement and hallucinations," he said. Lerner said he believes the average for "first use" is about 14 years old.

Los Angeles assistant district attorney Richard Neidorf cautioned all investigators attending the conference to be meticulous in gathering evidence in future, saying, "the PCP diminished capacity defence is being used all too often."

Brenda wrote boastful letters saying she was in bad shape and was coming down from all the drugs she was on. None of these claims were believed at the time. What may have been a cry for some sort of help was ignored.

Police at the time continually questioned the ease of obtaining hard drugs. But Brenda always said that you could get anything you needed from school and once quipped that it was easier to get drugs than chewing gum at Patrick Henry High.

Police knew about drug problems at Patrick Henry. They assigned undercover operatives.

Shelly Zimmerman, who later was to become San Diego's chief of police, was 24 and a young officer in 1983, but she looked more like a 12-year-old. With her Ohio accent, she posed as a Midwestern transfer student and enrolled in the school.

Zimmerman managed to infiltrate druggy groups and targeted the sellers. She netted more than 70 arrests. Prosecutor Bill Holman was so impressed with her, saying, "it was so easy for her to buy dope from these people."

It is reasonable to argue that if an undercover police officer could buy drugs at Patrick Henry High, then it is not too far-fetched to think Brenda could have done the same. Brenda received $5 a week lunch money, and she claims to have also traded or sold stolen items for drugs.

Dr. Robert Smith evaluated Brenda in June 2005, saying, "certain substances may no longer have been in her system because of the time she had been tested."

And "even if inmate Spencer was not under the influence of drugs and/or alcohol at the time the offence was committed, the use of illegal drugs and intoxicants would have exacerbated the serious emotional problems that she was already experiencing during her adolescence".

I believe it is entirely possible that Brenda was on drugs and alcohol at the time of the shooting. Whether or not they were enough to cause full-blown hallucinations is open to question. Brenda had alcohol and drugs at her fingertips the morning of the shooting. It is most remarkable that traces of both were not found in her system.

Brenda has spent more than 40 years trying to explain how the police toxicology report was negative. If she were on drugs at the time of her offence, she maintains, then she would definitely have had diminished capacity and never would have plea bargained.

SUICIDE BY COP

Officer Marty Duitz had his weapon fixed on the front of the house but never had Brenda in his sights. Brenda was clearly of sound enough mind not to go near any windows. If she had, one of two things could have happened. Either, she would have seen an abundance of targets at the condo complex, or she might have taken a bullet from the police SWAT team.

In 1970s crime shows, the hostage taker or sniper is almost always taken to jail without injury. Brenda was a big fan of these shows and would have known that police would shoot her only under extreme circumstances.

San Diego Police's special weapons and tactics team, like the TV show SWAT, had never taken a life in these types of situations and Brenda would have known this. Instead, she would be fully aware that she would be on TV and seen by millions.

The suicide-by-cop phenomenon did not hit scientific journals until the late 80s. Brenda has said that somewhere between opening fire and speaking to Det. Olson, she lost her nerve. There does not appear to be any evidence that she wanted to end her life that day.

PLEA BARGAIN AND DRUGGING IN PRISON:

Brenda joined a group of inmates called "Women Prisoners Convicted by Drugging" to protest the use of psychotropic drugs being used on county detainees during their trials. She claims she was drugged while at the Youth Authority and was unable to make clear decisions.

McGlinn and doctors noted she was docile and uncooperative

during psychiatric examinations leading up to the trial. Wally had also given her strict orders not to rumble him for starting a relationship with a 16-year-old. Brenda has shown over the years that she carries many of her families' issues as her own. She goes quiet, and in later years, she has self-harmed.

Sheila McCoy was her cellmate at the CYA and did not report any use of any extra drugs. It is possible that Brenda received heavy doses within her seizure medications.

Brenda attended alcohol and narcotics anonymous organisations once she entered the CIW, and eventually, she became clean in 1989. All officials and the judiciary had determined that she was not a drug user or was not impaired by any chemicals when committing the crime.

It may never be known when Brenda became a drug addict, but there is evidence to say that at one time she was. What is certain is that Brenda had no idea that making a plea deal would give her a longer stay in prison.

37

INFLUENCES

EARLY LIFE AND ABUSE

Brenda's upbringing was certainly different to most people's but is not remarkably strange. Her parents divorced, but the siblings stayed together, living in the same area.

During the separation, Wally pleaded poverty when dealing with early child support payments. Dot harshly criticised the father for being too stingy to make these payments and often called Wally "weak". This tactic backfired, and the kids left.

Brenda's mother was angry at her ex-husband and was spiky to the kids after they abandoned her. Dot threw herself into her work and would try to make time for the children in evenings and on the occasional weekend.

Wally let the kids run riot and was often absent when it came to parenting. Scott would argue with Wally, continually moving in and out over the years. Teresa took her first opportunity to leave the house and never came back. Brenda was essentially left behind.

As a young girl, she exaggerated wild stories to get attention. She befriended a younger boy and became his leader. Brenda watched TV and fantasised what those scenarios would be like in the real world. Millions of kids do this, and it is not unusual.

The Spencer's were not poor or in poverty as was often reported.

Wally had a decent job and low mortgage. He also managed to buy two vehicles and additional property in Potrero. They certainly lived in filth but were not needy by any means.

The case for Brenda being a loner and without friends also is not true. She introduced the Minors to at least four friends and two who called her a best friend. She was also close to her brother and there was trusty Brant for friendship.

Brenda was expelled for truancy during her first year at Patrick Henry and had been back from Garfield alternative school only for four months when she attacked Cleveland Elementary. It is quite possible that many students did not know her because she was rarely there.

Brenda crashed her bike at a young age and soon began to have seizures. At the time, Dot knew of the head injury but chose to leave all responsibility to Wally. Neither of Brenda's parents took her to the hospital; it was her older sister, Teresa, who took control the following day.

Wally was simply oblivious to Brenda's needs, and Dot was cold and angry. Dot knew that husband and daughter shared a bedroom and that abuse was possible. But Brenda never confided in her mother, and Dot did little to build trust with her daughter.

When Dot was first told that Brenda was the shooter, she initially told police she could not attend the scene right away.

She may have done this because she thought the matter was Wally's problem and she had washed her hands of the kids.

Almost every neighbour or acquaintance I interviewed mentioned they thought there might have been abuse. A victim's father, Norman Buell, had also considered abuse long before it was mentioned in parole hearings.

McGlinn, her court-appointed lawyer, was an expert witness in a previous child-abuse hearing but did not pull any of this evidence into play. He spent countless hours with Brenda and her father as her guardian. Wally visited his daughter in detention every week, and Brenda kept quiet.

At the time of the trial, Wally was secretly keeping little Sheila as his mistress. He pushed Brenda and McGlinn to plea bargain and avoid an invasive trial. The Spencers were an insular family and did not respond well to any invasion.

I contacted McGlinn to get his comment on new information about Brenda and her possible parole. This was his response:

> *I am not interested in participating in your endeavour to relive the events of the tragic day when Brenda fired a gun from her home at the Cleveland Elementary School.*
>
> *It was tragic for the school, especially for the principal and custodian who were killed, for the children, and the police officer who was shot. The families of those killed and injured will be forever scarred by this terrible event.*
>
> *The legal system assessed guilt, responsibility, and an adequate punishment for what took place. There was no dispute as to the facts on the day of the incident. The actions of the police and the school personnel were described in detail in the local papers. The DA had all the police reports and had ready access to the detectives and officers involved.*
>
> *The police interviewed the reporter who had spoken with Brenda.*
>
> *I recognise you have a personal interest in revisiting the tragic events of that day especially as you say Brenda might be paroled in a year or so. But I respectfully decline to participate in your endeavour.*
>
> *Michael McGlinn*

I respect McGlinn's right to move on. He worked tirelessly to help Brenda and did all that he could make sure she was represented responsibly. It will never be known why he did not bring attention to Wally's illegal relationship with a minor.

The biggest evidence to support Brenda's abuse claims is that her father was a known paedophile. To avoid apprehension, he was forced to marry a pregnant underage girl with a similar appearance to his own daughter.

Brenda told me she eventually forgave her father saying, "Dad, well me and him would go round and round in the visiting room over the abuse. Finally, he apologised for all he had done. At that point, I told him we would let the past stay in the past and move on from there. We began a friendship and moved on. I guess in some way I did love him."

THE WEAPONS

At the time Brenda was arrested, she left two knives in the entranceway and set two guns down outside on the pavement. She had broken two small windows out of the front door and kept the knives close to hand.

The two guns recovered by SWAT were her new .22 calibre rifle with scope and her trusty pellet gun.

Both rifles are not the first choice for shooting anything but very small prey. The .22 is not a large weapon and must be fired accurately to kill. The pellet gun was slow in loading and would only hurt small animals at close range.

Brenda was a good shot and took time to hit each target with her .22. Modern-day school shooters have learned from Brenda's example and use far bigger weapons for maximum damage in a small amount of time.

Owners of .22 rifles often say, "if you poke enough holes in something, it'll go down." I don't believe Brenda started out trying to kill anyone with her small weapons. She would have known what kind of damage her rifles would inflict from shooting birds and hunting in Arkansas.

What was her state of mind when she made two rifle positions in the door? She clearly intended to use both weapons.

I believe she tried to shoot her pellet gun first but discarded it when she did not get the desired reaction. Witnesses said they heard noises in the bushes before they heard gunshots. They said they looked around for where it was coming from. Brenda then put down the pellet gun, changed windows, and took aim with her .22.

The biggest controversy with the rifle is how she obtained it. Wally was proud of Brenda's ability to shoot a gun, the whole family bragged about it. Brenda was a dead shot with her pellet gun and proved she could be trusted with a bigger weapon.

Before Christmas 1978, the entire family knew Brenda wanted a rifle. Her brother had discussed the matter with their father and bought her a trigger lock for safety. Her mother and sister also were aware she had asked for a rifle for Christmas and made no effort to block it.

None of the Spencers, including the mother, felt they were in any danger when Wally bought the rifle. Brenda's later statement, "he bought the rifle so I would kill myself" makes no sense. Brenda could just as easily have shot her father as she could herself. But she did neither.

Wally left ammunition in his unlocked van for Brenda to use anytime. His van was as dishevelled as the house, and missing ammo would not have been noticed for some time. Any statement suggesting Brenda took his keys and stole the ammo is likely untrue.

A year before the shooting, Brenda and Brant were arrested for vandalising the school. Despite reports in the newspapers and neighbours' recollections, Brenda did not bring her BB gun or pellet rifle with her. None of the witnesses saw her with a gun, and the police report does not mention any weapons. The internet is full of armchair sleuths saying the event could have been forestalled because she had already shot up the school once. This is untrue and without evidence.

Brenda was a poor student and had been seeing a school counsellor for truancy. None of the family felt these issues were severe, and they were unaware of any homicidal or suicidal tendencies.

"I asked for a radio and got a rifle" is a statement taken from parole hearings to deflect guilt and is untrue.

INFLUENCES

The political climate and music of the 1970s had an influence on Brenda as it did with all teenagers. It is worth considering but is not a major factor in her choice to shoot at the school. There are many environmental and emotional reasons closer to home that had larger influences.

From Brenda's bedroom you could hear and see the school quite clearly. She would have woken up each morning with the sound of screaming kids. Maybe she just had enough?

I was 10 at the time and remember my teacher saying Brenda was born on the Pisces-Aries cusp and they tend to be great planners. My teacher also said that if she lived across the street from the school, she would go crazy too.

My friends thought she looked like the Stephen King character "Carrie" and was destined to do bad things. We all knew that she had just repeated the Garfield cartoon catchphrase, "I hate Mondays." The cartoon strip was popular, and it had just become a Saturday morning cartoon show that September.

Officer Robb thought the film "Deadly Tower" with Kurt Russell had aired the weekend before, and she took inspiration from that. It was a TV drama about the 1966 Austin, Texas, sniper Charles

Whitman. But the show actually aired on Nov. 28 at 3pm in the afternoon – two months before Brenda's rampage. It was strangely scheduled just as kids got home from school.

Maybe the Jonestown Massacre in Guyana gave Brenda criminal thoughts. Nearly 1,000 cult followers of a crazed man named Jim Jones had ended their lives by drinking grape Flavor-Aid laced with cyanide just two months before.

Perhaps it was what happened the weekend prior before the shooting? Brenda would have seen this story on the news or in the papers.

A female hijacker took control of a Boeing 747 at Los Angeles International Airport. Dressed in casual clothes with a white headband, 49-year-old Irene McKinney claimed she had nitroglycerine in her handbag. She said she had invented a "technological heaven" that would save the world and demanded Charlton Heston or Lindsay "Bionic Woman" Wagner be brought to the plane. McKinney wanted the Hollywood stars to read her list of demands on national TV.

Heston was rushed to the airport, but it was all over before he could help. Passengers drank wine and sang songs on the plane as they waited for events to unfold. After 11 hours, FBI agents subdued McKinney and found no trace of explosives.

But investigators said she was angry after a bad divorce in which she lost custody of her children. This may not have influenced Brenda, but it was a bloody good story and a sign of the times.

I feel Brenda was more intrigued than influenced by local murderer Danny Altstadt, an 18-year-old who killed both his parents and sister with a hatchet in 1975, and the *other* Brenda in Arkansas. There are slim similarities between all three cases, but these would have had an impact on Brenda's teenage years.

She had dressed as an axe murderer for Halloween and joked about Altstadt's younger brother's injuries, the sole survivor of the

Alstadt murder who was left paralysed. Scott was friends with the family, and she spent a lot of time talking about it to him. Brant told police she dreamed of using an axe on a cop.

Brenda told me, "My favourite Halloween costume was an axe murderer. I scared the hell out of my dad with that one. He almost had a heart attack. I guess he thought I was going to pay him back for all the shit he'd done to me. I'd never seen him so scared before."

Like the *other* Brenda Spencer in Arkansas, she also made a series of false claims during her stand-off, shot a single policeman and eventually gave herself up. The crimes of the Arkansas Brenda Spencer flabbergasted her relatives there, who joked that the criminal had the same name as their California niece.

Considering all the evidence and speaking with Brenda, I still come back to this conclusion: If Brenda was of sound mind and being abused, why didn't she shoot her father? If Brenda was on drugs, not of sound mind and being abused, the shooting makes more sense.

We will never know her reason for wounding nine and killing two at Cleveland Elementary School that day. Brenda may not even know herself. Maybe she just really didn't like Mondays.

ACKNOWLEDGEMENTS

THERE ARE MULTIPLE people who contributed to this book and many I need to thank.

School faculty members, Michael Guerrero and Mickey Miyashita were instrumental in giving context and insight to the day to day running of the school. Thanks to you both.

The San Diego Police officers are heroes, and I'd like to thank Steve Zazueta, Marty Duitz, and the late Dick Thwing.

Detective Paul "Ole" Olson and Ted Kasinak deserve a special mention for their honesty and professionalism. I owe you all a drink.

I need to give a big thank you to SD Fire & Rescue dispatch expert and Nottingham Forest fan, Tim Robinson. The book started with you. Thanks, Tim!

San Carlos residents Cassie and Colleen require a major thank you too. The two of you were so pleasant to speak with, and I hope your families are well. Thanks for your information.

I'd also like to thank the fantastic folks from the San Diego Evening Tribune, the last great newspaper in the region. Steve Wiegand shared all that he could from that fateful day. Thank you, my friend.

Bernie Hunt, my father, was one of the Tribune's editors on duty that day, and he went above and beyond to support this project. Thanks for the guidance, but most importantly, thanks for pointing out the obvious.

Finally, Brenda Spencer herself shared personal details and

insights into her life that was an enormous help in understanding why things turned out the way they did. She will always be a notorious figure and is prepared for this eventuality with or without freedom.

PHOTOS

Brenda Ann Spencer, mugshot

Brenda as a child with her pets *(above and below)*

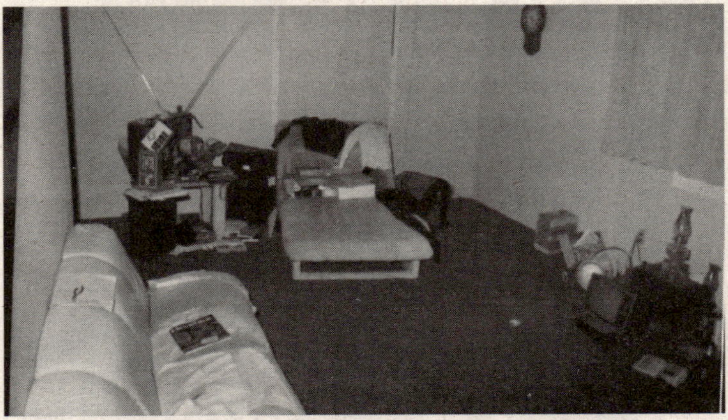

Wally Spencer's unkempt bedroom *(top)* and the family room of Brenda's childhood home *(bottom)* – note the lack of alcohol

School photo around the time of her parent's divorce *(above left)*
and Brenda as a child *(right)*

Brenda pictured with her father Wally

Brenda's house during the shooting, far right obscured by another roof. Members of the San Diego SWAT team can be seen at left

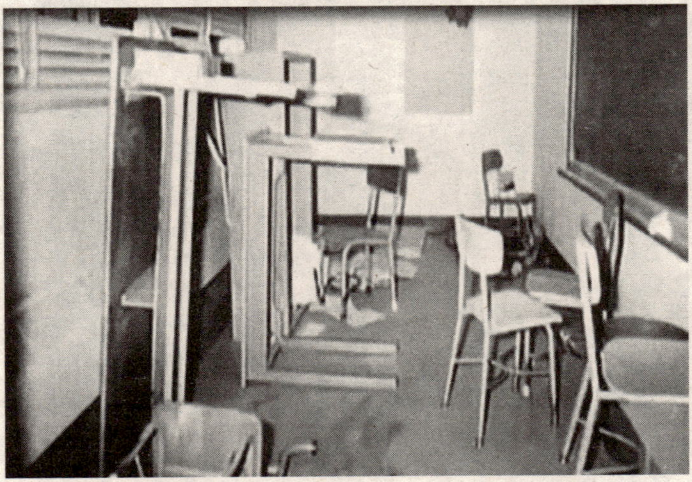

Classroom in Cleveland Elementary School 1979

Sheriff deputies escorting Brenda

Brenda Spencer, mugshot from 1996

Brenda Spencer arrest

Boomtown Rats, November 1979

Brenda leaving court in October 1979 after pleading guilty

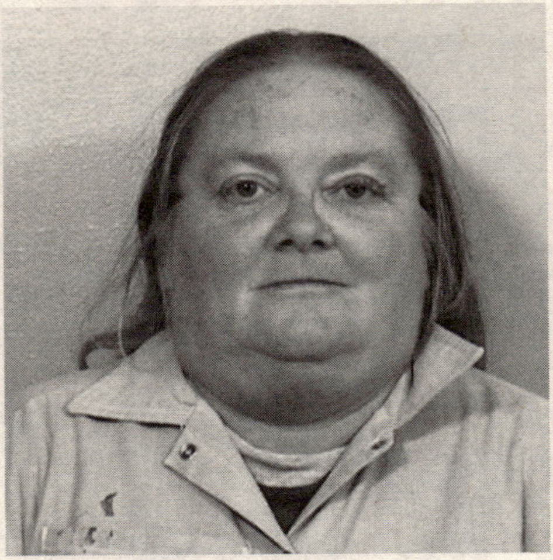

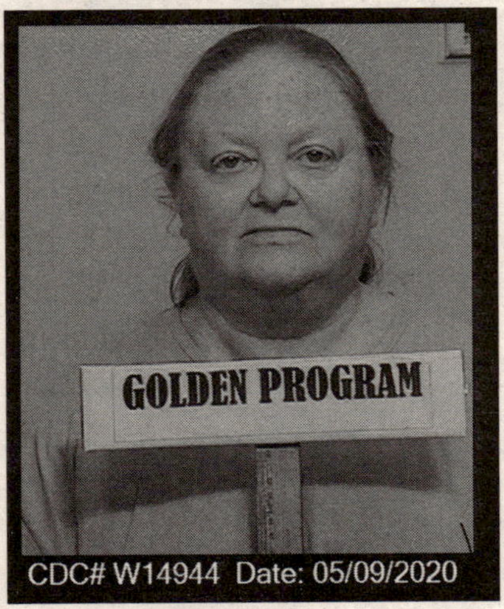

Golden Girl Brenda pictured in 2018 *(top)* and 2020 *(bottom)*.
Credit CDCR